DATE DUE

SEP 2 3 1986		
JAN 0 4 1988		
APR 2 7 1988		
OCT 1 9 1989		
OCT 10		

THE
YOM KIPPUR
WAR

Also by Peter Allen

One More River: The Rhine Crossings of 1945

THE
YOM KIPPUR
WAR

DISCARDED

PETER ALLEN

Charles Scribner's Sons
New York

Library of Congress Cataloging in Publication Data

Allen, Peter, 1937–
    The Yom Kippur War.

    Bibliography: p.
    Includes index.
    1. Israel-Arab War, 1973.   I. Title.
DS128.1.A64   1982   956'.048   82-3183
ISBN 0-684-17488-X   AACR2

1 3 5 7 9 11 13 15 17 19   F/C   20 18 16 14 12 10 8 6 4 2

Printed in the United States of America.

Acknowledgments

In writing this book about what is forlornly hoped to have been the last outbreak of open warfare between Israel and her neighboring Arab states, I have been left only too conscious of the enmity and mistrust that still remains at the public level. But beneath the all-too-familiar and popularized face of Middle East politics, at the level of the individual, there is often a real sense of sorrow. The Arab who expressed to me his horror at seeing Israeli soldiers burned beyond recognition and his realization of the futility of it all, and the Israeli soldiers who recorded their revulsion at the slaughter they had inflicted, were concerned for their fellow men. Religion and politics had no place in that concern.

Nevertheless, there remains in governments, official bodies, politicians, soldiers both active and retired, and even in ordinary people who stayed on the sidelines in the warring states, a reluctance to have their opinions and recollections openly attributed to them. Therefore, in compiling this acknowledgment to all who corresponded with me, discussed their experiences, or otherwise aided me in writing what I sincerely hope is a faithful account of that bitter yet significant conflict, my list of names is somewhat attenuated. I have also refrained from detailing the occupations or titles of my correspondents and informants.

To those here listed, and those who prefer to remain anonymous, I wish to express my sincere thanks for their time and efforts: H. Meer Alamiri, Jonothon Denton, A. Fawzi, P. Gorshkove, R. S. Greenbaum, N. Jopling, H. el Konayessi, J. I. Krilof, S. Michaelson, M. Milner, J. Moonman, H. Omari, M. M. Rehzan, R. Salmon, R. Sanderson, A. E. Sarhan, O. Shazli, M. Shimon, Col. Y. Simon, D. D. Stone, H. P. Sullivan, A. Wahby, J. S. Zeiklin, and finally, but no less for that, my son Andrew who prepared the draft maps and helped in my research.

For the photographs, I am indebted to H. el Konayessi, Terry Fincher of Photographers International, and to the Israeli Government Press Office.

I also wish to thank *Newsweek* for permission to quote extracts from their November 5, 1973, issue, and *Time* magazine for permission to quote from their issues for October 22, 1973, and October 29, 1973.

Contents

Contents

Maps

Introduction

*And he gathered them together into
a place called in the Hebrew tongue
Armageddon.
And the seventh angel poured out his
vial into the air; and there came a
great voice out of the temple of
Heaven, from the throne, saying,
It is done.*
— Revelation XVI

Armageddon, according to the Apocalypse, will be the scene of
the battle of the great day of God. Its most likely location is
thought to be at the site of the previous great battle—Megiddo,
a city of ancient Israel. There is, however, another possibility.
"Armageddon" could be a corruption of the words "har mo'ed,"
which mean "the mountains where the Gods meet." In modern
terminology that is Mount Hermon—the Golan Heights.

Of all the conflicts that have occurred between the Arabs and
the Israelis since 1948, the aggression that erupted on Yom Kippur, Saturday, October 6, 1973, most astounded the world and
threatened Armageddon.

It seemed unthinkable that the Arabs, who had been defeated so swiftly and decisively only six years before, should attack "Fortress Israel," powerful and secure behind the physical barriers won in 1967—the Suez Canal, the Jordan River, and the Golan Heights. But when the war erupted in full fury that hot Saturday afternoon, Israel was at prayer and fasting on the most holy day of the Jewish year. So unexpected was the conflict that it barely made headlines in the Sunday papers in the West. By Monday, when most Western observers expected the Israelis to have retaliated and started to give the Arab invaders a thrashing, the news instead was of brilliant Egyptian and Syrian successes and of the Israelis reeling in broken disorder. The vaunted Israeli Air Force, far from controlling the war, was being clawed from the sky by Arab missiles.

As the days passed, it became obvious that a new era in warfare had arrived, in which mighty 40-ton tanks could be destroyed by a single soldier with a throwaway weapon, and multi-million-dollar aircraft stood virtually no chance against surface-to-air missiles that trundled along on their own tracked vehicles. It was a war in which courageous advances were checked by electronic weapons, and the traditional timidity of the Arab soldier was replaced with newfound intrepidity.

Soon it was the fate of Israel that hung in the balance. She had been caught on the wrong foot and foregone her traditional military response to the overwhelming superiority of her Arab neighbors—a preemptive strike—in the belief that world opinion would swing to her support. She was wrong, and the novel and brave political move did nothing to prevent her condemnation by the swaggering Third World hangers-on to Soviet policy. Even within Israel's own armed forces there were powerful pressures that did little to remedy the fundamental misperceptions. As her losses mounted and the Arabs were seen to be winning, other states began to pour in aid to deliver the coup de grâce.

But the Israeli commanders pulled themselves together and struck back. First, a stunning low-level air raid into Damascus destroyed the electronic nerve center of Syria's air defense system and allowed the Israeli Phantoms to take to the air again over the Golan Heights just when Israel's armored reserves were flowing into battle. The Syrians were trapped in the Hushniyah pocket, decimated, and the remnants shoved back over the cease-fire line.

Using all their ingenuity and dogged courage, the Israelis won a corridor straight through the Egyptian lines on the East Bank of the Canal down to the water, and even before the Egyptians realized what was happening, the Israelis had hauled bridges right through the battlefield and placed them across the Canal. Soon their forces were rampaging in the Egyptians' rear, cutting off their Third Army and even posing a threat to Cairo.

By then the superpowers, who, like master puppeteers, had manipulated the satellites and the spy planes, allocated the tanks and replaced the missiles, found themselves heading toward a collision. Suddenly they were no longer just victualing the battle and proving their latest weapons; they had moved a vital step nearer confrontation. The world held its breath as Soviet parachute divisions were loaded into giant transports, B-52 Stratofortresses stood loaded and ready to go, the battle fleets of both powers were arrowed toward the Israeli coasts, and the missiles in their silos thousands of miles away stood armed and waiting for the final signal . . .

CHAPTER
1

The Six Day War

Dawn came quickly over the desert. Hardly had the first grayness flushed to pink than the sun edged with unseemly haste over the eastern horizon and flashed its rays long across Egypt. Sounds rose from the awakening Nile villages as they had done for four thousand years. There was a plaintive, irritating squeak, suggesting the chirp of grasshoppers, but in reality the lament of wet pulleys creaking from the first moment of sunrise. The timeless Egyptian villages were at work.

At a stark utility military airfield outside Cairo, the bustle had begun before first light. Guards were changed with much stamping and yelling of repetitive well-known commands, the harsh voices echoing across the open expanse of the airfield. Gasoline trucks, painted to match the dun landscape, rolled toward the orderly rows of MIG fighters and Ilyushin bombers that glinted silvery in the first sunlight; all bore the red, white, and black emblem and three stars of Egypt. They cast ungainly early morning shadows across the dusty expanse of bleached concrete runways and hardstandings. At the airfield perimeter, antiaircraft guns quartered the deepening blue of the sky, probing the depths in case the enemy should appear.

On eleven Egyptian airfields similar scenes were being enacted as a much rehearsed operation began to gain momentum. Here and there a devout Muslim airman would kneel and briefly pray for succor during the coming battle; for this day, many belatedly realized, was no rehearsal. On Monday, June 5, 1967, the combined Arab armies of Egypt, Syria, and Jordan were going to launch a sudden, powerful attack to set their forces rolling from west, north, and east into Israel until they met in Tel Aviv and Jerusalem and expunged the Zionist intruders.

Away to the east of Cairo, across the Nile with its lateen-rigged rivercraft and beyond the shimmering waterway of the Suez Canal, in Sinai, Egyptian armored forces were ready. Soviet-supplied T-34 and T54-55 tanks squatted on the sand and rock like so many ungainly, drab olive sandbugs in the waterless shifting expanse. Already the tank hulls were almost too hot to touch. Behind them, rows of trucks and support vehicles were arranged for the assault, and groups of heavy guns pointed their long barrels high to the east and northeast, awaiting only the word of command when they would crash and recoil as their heavy shells were hurled toward the thinly deployed Israeli Army, guarding its ill-shaped, misborn, and indefensible country.

The planning, the training, the deployment was done. Long and often acrimonious negotiations and confrontations between the ill-matched, mutually jealous Arab partners had eventually brought forth agreement on the day and objectives of the assault. Egypt, the strongest partner, would smash across the indistinguishable desert borders from Sinai; Syria would pour her armor and troops down from the commanding ridge of the bramble-covered Golan Heights to overwhelm the Israeli northern settlements as they drove for the sea clearly visible from the rocky escarpment; and Jordan's elite Arab Legion would crash out of its salient to sever the 10-mile waist of Israel, cutting the misshapen foundling state in two.

By 7:00 A.M. the Egyptian commanders were satisfied that all was ready. Field Marshal Abdul Hakim Amer, the commander-in-chief of the armed forces, arrived at a closely guarded airfield a little way from Cairo. There, amid much saluting and felicitation, he met his subordinate commanders for a final briefing. He then prepared to leave for a tour of inspection of the Egyptian forces prior to the launching of the attack. His aircraft was ready on the hardstanding, and he went quickly aboard after a brief talk to the pilot. The rest of the commanders who were to accompany him followed Amer into the aircraft. Clearance from the control tower was requested and confirmed, and at 7:20 A.M. the commander-in-chief's aircraft was rolling along the runway. On the ground, the remainder of his entourage and the station commander and his guard stood at attention as Amer's aircraft rose, bearing with it all Egypt's aspirations for a quick and decisive victory over Israel.

As Amer's aircraft left the airfield near Cairo and turned east, a signal was flashed to the commander of the country's line of Soviet-built and -equipped radar installations, antiaircraft batteries, and surface-to-air missile sites that guarded the borders, telling him to hold their fire as the commander-in-chief was in the air.

But even as Amer's lone aircraft cruised eastward, 183 aircraft were heading westward, rocketing low across the Sinai Desert, seeking the cover of the hills that masked the radar scan and hid their approach. These aircraft bore the Star of David, and all were loaded with bombs, rockets, and cannon. They streaked over the Israeli-Egyptian border, through the silenced line of guns and rockets, and past the unwatching radar stations.

The previous afternoon the commander of the Israeli Air Force, Maj. Gen. Mordechai Hod, had told his wing commanders of the plan for a preemptive Israeli strike before the Arabs launched their massive, overwhelmingly powerful attack across Israel's virtually indefensible borders. They were to attack at H-hour, which had been set for 7:45 A.M., when the Israelis correctly assumed the senior Egyptian officers would be in transit from home to headquarters or to their units. At 8:00 P.M. the same evening the wing commanders had briefed their squadron leaders on the plan, and emphasized the need for a low-level approach and absolute radio silence; not even in the event of an Israeli aircraft crashing was radio silence to be broken.

In the stillness of the early morning of June 6, the Israelis, too, had prepared. The pilots had been awakened at 3:45 A.M. and given their final orders, while outside the Mirages, Skyhawks, and Mystères were prepared. Then, just on 7:00 A.M., the first wave of aircraft had set off in clouds of white dust. In the Israeli Air Force command post, recalled Moshe Dayan, then the Israeli commander-in-chief, the tension was almost tangible. "Not an eye moved from the war table, not an ear from the radio network."

At 7:14 A.M. the first wave of Israeli jets screamed in over Egypt's main Bir Gafgafa air base in Sinai. A second wave of twenty-seven aircraft that had left a minute later swept across the Suez Canal and shrieked in over the great Abu Suweir base, where they roared back and forth machine-gunning the neat lines of parked MIGs and Ilyushins, and loosed bombs and rockets at the workshops, buildings, and control facilities. Belatedly the antiaircraft guns swung to open fire on the Israeli planes, but by then the jets were zooming away low over the desert. The air filled with bursts of flak amid the drifting smoke trails from the rockets. Great plumes of flame-flecked oily smoke rose from shattered Egyptian aircraft, many totally engulfed in flames, others just crazily collapsed on broken undercarriages or shattered wings.

Between 7:14 and 8:55 A.M. the Israelis attacked 11 airfields, destroying 189 Egyptian aircraft on the ground. Of the few gallant pilots who did manage to get airborne and attempt to drive off the attackers, another eight were sent spiraling to the desert. Six of the airfields were totally destroyed and left inoperable, four of them in Sinai and the others west of the Canal. Sixteen radar stations were put out of action. Eventually, as the Israeli jets faded away over the Canal and Sinai, the Egyptians began to pick up the pieces and gazed in dazed horror at their wrecked war machine. But even before they could begin to assimilate the extent of the disaster, a second wave of Israeli jets screamed in from the Sinai Desert.

The second wave had taken off at 9:34 A.M., after a delay to allow alterations in the operations as a result of the first attack. On some Egyptian airfields all the aircraft had been destroyed, while from others, surviving aircraft had been scattered to airfields not originally included in the attack. On the more distant bases at Helwân, Mantzura, Bilbis, Minis, Luxor, and Gardake, Egyptian crews who had escaped with their remaining aircraft were thunderstruck when the Mirages and Skyhawks pursued them and left their planes, too, burning wrecks. Of the 164 Israeli aircraft making the second attack, 115 went for air bases, 13 went for radar stations, and the remainder patrolled or supported the assault. Again Abu Suweir was pounded and an additional 61 Egyptian planes were destroyed there.

The unbearable tension at the Israeli command post had finally broken at 7:30 A.M. when the coded message, "Nahshonim—Action. Good luck," had crackled through the loudspeakers and the waiting men knew their planes were attacking. They had succeeded in their gamble, and were through the radar and missile screen. At that moment, too, another command was given and the Israeli armor began to move from its assembly areas. With the knowledge that the Egyptian armor had lost its air cover, while their own was virtually intact, the Centurions and Pattons began to grind forward across the sand. As Dayan recalled, "So we had crushed the enemy's air strength. But this was only a part of the enemy's armed might, and our tanks had not yet encountered the Egyptian armor. However, already, within a few moments, the nightmare of the previous weeks had vanished. True, the war had only just begun, but it was the kind of start which augured well for the remaining phases. Egypt was left without an air force."

Anwar el-Sadat, then the Egyptian vice president, learned of the Israeli air attacks from the radio on the morning news. He recalled thinking: "Well, they'll be taught a lesson they won't forget." He was confident of his country's ability to retaliate, so he went to have a shave, took his time changing, and made a leisurely progress down to the command headquarters. He arrived there at about 11:00 A.M. and later remembered that the Soviet ambassador's car was already there. On entering, Sadat asked what was the news, and was told that forty enemy aircraft were down. Feeling elated at such splendid tidings, he went to Field Marshal Amer's office, only to find him standing in the middle of the room, "looking about with wandering eyes." Several times Sadat greeted him, but Amer didn't seem to hear. It was at that moment that a nasty suspicion began to dawn on the vice president. He promptly sought information from those others in the room and to his horror was told: "Our air force has been destroyed on the ground." Later on, Sadat found out why the Soviet ambassador had arrived so early; Amer had learned of the disaster on landing, panicked, and immediately asked the Russians to arrange a cease-fire. The war was then barely an hour old.

Just in time for what was to become known as the Six Day War, the Israeli Armored Corps had been reequipped with Centurions armed with the latest 105mm guns, and a large number of M-60 Patton tanks, many of these ex-West German Army equipment. The tanks, together with several brigades of elderly thought updated wartime Shermans, some over twenty years old, proved more than a match for the Arab armored forces. In one notable action, a reserve battalion of Israeli-engineered M-50 Shermans virtually destroyed the Jordanian 40th Armored Brigade's more modern Pattons.

Events moved with such breathtaking speed that only the television and radio news reporters could keep up with the developments; the press reports became outdated even as they were written. The sheer audacity of the Israeli assault left the Arabs dumbfounded, and, inevitably, wild rumors were deliberately circulated to account for their calamitous failure. Anwar Sadat recounts how at the very outset of the disaster, Amer tried to put the blame entirely on the Americans, claiming, "It was the U.S. Air Force, not the Israelis that had dealt us that blow." Apparently Egypt's President Nasser retorted that he would not believe this, "until you've produced at least one aircraft with a wing showing the U.S. ensign." Nevertheless, this was good propaganda and readily accepted by the volatile and confused citizens of the Arab countries. A Damascus radio broadcast screamed that British aircraft had raided their positions after the failure of the Israeli Air Force, and claimed that RAF Canberra bombers had been identified. Not to be outdone, King Hussein of Jordan claimed personally to have seen the British bombers that attacked his palace.

By the evening of the first day, the Israelis had captured the vital Egyptian position at El Arish, the capital of Sinai, commanding the approaches to the Sinai passes leading to Suez, and their armor was plunging deeper into the Sinai peninsula. The correspondent of *The Times* (London) wrote of the feeling in Tel Aviv. "Today's fighting has taken everyone by surprise. Its efficiency bears the mark of great preparation but there is no evidence that it is really premeditated." Premeditated it might not have been, but the situation in which Israel would have to strike first had been foreseen, and in their war games the Israeli commanders had learned what had to be done.

Indeed, the speed and sweep of the Israeli armor across the Sinai Desert was even then ensuring the campaign a place among the masterpieces of mechanized war. First, the Gaza Strip was taken by quick thrusts either side of the main populated area. Then, with his rear secure long before the earliest time that even the most optimistic estimates suggested, Dayan was free to accelerate his main thrust across Sinai to a level at which only the most masterful planning could possibly have provided supply. That first day's preemptive air triumph was dictating the entire course of the battle.

Britain's painful experience of what could happen to armor in the desert when air supremacy was lost was well known to Israel's commanders, some of whom had served with the British during World War II. It provided a background of knowledge that was put to good use in those scorching June days. The morale of the Egyptian Army, which had not indicated at any time in the recent past a patient endurance of sustained and unrelenting air attack, began to crumble. Time and again, Israeli jets swept out of the dazzling sun and ripped open the Egyptian tanks with rockets, leaving the thin-skinned vehicles in long blazing columns that marked their dismal flight from Sinai as surely as Napoleon's litter traced his retreat from Moscow. In fairness to the hard-pressed Egyptian troops, it must be recalled that Nasser's adventures in the prolonged Yemen campaign were estimated to have cost around 50,000 of the army's best troops; the troops in Sinai were the residue, frightened and demoralized, and they started to crack under the remorseless air attacks.

Israeli armored columns began to race ahead of the Egyptian forces, and by the time the latter reached the vital Mitla and Giddi passes, which held the key to the domination of Sinai, Israeli armor had got around their flanks and reached the passes ahead of them. The defeat became a rout, for as the columns of surviving Egyptian armor and trucks reached the passes, they were set upon by the Centurions' guns. Deadly accurate, the long-range weapons picked them off as they approached, until the passes and the desert to either side resembled a smoking and burning scrapyard.

Sadat recalled becoming "even more dazed and broken-hearted as I watched the crowds flocking in from al-Tahrir Province in big trucks, or filling up the vast Pyramids road as they marched in 'companies,' chanting, dancing, applauding the faked-up victory reports which our mass media put out hourly." Loudspeakers in public squares blared out news bulletins and anti-American invective. People in the city gathered in little knots along the streets to listen to transistor radios for the latest bulletins from the battle zone. "We are not afraid of President Johnson!" bawled one Cairo commentator.

Nevertheless, the full extent of the disaster could not be hidden forever, for, though few among the chanting masses in the darkened Cairo streets realized it, the battle zone was getting uncomfortably close. As the Egyptian military command put out communiqués throughout the day, veiled and cautious though they were, the Cairo crowds began slowly to comprehend that the news was bad.

Late on the second day, those Egyptians who had not been trapped in the forward positions were in full retreat. When the Israeli General Staff learned that the Egyptian force at Sharm el-Sheikh, guarding the entrance to the disputed Straits of Tiran, had begun to abandon its position, a paratroop formation was ordered to capture the vital positions. At 1:00 P.M. on June 7 they set off in helicopters, but found on arrival that two Israeli torpedo boats had already claimed Sharm. The Israeli flag was fluttering above the quay.

By the third day, June 7, the signs of impending adversity had become more palpable, as reserve troops began to dig in on Cairo's outskirts and construct more strongpoints on the Nile bridges. Rumors filtered back to the Egyptian capital that troops were digging in along the Nile Valley, some 40 miles west of the Suez Canal. The city was gripped with fear and apprehension as it was learned that Egyptian troops were falling back rapidly before an unbelievably ferocious Israeli onslaught. Then in the blacked-out city truckloads of troops began to arrive, all in battle dress and steel helmets, but tired, bedraggled, and unshaven. Utterly exhausted and bewildered, they rolled into the city center, many of their trucks towing field kitchens. They were greeted by wildly cheering crowds who simply couldn't comprehend what was happening. The radio bulletins told of startling victories while about them armed home guards patrolled the streets. Shops remained open far into the night and queues began to form at the food stores.

On the bramble-covered, volcanic slopes of the Golan Heights, the Syrians fought hard but were inexorably pushed back. The Jordanians, too, put up a stiff fight, but in the end, with their air force wiped out, they began to fall back as tough Israeli paratroopers, closely supported by skilled and daring tankmen, closed in on their positions in Samaria and in Jerusalem.

By that evening the Egyptians had had enough. At the United

Nations, the Soviet delegation pressed the Security Council on their behalf to meet in emergency session, and it seemed very likely that they would impose a cease-fire the following day. In view of this, after hurried discussions, the Israelis dispatched two divisions to advance immediately to the Suez Canal and to Ras Sudar, the position commanding the Gulf of Suez. An hour after midnight the advance began, and by dawn one division's parallel columns of armor were within 10 miles of the Canal. Behind them followed a paratroop brigade. Across their path, however, was entrenched a strong Egyptian force of commandos, paratroops, tanks, and artillery, determined to prevent the Israelis from reaching the Canal while the cease-fire was being arranged. For hours a fierce battle raged as the long-range Centurions slammed away at the Egyptian tanks and infantry positions, and towering 155mm guns spewed huge shells into the Egyptian lines. The Israeli Air Force pounded the enemy positions, and under the relentless pressure the Egyptians finally gave way.

By nightfall the Israelis had seized East Kantara on the Canal, and by 7:30 A.M. on June 9 they were swinging south to reach the important Ismailia crossroads and the Firdan Bridge. Meanwhile the other division, under Maj. Gen. Israel Tal, had captured the great air base at Bir Gafgafa, smashed the Egyptian armored concentrations in the area, and joined the force already at the Firdan Bridge. The Canal line was secure, the retreat sealed off for Egyptian troops still fighting their way across the Sinai Desert.

The main attack had in a sense been predictable. Whether in less favorable circumstances General Dayan would have felt free to use all the three main routes across Sinai to the Suez Canal is open to discussion. In other situations he might have felt obliged to draw part of the Egyptian forces to one road while exploiting the other two across Sinai. But in fact he went flat out along all three routes once the initial breakout from El Arish had been achieved.

By the time the United Nations imposed their cease-fire, the Arabs had been decisively beaten. Vast quantities of discarded weapons littered Sinai. Many tanks and guns had not been fired, and some still had muzzle covers in place. Egyptian troops had even discarded their boots in their headlong flight. Drawn up along the Suez Canal, along the Jordan River, and atop the Golan Heights commanding the route to Damascus, the elated Israelis just could not believe what they had done.

But in the Arabs' hour of failure and utter despondency lay the seeds of revenge and a determination to erase the humiliating defeat. Already the Soviet Union, ever eager to exploit a situation for its own opportunist ends, was pouring military aid into the open arms of the Arabs. Next time, they assured their humbled clients, they would be guaranteed victory by the training and dazzling military hardware that the full resources of the Soviet Union would put at their disposal. The Six Day War had ended in defeat for the Arabs, but the battle was not over.

CHAPTER

2

No Substitute for Victory

Hovering against the breeze like a falcon, the Israeli helicopter struggled to maintain position while its crew winched in the downed Phantom pilot from the sparkling blue of the Mediterranean. As soon as the dangling man was snatched into the gaping doorway, the pilot opened the throttle to send a burst of power into the whirling rotor blades. The downblast of the great scythes flattened the surging waves as the rescued pilot blew into his steaming coffee. The helicopter swooped away, leaning into the wind and heading back along the whitened coast toward its base in Israel; above it, a flight of Phantoms hawked to and fro lest the Syrians try again from their bases behind the port of Tartus. Below, the waters resumed their timeless motion, hiding forever the wreckage of the Phantom and thirteen Syrian MIGs.

This incident — in September 1973 — was one of the most serious that had taken place in several months between Israel and her Arab neighbors, especially Syria and Egypt, and it reflected growing tension. It also coincided with an Arab summit in Cairo, and many observers thought it was an open Israeli warning to her enemies never to forget what Israel could do.

The tension had been building up over six years since the Six

Day War. And just as the over-taut strata of rocks in the Middle East every so often reach breaking point to produce a cataclysmic earthquake, so too the political bedrock was about to snap again, plunging the region into another Armageddon.

The Six Day War had ended on the Egyptian front on the morning of June 9, 1967. On the Syrian front, the fighting had slowly petered out the day after, leaving both sides exhausted. But whereas the Arab exhaustion was the result of a shattering defeat, for the Israelis the tiredness was that of elation and sheer stupefaction. It was only when the guns had fallen silent that the Israelis realized the full magnitude of their victory. A week before their very survival had been at stake, as they faced surrounding enemies who had sworn to throw the Jews into the sea. Militarily outnumbered by a huge margin, the Israelis had not imagined in their wildest dreams or most fervent prayers that the formidable armies threatening them would be routed in a matter of days. Not since Judah had defeated the Ethiopian hoards of Zerah had the Jews scored such a victory.

With the advantage of hindsight and its comfort, some Israeli generals and politicians argued that their apprehensions of the prewar days had not been justified, and the existence of the state had never really been in danger. The majority of Israeli commanders had indeed been confident on June 5, when they launched their devastating preemptive strike, that their quality would prevail over the enemy's massive forces and that better Israeli training would be decisive.

The shock of the defeat to the Arabs had been great, for only a day earlier they had exchanged salutory messages that they would soon meet again in Jerusalem and Tel Aviv. In the eyes of the Arab leaders, Israel was doomed, and none conceived that she could defend herself. Although the nidifugous state had resisted attack after its traumatic birth in 1948, then, they reasoned, it had faced only the small, uncoordinated forces of King Farouk, King Abdullah, the Iraqi Hashemites, and incompetent Syrian politicians. When, in 1956, the Israelis romped to the

Canal after a few days of fighting, they did so in collaboration with the British and French. In 1967, Israel was alone to cope with the martial soldiers of several Arab countries, who were fired with a new spirit of Arab revolutionary nationalism. But on June 4 of that year, the Israelis, faced with the closing of their sea artery at the Straits of Tiran (left unguarded when the Arab states bullied U.N. Secretary General U Thant into withdrawing the U.N. troops) and threatened with imminent extinction, had resolved to go down fighting.

The military losses to Egypt had, in truth, been staggering. At a cost of 679 Israeli soldiers killed and 2,563 wounded, the Egyptian casualties were more than 11,500. That early air strike had cost Egypt two thirds of her air force, and during the close-packed hours that followed through desperate days and nights of action, 800 of her 1,000 tanks and most of Egypt's guns had also been lost.

In the first weeks after the Arab defeat, a shattered and bewildered President Nasser said that he felt "like a man walking in a desert surrounded by moving sands, not knowing whether, if he moved, he would be swallowed up by the sands or would find the right path." Nevertheless, the confused Egyptian people, who had believed themselves victorious, still rallied to the charisma of his leadership. When he resigned on the evening of June 9, the streets of Cairo soon filled with an emotional throng, crying: "Nasser, Nasser, don't leave us, we need you!" He changed his mind and stayed on, for while the generals had been disgraced, there was little popular blame for Nasser.

It was at this critical time that the Soviet Union had appeared, with its usual bland opportunism, as the real friend of the Arab cause. The Soviets established an air bridge almost at the moment the cease-fire went into force, and quickly followed that with ships crammed with warplanes, tanks, guns, and war stores of every kind. Those billions of dollars worth of modern Soviet war materials were as vital politically as they were militarily: an important antiimperialist gesture and a means of securing a dominant Soviet presence in the region. The uncompromising Egyptian demand to reclaim Sinai (a territory that, in fact, had been a part of modern Egypt for only sixty years) was to open to the Soviet Union a key foothold in the country and naval bases from which it could dominate the eastern Mediterranean and threaten NATO's southeastern flank. Since the time of Catherine the Great, the Russian policy of expansion had not changed; she still coveted a warm-water egress from her landlocked mass, apart from the oft-frozen northern ports and the NATO-observed Black Sea. The great Soviet submarine fleet, in particular, needed supply bases far from the ever-watching eyes of the West, whose long-range aircraft followed them whenever they left ports. Since the Soviet Union's confrontation with China, the East offered little attraction, and in 1967 its clients in Southeast Asia were still battling for Vietnam. But the Russians were well advanced in their domination down Africa's east coast, and possession or at least control of Egypt was a mouth-watering goal.

In the summer of 1967, Anwar Sadat, then Egyptian vice president, was convinced that the Egyptian Army had been betrayed by its commanders, defeated through lack of fighting ability or spirit. His attitude, not unlike that of Hitler in 1945, who also blamed his generals for the crumbling Wehrmacht's defeat, led to an uncompromising determination to fight on, whatever the cost. By November 1967, Sadat regarded the Soviet-reconstructed Egyptian Army as a new-forged weapon that should be swiftly used lest its bright cutting edge deteriorate. Indeed, as Sadat said, "Our assimilation of the new weapons took exactly five months, although the Soviet Union had calculated it should take three years, during which they estimated the situation would have calmed down." The Russians, in Sadat's view, did not really want Nasser to use his new weapons, for a conflict in the area could only lead to United States intervention.

International efforts to restore peace in the Middle East once the Six Day War ended were to be lengthy, highly complicated, and ultimately futile, for the divergent Arab and Israeli demands were quite irreconcilable. The weary rounds of negotiations began in the towering glass block of the United Nations in New York City, when the General Assembly convened at Soviet initiative on June 19, 1967. But the many sometimes ingenious formulae were to lead nowhere. The antagonists remained implacable: the Arabs refused to recognize Israel, guarantee her borders, or afford passage of the Tiran Straits and the Suez Canal to her ships; the Israelis would not evacuate the Arab territories they had won by military prowess and which gave them strategic advantages hitherto unattainable.

The skirmishes along the Canal, which had gone on intermittently since the cease-fire, were, by 1968, assuming more dangerous proportions and beginning to escalate. In September of that year, Maj. Gen. Ahmed Ismail, who had succeeded Amer as Egyptian commander-in-chief (Amer had shot himself), completed the building of a series of Egyptian defense lines along the West Bank of the Canal, and Nasser instituted his "war of attrition."

Nasser was desperately frustrated, having promised his people with irritating frequency that he would soon liberate the occupied territories. He was seeking a way to put pressure on the Israelis, who, with their limited regular forces, were being forced to maintain a high proportion of reserve troops at readiness, thereby weakening their economy. A pattern was emerging in which Egypt's artillery ranged along the 100 miles of the Canal would open fire, hurling shells across the still waters in which almost two dozen trapped merchant ships lay rusting under the brazen sun, their progress ended by sunken blockships at either end of the Canal. For several hours on end, shells zoomed over flimsy Israeli slit trenches and rudimentary observation posts, exploding in cascades of sand and rock splinters. Eventually the shelling and mortaring would cease, leaving the blazing sun to beat the stilled desert into a dazzling, shimmering silence, in which isolated military observers put scorching binoculars to their watery eyes and stared at one another across the green water. Then, in due course, the Israelis would retaliate with helicopter-borne paratroopers whirring behind the Egyptian lines, attacking gun emplacements, destroying radar installations, and striking fear into the enemy.

By early 1969, the Israelis were getting deeply concerned at the persistent and powerful Egyptian artillery concentrations and the periodic forays Egypt's commandos made across the Canal, forcing vicious hand-to-hand pitched battles on the Israelis before they threw their enemy back. Their own cross-Canal skirmishes and deeper raids into the Egyptian hinterland were worrying the Israeli High Command, too, and compelled them to do some military soul-searching while they rethought their strategy for the first time since the Six Day War. Their response was to place the small Israeli Defense Force in a basically defensive attitude and resort to the building of a line of fortifications — decisions which, in the fullness of time, were to have near-fatal consequences for Israel's security.

Maj. Gen. Avraham Adan, usually known as "Bren," was appointed by Lt. Gen. Chaim Bar-Lev, the Israeli chief of staff, to lead an interservice team charged with creating a defensive system to cover the Israeli positions in Sinai, based on a fortified line along the East Bank of the Suez Canal. However, even before the team arrived in Sinai, the problems posed by the defense of the Canal had been already considered by Maj. Gen. Yeshayahu Gavish, who had led the victorious forces in the Sinai campaign.

Gavish had already concluded that the Israeli troops needed adequate cover in strongpoints to protect them from the Egyptian shelling. His dilemma was whether to hold the Canal bank itself or to maintain his forces in depth some way back. In 1968 the Israelis had analyzed this problem by holding war games in which Maj. Gen. Mordechai Gur played the role of the Egyptian commander. His forces had "crossed" the Canal along its entire length, advancing all along the major axis with helicopter-borne troops deployed in depth behind the Israeli front line. With that experience in mind, Gavish thought it advisable to establish strongpoints to cover all possible crossing areas since it seemed the Egyptians would be likely to cross along the entire length of the Canal.

After examining the situation in Sinai, and with Gavish's experiences to draw on, Adan recommended building fortifications along the Canal that would give maximum observation by day and electronic observation by night to warn of any Egyptian intrusion. These positions would, moreover, expose only a minimum number of troops to Egyptian shelling, while giving immediate warning of enemy penetration to the forces holding a static defense line 7 miles back from the Canal. The static line would provide artillery and armored support in the event of an attack, but there would also be mobile armored troops patrolling between the observation points themselves. When this idea was put to Gavish, he accepted the concept of a warning outpost system, provided that at the northern end of the Canal—which he thought especially vulnerable—all possible crossings would be protected with groups of fortifications. In his view, the line of observation points should be fortifications that would, in the event of a major attack, hold up the enemy before they reached the defensive infantry brigades in the rear, and so give time for the armored forces to deploy across the front from Baluza in the north to the vital Mitla Pass in the south.

When Adan submitted his proposals to the General Staff, however, he was opposed by two influential senior officers, Maj. Gen. Israel Tal, who was attached to the Ministry of Defense, and Gen. Ariel ("Arik") Sharon, the chief of Military Training. Both of these men argued that Adan's proposals would not provide the essential flexibility the limited Israeli forces needed in their defense. They proposed instead to keep the observation points on the Canal, as Adan suggested, but maintain armored divisions as mobile forces, able to deploy swiftly to whatever point of the Canal line was threatened. Additional armored forces would patrol along the Canal itself. This, they insisted, would ensure a flexible defensive system in which the armored striking forces would make the most of their mobility, able to move immediately to oppose an enemy incursion. This concept paralleled the Germans' use of the limited *Panzer* forces behind the outpost positions of their Siegfried Line in 1945.

But, General Adan riposted, his plan was both a political and a strategic concept. Politically, the Israeli Defense Force had to

ensure that the Egyptians could not cross the Canal with substantial forces. Therefore, Israel had to adopt a defensive posture,
with her fortified observation points backed by the static defensive line. A military road would be constructed as well, to provide lateral communications enabling tanks to move rapidly to
annihilate any Egyptian forces that managed to break through
the Canal bank line and get inland.

General Gavish had long held the opinion that if the Canal
was to be considered a physical barrier, Israel had no alternative
to establishing a physical presence along it. With uncanny clarity
of vision, he saw the danger of a sudden Egyptian move to seize
a foothold on the East Bank and dig in while an immediate
attempt was made to get an internationally agreed cease-fire. He
also drew his colleagues' attention to the Israeli concept of a
counteroffensive into the enemy's territory, which demanded the
presence of her forces along the Canal itself. Otherwise, they
would have to fight their way through the enemy to it once
more.

Sharon and Tal shook their heads in disagreement and pointed
out that Adan's proposals would be expensive in both men and
materials. They both favored leaving the Canal open to an Egyptian invasion, which would be dealt with by swiftly moving
Israeli armored and air forces. In this suggestion, they were
drawing conclusions based on the experience of the Six Day
War, which evinced little Egyptian determination, and did not
envisage a situation in which the invader might be much more
resolute. In spite of the erudite arguments of Sharon, Tal, and
their supporters, General Bar-Lev finally decided in favor of
Adan's fortifications. The latter's team proceeded to oversee the
construction of the defense line, upon which too many hopes
were to be pinned.

The future would reveal the faults of both plans. Adan's
defenses were to prove untenable when the Egyptians attacked
in force, and, as he predicted, though for the wrong reasons, they
would indeed have to battle to the Canal once again.

The fortifications, which were quickly built in January and

February 1969, were, in any case, only one element in what became known as the Bar-Lev Line. Although the Line was to become identified with the French Maginot Line concept of a continuous, heavily fortified defensive system—especially after the Egyptian breakthrough in the Yom Kippur War—it was not so. A better comparison is with the northern sector of the German Siegfried Line, which was a series of defensive positions backed by a succession of lay-back defenses where the artillery and armor were deployed in readiness to plug penetrations. Each fortification in the Bar-Lev Line controlled an area extending 0.5 to 1 mile on either side, which, nevertheless, left a gap of 5 to 6 miles in between to be covered by observation points and armored patrols. However, in the critical anchor positions at either end of the Line, or in isolated strong points, tanks were established for added firepower and support. Behind these outposts were tank concentrations, while troops of tanks were deployed within the areas of the fortifications themselves, their ramps so sited that the tanks would be able to give enfilading fire along the Canal in case of a water-borne crossing attempt. The whole complex was supported by a huge infrastructure of underground headquarters, connecting roads, water and communications systems. Repair and stores facilities were also provided, which were particularly important since the Israelis could not rely on anyone else to make good their armored combat losses.

The Bar-Lev Line had hardly been completed when the conflict again erupted with prolonged artillery duels on a daily basis. In one such particularly vicious outburst, a powerful Israeli concentration crashed down about an Egyptian command post, killing their chief of staff. This prompted the Egyptians to enforce a strict blackout throughout the country, and on April 1, 1969, Nasser bitterly declared that the cease-fire was null and void. Orders were given for his forces to escalate the confrontation with Israel into virtually open warfare, which Nasser confirmed in June when he officially announced that the war of attrition had begun. This, he saw, was the only way by which he could compel the Israelis to evacuate the occupied territories. Since all-out war and an invasion of Sinai were thought impossible, the best alternative was to force the Israelis to weaken their economy by maintaining a large part of their manpower under arms. Early in June, the U.N. Secretary-General reported that the cease-fire had definitely broken down — open warfare was being waged on the Canal front.

The real escalation was nevertheless still to come, and in the following weeks the fighting intensified and spread like a stubble fire along the fringe of the waterway, reaching a climax on July 20, 1969. On that day the Israelis unleashed their much touted air force to strike at vital military installations in Egypt on a massive scale. Their new and powerful F-4 Phantoms attacked Egyptian gun and missile positions with devastating effect. Furiously, Nasser announced that the final stage of liberation had been reached, leading to the crossing of the Canal. But he spoke without considering the full effect of the Israeli air offensive, which had destroyed many of the key antiaircraft gun positions and surface-to-air missile (SAM) sites, without which an Egyptian Canal crossing was impossible.

While Nasser's offensive was intended to pin down Israel's forces, Defense Minister Dayan's strategy was to ameliorate Egyptian pressure with a limited Israeli air offensive. The war of attrition was getting out of control. By December 1969, eighteen months after the Six Day War ended, a peace settlement was no nearer, despite the strenuous efforts of the United Nation's peripatetic representative, the Swedish diplomat Dr. Gunnar Jarring. After a Soviet six-point peace plan had been rejected by the Israelis, the Americans had submitted their Rogers Plan, which called for almost total Israeli withdrawal from the occupied territories. Israel's rejection of this plan might have jeopardized her relations with her sometimes demurring protector, but for Nasser's implacable resolve to continue the confrontation at all costs. He too loftily rejected the plan, which even pro-Egyptian observers regarded favorably. Much to Washington's chagrin, the Russians then spurned the plan after having initially supported it.

Dayan had no exaggerated political expectations about the

eventual effects of the Israeli air offensive. Military experience in other parts of the world, he pointed out, had shown the political and military effects of saturation bombing to be almost always below expectations. But in both Israel and Egypt, there was the feeling that something had to be tried. In Israel, the political risk was thought to be small, since Nasser was already at his most obdurate and there were already several thousand Russian advisers and technicians in Egypt. So when on January 7, 1970, the Israeli Phantoms made the deepest raid yet, striking at targets well inside Egypt, including Cairo's suburbs, Nasser promptly summoned the Soviet ambassador and their military experts. He told them that he desperately needed the SA-3 missiles, which had been promised for June, insisting it was the only way to counter the Israeli air strikes. In response, Nasser was invited to Moscow for a secret four-day visit, beginning January 20. There, he impressed upon the Russian leaders the gravity of the situation. According to Sadat, he asked for Soviet intervention, including "a Soviet air commander to take over our air defenses," which were particularly weak. He also wanted the TU-16 "Badger" bomber, a big turboprop aircraft capable of delivering a guided rocket-bomb.

The *Strategic Survey* for 1970, published by the London Institute of Strategic Studies, stated that "the sheer volume of Soviet military support for the United Arab Republic [Egypt] during 1970 was without precedent. Never before had the Soviet Union injected anything like the quantity of sophisticated military equipment into a non-communist country in such a short time." Not even a Warsaw Pact country received such quantities of weaponry. At the beginning of 1970, when the deep-penetration raids began, there were no Soviet pilots or missile crews in Egypt. But by the end of the year more than 200 Soviet pilots were flying MIG 21-J interceptors, and 12,000 to 15,000 Soviet officers and men were manning some 80 surface-to-air missile sites. Six airfields were exclusively manned by Soviet personnel, and there were another 4,000 Soviet instructors in the other branches of the Egyptian Army.

The decision to engage in deep-penetration bombing, which

was discussed at length by the Israeli government and even found advocates among the "doves" there, was directly responsible for this massive Soviet intervention. Although Russian personnel had been in Egypt since the Six Day War, it was the death of civilians in Cairo suburbs that panicked a distraught and frightened Nasser into asking the Russian bear for aid. For more than a hundred years it had been the unchanging Russian policy to break out to the south, but such moves had been thwarted by British power in India and the eastern Mediterranean. Now, with that power totally eroded, the Egyptians had opened the door to the Russians, and they needed no second bidding.

The regional power politics, nationalism, and religious enmity of the "Balkanized" Middle East were leading the two superpowers surely and inevitably toward a frightening confrontation, just as the Balkans had led the European Great Powers into cataclysm a half century before. Perhaps the inevitable might have been averted with a stronger warning by the United States that the Soviet presence, having gone thus far, should go no further. But they, like Britain in 1914, hedged and tried to be fair-minded, using the same brand of kid-glove diplomacy against Soviet military might that Britain had used so ineffectually against both Kaiser and Führer. Messages flew between Washington and Moscow, and the United States rejected an Israeli request for additional interceptors and strike aircraft in the hope that the gesture would halt or at least slow down Soviet involvement in Egypt. But the Russians were too heavily committed to stop midway, and their intervention was having dramatic military and political results.

Both Egypt and Israel were getting punch-drunk after five months of punishing strike and counterstrike, and a slight shift could be detected in the attitude of each side. Despite the arrival of Soviet personnel, the Egyptians were far from satisfied with the delivery of aircraft, and in April they repeated their request for more. Nasser was both disillusioned and angry at what he saw as Soviet procrastination, for it was clear that having established important military bases in Egypt, the crafty Russians were not going to deliver the weapons with which the Egyptians might finish off Israel; that, after all, would make the Soviet presence no longer necessary. In exasperation, Nasser turned to Sadat. "Listen, Anwar," he said, "whether we like it or not, all the cards in this game are in American hands. It's high time we talked and allowed the U.S.A. to take part in this."

As a reflection of this view, Nasser's May Day speech, while bellicose enough to satisfy his people, also contained some appeals to reason. Where do Israel's borders start, he asked; what do they really want? Why were they not willing even to mention the term "withdrawal"? Nasser had told Jarring, the United Nation's mediator, that Egypt would agree to a package deal covering all provisions of the Security Council resolution, which could be signed before withdrawal began. But he also made conditions, including no direct negotiations with Israel and no formal peace treaty or diplomatic recognition. Israel would have to give up all the occupied territories. The diplomatic technique implied Nasser's wish to talk with the United States, who would speak for Israel.

Israel's demands remained as before: No withdrawal without a peace treaty, no total withdrawal in any case, freedom of passage for her ships through the Canal and the Tiran Straits, a united Jerusalem under Israeli rule, and the settlement of refugees in Arab lands. Nevertheless, Mrs. Golda Meir, the Israeli prime minister, did say in a speech on May 5 that for true peace, Israel would make concessions that might "surprise the world."

For a short while it seemed that the war of attrition was drifting into another stalemate as both sides licked their quite considerable wounds. Egypt is estimated to have lost up to a third of her first-line combat aircraft, and had been forced to evacuate half a million inhabitants from the war-ravaged Canal Zone. Israel sustained more casualties in the clashes across the Canal than she had in the Six Day War itself. Conditions, therefore, seemed auspicious enough for a new American peace initiative, which Nasser again rejected, before setting off apprehensively for Moscow on June 19, 1970.

In the bright sunshine of the Soviet capital, Nasser spent his time desperately trying to persuade the Russian bosses to send a "deterrent" weapon to counter the Israelis' growing strength. But to his fury the Soviet leaders refused, and when Nasser angrily declared that he had been obliged to accept the American peace plan, it was the normally phlegmatic Russians' turn to react angrily. "Brezhnev was beside himself with rage," according to Sadat's account. The craggy countenance of the Soviet leader darkened with disbelief, demanding how Nasser could accept an American solution. Nasser retorted that he would accept anyone's solution — "even if it came from the Devil himself!"

The angry exchanges had some effect, for that very same night, under cover of darkness and making as little noise as possible, Soviet-built, -supplied, and -manned tractors successfully moved a considerable number of SA-2 and SA-3 missile sites forward to the edge of the Canal. The effect of this was not only to increase the protection of Egypt's territory but also to threaten Israeli aircraft operating up to 12 miles inside Sinai. A few days later a surly General Bar-Lev glumly admitted that the military balance had shifted seriously against Israel. But even at that stage no one could fully comprehend just how dangerously the balance had indeed swung in Egypt's favor.

The Israeli deep-penetration raids soon became increasingly costly — seven aircraft were lost between June 30 and August 7 — and the Israelis were growing apprehensive of a head-on collision with Soviet forces. In spite of caution, nevertheless, they did clash occasionally when their Phantoms and Skyhawks ranged along the Canal, loosing their bombs and rockets before streaking away. On July 30 they encountered a flight of MIG 21-Js piloted by Russians and were forced to join in a whirling, high-speed dogfight, at the end of which five Russian-piloted MIGs had been sent spinning down. Elated but definitely apprehensive, the Israelis beat a hasty retreat and waited for developments. Despite continuing Israeli air strikes, however, the Soviet troops were still inching forward more of the wickedly potent SAM sites, and the Israelis could not stop them.

For six months Israeli jets had had their way, roving far and wide over Egypt, before the Soviets became directly involved during August 1970. Ten squadrons of MIG 21-J fighters then began operating, all manned by Soviet pilots as a part of the Egyptian air defense system. But while the Israelis were rightly apprehensive of a major collision with the Soviet Union, they refused to be cowed. Defense Minister Dayan responded with an article in *Ma'ariv:* "Let's hope the Soviets do not intend to do what they have in mind, and let's hope the Americans will not have to do what they have in mind, and let us not believe that the Arabs will receive what they do not want."

The Israelis, Dayan made clear, would fight any military force, regardless of its identification, in protecting Israel's front line on the Canal. More directly he declared: "We shall not allow the establishment of a Soviet missile system within fifty kilometers of the Canal." As if to make this absolutely clear, Israel's chief of staff, Bar-Lev, stated: "The road deep into Egypt is open to our air force."

The incident off Tartus in Syria that occurred in September 1973, then, when Israeli Phantoms shot down thirteen Syrian MIGs for the loss of one Israeli aircraft, was the final direct warning of what Israel could and would do. It coincided with the Arab summit and, according to Israeli sources, came about when two Mirages flew off the Syrian coast, trailing their "coats" as bait. The Syrians took the bait and sent up interceptors, which were pounced upon by the waiting Phantoms. It was the clearest warning that could be given of Israeli airpower. But it was provocative, and misguided, for although they could operate over the sea, the coming battle would be fought over land, and both along the Syrian and Egyptian frontiers those missile sites would remain for the time being a checkmate to Israel's airpower.

CHAPTER

3

The Eve of Yom Kippur

The decision to attack Israel was made in Cairo in the spring of 1973. It was no sudden decision, nor the first such resolve.

The Arabs fully realized that only America could possibly bring pressure to bear on the Israelis, and it was after the failure of a mission by Hafez Ismail to Washington in March 1973 that the idea of a new war began to preoccupy the Egyptian president. According to the Egyptian version, Hafez Ismail, Sadat's adviser on security affairs, was told by President Nixon that he was willing to influence Israel only if Egypt would make a public declaration to the effect that she would accept concessions that went beyond the Rogers Plan. Meanwhile, Ismail was told, the supply of Phantom aircraft to Israel would continue—a threat that caused much worry to the Egyptians.

Anwar Sadat had succeeded Nasser as president of Egypt on the latter's death in 1970. His presidency got off to a shaky start, with an attempt to overthrow him—sponsored, it was rumored, by the Soviet Union. But by mid-1973, Sadat was firmly entrenched.

The Rogers Plan had been very favorable to the Arabs, envisioning, as it did, a total Israeli withdrawal to the former international frontier between Israel and the three states on which she bordered. Only the future of Sharm el-Sheikh and the Gaza Strip was to be left to negotiation. Although Nasser had rejected the Rogers Plan in December 1969, three years later Sadat seems to have been willing to accept it, provided that further modifications could be made in Egypt's favor. But, by then, Washington felt itself no longer bound by the plan, and a new stalemate ensued.

At that point Sadat concluded that there was no way to break the deadlock other than a war in the imminent future. On March 26, he announced in the Egyptian parliament that he was taking over the premiership in order to prepare Egypt for total confrontation with Israel. He followed that bellicose announcement with a statement to Arnaud de Borchgrave, a senior editor of *Newsweek*, in April 1973, that "everything in this country is now being mobilized in earnest for the resumption of the battle, which is now inevitable." This determination was to recur in countless speeches and interviews; on Libyan television, he said: "It has always been our conviction that what has been taken by violence can only be restored by violence." War had become a necessity for Sadat's regime to overcome the credibility gap created by the failure of its repeated promises to the people to regain the occupied territories.

The Egyptian Army was prepared for war, although no one really had any illusions that it was strong enough to tackle the Israelis single-handed. Israel still had an undeniable superiority which, while it could be partly offset by a surprise attack, nevertheless would have made war suicidal for Egypt without the help of Syria, Jordan, and, if possible, other Arab states. Egypt was also seriously concerned about the effect of détente and whether it would limit help from the Soviet Union in the case of an Egyptian attack. Sadat was furthermore unsure whether the contemporary international climate favored Egypt or not.

Egypt's leaders were well aware of America's growing energy problem, which centered on oil, and they wondered how much pressure the Arab world could exercise. However, whereas King

Faisal of Saudi Arabia wanted to wait until Western dependence on Arab oil increased to the point where it could be used more effectively as a political weapon, Sadat was too impatient. The superpowers were exercising increasing control even on regional conflicts, and as Mohammed Hassanein Heykal, the influential editor of *Al-Ahram*, warned in his column in July 1973, it was wrong to overrate the effectiveness of the oil weapon. The world financial crisis would be solved, he said, and energy sources other than oil would be used by the main consumers. "We have altogether between three and five years to join forces and to develop a unified Arab policy." According to some reports, the Russians, too, told Sadat not to put too much trust in the oil weapon, and Brezhnev informed Sadat in a personal message that détente was there to last for perhaps three decades. There was, therefore, a real danger as many leading Egyptian politicians saw it that the status quo in the Middle East would be maintained, including Israel's contemporary borders with her Arab neighbors. Sadat was still far from secure in his rule at that time, and, no doubt, he needed some major political coup, such as fulfilling his promise of regaining those lost territories, to keep the political wolves from his presidential door.

Egypt's relations with Moscow then became of crucial importance. A communiqué published at the end of the Egyptian foreign minister's visit to Moscow in late May 1973 pledged Soviet support for the Egyptian efforts to "liquidate the consequences of aggression," and did not rule out the possibility of military action. That Soviet pledge was to Egypt what the Kaiser's offer of aid to the outraged Austro-Hungarian Empire had been in 1914—an open encouragement to aggression if accepted promptly.

Moves were also being made to patch Egypt's shaky alliance with the Soviet Union, which had been soured since the attempt in 1971 to overthrow Sadat, and following a talk with Brezhnev in Moscow in mid-June, Hafez Ismail announced that there was agreement with regard to the latest steps to be taken. Sadat, however, made no secret that he still had certain reservations about

Soviet policy. "I told the Soviet leaders back in 1971," he said on one occasion, "that the present situation cannot be maintained. For if Israel does not feel that we can hit back, it will cause an escalation of the situation." The Soviet Union had a global strategy and was insufficiently aware of the regional problems that interested the Egyptians. In spite of the honeyed words from Moscow, Sadat concluded that "In our calculations we shall not consider the meetings of the superpowers and their discussions."

Even after Soviet leaders had promised that military assistance to Egypt would continue, Sadat complained: "We are not altogether satisfied with the arms deliveries but this is perhaps God's Will . . ." Sadat had in his mind the effect of the much publicized détente between America and the Soviet Union, which, as he saw it, threatened to stop Soviet aid short of what he felt was absolutely the minimum to ensure success in another war with Israel. He was rather in the mood of the would-be hunter who, when asked what size gun he wanted, replied that it should be big enough to kill an elephant if he hit it in the toe. The Egyptians wanted strategic weapons, or an assurance of Soviet aid up to, and including, intervention if it became necessary. Sadat was not against détente, only against its consequences in the Middle East. Egyptian journalists were, nevertheless, more outspoken, and articles in *Akhbar al Yom*, in August 1973, maintained that the Soviet Union had changed its foreign policy so that it no longer corresponded with the interests of the Arab countries. This was short of direct military intervention; in their reply to Egyptian critics, Soviet spokesmen pointed to the Aswan High Dam, the Helwân steel plants, the Alexandria docks—not to mention the modern planes defending Egypt's skies.

In the months before the 1973 War, then, although there were still tensions in Soviet-Egyptian relations, these in no way were to prevent a close military collaboration. The Soviet Union, despite Egyptian complaints, remained Cairo's most important arms supplier, would support Egypt in the United Nations, and could be relied upon to put pressure on the United States. While

Moscow regarded Sadat's government as far from ideal, and unreliable as far as Soviet ambitions in the region were concerned—Sadat had given military aid to the Sudan to suppress a Communist coup—any failure to support Cairo would have greatly harmed the Soviet position in the Arab world. No doubt they hoped that one day a more trustworthy regime would emerge in Cairo.

Throughout the summer of 1973, spokesmen of American oil companies had impressed upon their government the crucial importance of the Saudi Arabians' increasing their oil production, without which the United States, most of the Western world, and Japan would face an acute oil shortage in the near future. They argued that the Saudis would be willing to do this only if the United States changed its policy with regard to Israel. Hitherto the Saudis had always refrained from mixing oil and politics, but as the West became more and more concerned about the predicted energy shortage of the 1980s and 1990s, a shift in Saudi attitude was detectable. King Faisal was under growing pressure by his fellow Arabs to impose an oil boycott, and while he had no intention of cutting production as the Libyans had done, he could not increase it to the extent the Americans wanted.

If the Americans needed Saudi oil, the Saudi regime required the political and military help of the United States even more badly if it was to survive. Still, the demand for oil ensured that Faisal was bound to carry weight in Washington. The Saudis, in turn, cautioned that the Arab policy should be to threaten nonexpansion of oil production rather than sudden cuts, since these might cause the Americans and Europeans to take drastic action, perhaps even seize and internationalize the Arabian oil fields. Applying gradual pressure, on the other hand, would probably induce greater willingness on the part of the West to fulfill the demands of the Arabs. Sadat, it seems, accepted this viewpoint and did not press then for cuts in supply.

It is not known to what extent Faisal was drawn into Sadat's confidence about his war plans, and it is probable that he discussed the October campaign only in terms of a possible war in the not-too-distant future and what eventualities could arise in that event. Some, like Heykal, suggested that Egypt should try to evince Saudi support, while carefully avoiding any suggestion of a Cairo-Riyadh axis, which was bound to cause problems with the more radical Arab states such as Syria, Libya, and Algeria.

Central to the concept of the war against Israel was the notion of reactivating the eastern front. King Hussein had effectively restored his rule in Jordan after his "crack" Arab Legion soundly defeated the Palestinians, who had become almost an alternative government in his small desert kingdom. He was, however, still ostracized by most of the Arab world as a result of what was called "Black September." Throughout his struggle, Hussein had retained the tacit support of the Saudis, who wanted to bring about a reconciliation between him and the Palestinians; and they might have succeeded but for the murder in Cairo of the Jordanian prime minister, Wasfi el Tal, by a group of Palestinians. The Egyptians arrested the culprits but later let them go free, which further estranged Jordanian-Egyptian relations.

A gradual rapprochement between the two countries began with visits by Jordanian envoys to Cairo in June and July, and to Damascus. In early August 1973, Sadat's personal representative, Hassan Sabri al Khouli, went to Amman, and upon his return declared that he had tried to create the conditions "for the sale of the cause for which we work on all levels—namely the battle." When Mustafa Tlas, the Syrian defense minister, went to Amman on August 29 to patch their own bad relations, it was evident to Israel that something was afoot. These contacts culminated in a Cairo meeting on September 12 between Sadat, Hussein, and Assad, the Syrian president, and diplomatic relations between them all were renewed.

The Jordanians commented on the Cairo meeting with considerable caution, stressing "national responsibility," "dialogue," and "consultation," but adding their gladness that relations with other Arab countries had again been normalized. While the war was certainly discussed at the Cairo meeting, it is doubtful whether Sadat in conversation with Hussein committed himself to a certain date and whether Hussein committed himself to any particular strategy. Jordan's army was small, though probably the best of the Arab armies for all that; it lacked heavy tanks and effective air support, though. With a long border to defend, Hussein did not commit himself in Cairo to taking an immediate part in the assault against Israel, although just by making threatening noises he would compel the Israelis to keep some forces in readiness along the Jordan River and south of Jerusalem. These forces would then be denied participation in the battles in Sinai or the Golan Heights. Thus Jordan would provide indirect assistance to both Egypt and Syria. According to Arab sources, however, Hussein also promised that his armor would attack the Israeli town of Bet She'an, a few miles across the border, once the Syrians had seized the Golan Heights.

After the Palestinian bases had been destroyed in Jordan and their freedom of action curbed in Lebanon, the Palestinians had been allowed to operate from Syrian territory, although they knew it would provoke Israeli retaliatory action. There had been heavy fighting on the Syrian-Israeli border in November 1972, and a day-long battle had been fought on January 8, 1973. Then Damascus Radio had called in vain to the other Arab states not to let Syria stand alone and take the enemy blows. It was, therefore, an embittered President Assad who was drawn into Sadat's confidence soon after the failure of Ismail's mission to Washington. The Egyptian security affairs adviser had visited Damascus on April 2, and again on May 8. In June, Sadat flew to the Syrian capital for talks with Assad, and then in July it was announced by the Syrian foreign minister that Egypt and Syria were agreed on a common policy.

During the weeks of August there were several meetings between high-ranking Egyptian and Syrian military leaders, and by the time the tripartite pact was signed with Jordan on September 12, the details of military cooperation between them had been worked out. The following day, however, had seen the spectacular disaster to the Syrian Air Force, in which it lost thirteen aircraft to Israel. It was a severe blow to Syrian prestige, particularly in Jordanian eyes, and to Assad personally, as the air force had been his own power base.

That incident also had repercussions among the Israeli forces. Their 4th Battalion, which was one of two regular battalions of the Barak Armored Brigade, had been in the front line along the Golan Heights for several months. Their tanks were distributed by platoons of three tanks each along the line, sited in close support of the fortifications established there, to deal with a possible Syrian breakthrough between them. On September 13, following the air battle off the Syrian coast, the entire 4th Battalion was alerted to watch carefully for any sign of Syrian retaliation, which usually happened after an incident. But apart from moving forward more troops to strengthen their front, increasing the number of artillery batteries, and moving forward their antiaircraft system to cover the area from Damascus to the southern Golan, the Syrians did nothing. Rather like Sherlock Holmes with the dog that didn't bark, the Israelis should have been alerted by the negative response that perhaps something bigger was being planned. Headquarters of the 4th Battalion in Kuneitra ordered an increase in their patrols, and plans were initiated to deal with the usual day's artillery and tank battles.

The Golan Heights overlook Israel's northern border, from the Upper Jordan Valley on the Sea of Galilee in the west, the Yarmuk Valley in the south, the Ruqqad stream in the east, and on the Hermon massif in the north, an area of over 400 square miles. The Golan plateau rises gently from 600 feet in the south to 3,000 feet in the north, its abrupt escarpments dominating the valley to the west and south. It is a rugged volcanic area where ancient lava flows from cracks and fissures have covered the plateau with a continuous layer of basalt. Volcanic cones, or "tels," stand out like so many giant anthills overlooking the harsh landscape, and make natural strong points.

Only a few routes lead up from the Jordan Valley in Israel to the escarpment, the main approach rising from Zemach to El Al on two roads, one via El Hamma and the second via Ein

Gev-Givat Yoav, known as the Gamla Rise. This route contin-
ues northeast through Ramat Magshimim and Juhader to the
Rafid crossroads; it was to prove one of the main invasion routes
for the Syrians. From the crossroads the route runs on north to
Israeli-occupied Kuneitra, the main town of the Golan, where it
joins the Kuneitra-Damascus road. A second route leads from
the Arik Bridge over the Jordan River near its confluence with
the Sea of Galilee in the Buteiha Valley. This road rises in a
series of gravelly hairpin bends through Yehudia to Kuzabia.
Here it forks, leading either northward to the strategically
important Nafekh crossroads—where there was an important
Israeli base—on the main Kuneitra-to-Damascus road, or to
Hushniyah, another major Israeli military area.

The ancient route connecting northern Galilee with Damascus crosses the Jordan River at the Bnot Ya'akov Bridge, whence
the road climbs breathlessly up the escarpment to the upper Syrian customshouse, then via the strategic Nafekh crossroads to
Kuneitra. To the north, another road from Kibbutz Gonen
climbs the escarpment to the Wasset crossroads, passing Kuneitra to the north along the main road to Damascus, or forking
north of that town and leading through the Druse village of
Masadah on the road to Mount Hermon, which dominates the
approaches from Syria. The essential difference between Sinai
and the Golan was the need in the north to control these roads
to enable armor to be deployed rapidly across the exposed and
barren Heights, either south into Israel or north into Damascus.
The Heights controlled the flow of forces both north and south.

The Israeli and Syrian front lines were separated by a strip of
no-man's-land only some 0.5 to 1 mile wide along most of its
length. This so-called "Purple Line"—established between Israel
and Syria after the cease-fire in 1967—is a good military line,
sited along a watershed. To the east the escarpment commands
the Syrian Valley, both for observation and fire, while in the
south the Ruqqad escarpment dominates the Yarmuk River
Valley.

In 1972, Maj. Gen. Yitzhak Hofi had been appointed commander-in-chief of Northern Command. In analyzing the military problem posed to him by his new command, Hofi realized that the main difficulty was that the Israeli and Syrian armies were facing each other on an open plain, without any physical obstacle to delay the advance of an invading army. The Syrians favored this situation, which conformed to the Soviet doctrine of an army that contemplated launching an attack.

For most of the year the Syrians maintained a fully mobilized army on an emergency footing, alerted, ready to go to war, and concentrated in the area stretching from the cease-fire line back to Damascus. The bulk of their forces was constantly in alert positions, although the Syrians did thin their line during the winter when the heavy snow and rain turned the soil into a morass, rendering it impassable at times even for armored vehicles. Then part of the Syrian force was moved east of Damascus to train.

Unlike that of the Egyptians, the Syrian Air Force did not have to alter any of its bases after the Six Day War, so the warning period available to Israel in the event of a Syrian air attack had not changed either, and was a potential danger to the civilian population. In addition, the Soviet Union supplied **FROG** (Free Rocket Over Ground) battlefield support missiles, which had a range of up to 55 miles and could easily reach the Israelis' population centers. The Golan Heights, with some fifteen Israeli civilian settlements, and the Huleh Valley settlements in Israel, remained within range of Syrian artillery, a problem which the Six Day War had eliminated on Israel's other borders. Most dangerous of all, the Syrian defensive system was constructed so that they could immediately deploy for attack without much movement of forces or warning of any kind.

The basic Israeli defensive concept was to hold the line with the comparatively small forces of her standing army, basing their operations on massive support from the air force to give time to mobilize the reserves. A system of seventeen solidly built fortifications constructed to take considerable punishment had been built along the "Purple Line," south from the Hermon. Manned by an average of fifteen soldiers each, they were well protected by mines and wire obstacles, and organized as fighting "hedge-hogs" with their own infantry support weapons. Behind each was a platoon of tanks. The entire system was designed to deal with major outbreaks of artillery and tank fire, and to act as a warning and blocking force in the event of attack. A brigade district was responsible for the line. The overall Israeli defense system was based on the assumption of advance intelligence warning, allowing for mobilization of reserves in time and enabling the forces assigned to the Golan to be in a position to meet any attack. This would have created the traditional ratio between the Arab and Israeli forces of roughly 2½ or 3 to 1 in favor of the Arabs. But, as will be seen, the system did not work that way when the time came, and very slender Israeli forces were left to cope with a massive invasion.

During 1972-73, Northern Command had built many new roads, as well as hundreds of miles of unpaved tracks to facilitate the deployment of artillery and the movement of tanks. On the suggestion of Brig. Gen. "Raful" Eytan, who assumed command of all the Golan Heights at the outbreak of war, the mobilization centers of the tank brigades intended to defend the Heights were advanced from rear areas to nearer the Heights; this was to greatly offset some of Israel's other failures. The action followed exercises which had revealed that the mobilization period required could be halved by these preparations. All the brigades in the command were put through exercises in order to gauge the exact periods of time required to move along the various axis built to the front line. Following major incidents in the winter of 1972-73, improvement and lengthening of an antitank ditch along the "Purple Line" was also carried out, to slow down any enemy advance and to channel their tanks into planned armored killing grounds. A series of tank positions and ramps was built to enable the tanks to cover the antitank obstacles by fire; these were to prove invaluable in due course.

Border fighting in the previous winter had given Northern Command real battle experience, and in the pitched battles that took place, Israeli tanks hit practically all the Syrian tanks that were deployed. In a second major flareup, however, the Syrians had introduced "Sagger" antitank missiles with which they succeeded in knocking out a number of Israeli tanks. Lessons had been learned, though, and mortars were allocated to the armored forces that dealt with the Syrian infantry operating the missiles.

So it was that in September 1973, the Golan was held by only a single brigade with two infantry battalions in the line supported by four artillery batteries, backed by the Barak Armored Brigade, with one battalion in the line and one battalion in the rear for training.

But after the 1967 War, the Syrians had also begun to apply the lessons they had learned, developing a highly concentrated system of antitank defenses from the "Purple Line" right back to Damascus. They carried out a series of large-scale exercises, which culminated in an exact replica of the Yom Kippur War attack. Israeli observers noted that Syrian training was being concentrated on the subjects of bridging antitank ditches, breaching obstacles and minefields, and making a major breakthrough. It was soon clear that the entire Syrian force had been geared to constituting one large antitank obstacle. The Syrians, meanwhile, had established positions designed to block Israeli penetration with static, almost obsolete T-34 tanks in built-in positions, supported by heavy concentrations of 57mm and 85mm antitank guns, dual-purpose 100mm guns deployed all along the line in massive fortifications, while the units all had the RPG bazooka-type antitank weapon at platoon level and Sagger antitank missiles at brigade level.

Early in the summer of 1973, the Syrians had thinned out their forces in the line—a reversal of the normal practice of strengthening the line in the summer months. The eight hundred tanks which faced approximately sixty Israeli tanks in the line were reduced to four hundred, and the eighty artillery batteries, opposed to a mere four Israeli ones, dropped to forty. But, on September 11, Israeli reconnaissance aircraft brought back photographs which showed that the line had been reinforced, and that there was a force of 550 tanks with 69 batteries of artillery.

The summer of 1973 had eventually given way to the halcyon days of autumn, and everyday life in Israel went on with an unaccustomed sense of well-being and a rare feeling of confidence. There was not even a great deal of excitement in their current general election campaign and the hustings were poorly attended. After work, or at the weekend, the average Israeli went to the local cinema to see the popular thriller, *The Day of the Jackal*. At the Habima Theater in Tel Aviv Tennessee Williams's torrid *Cat on a Hot Tin Roof* was playing, while, elsewhere, in a more cheerful mood, *The Merry Wives of Windsor* was romped through in true bucolic style.

Although it is not known precisely when the Soviet Union was told the exact date the war would begin, nevertheless their envoys and military advisers must have known about Sadat's preparations from the very beginning since they helped the Arabs work out their strategy. On September 22, certainly, Sadat called in the Soviet ambassador, Vinogradov, and handed him a note for Brezhnev; it seems very likely that this message contained the date that had been set for the attack. Although Brezhnev answered immediately, the contents were never disclosed. Therefore, the Soviet leaders had virtually two weeks to decide about their tactics with regard to the West, the United Nations, and the Third World. From then on events began to move against a background of increasingly strident Soviet broadcasts, accusing Israel of massing troops along Syria's borders and the Suez Canal. Because of increasing Israeli isolation in the face of Arab solidarity—the Soviet commentators intoned—Israel might launch a surprise attack. This was a clever, if not very subtle, Soviet move to throw dust in the eyes of all those easily duped Third World countries who could be relied upon for raucous support in the United Nations at the twitch of their strings.

Had they so desired, the Soviets could have forestalled a new Middle East war, simply by informing Washington in the best spirit of their own much acclaimed détente. Had they done so, Washington would have told the Israelis and, almost certainly, the Arabs would have backed away. That the Russians did not do so is indicative of their use of détente as an aid to Russia's long-term strategy and their collusion with the Arabs to destroy Israel. In all probability the overall Soviet strategy saw the war not as a means by which the Arabs would win back their occupied territories, but rather as provoking another Arab defeat, which would on this occasion provide a *raison d'être* for massive Soviet intervention to control the Middle East.

Their preparedness was further underlined when, on October 3, just three days before the war began, the Soviets began launching satellites. Cosmos 596 was the first, put into an orbit that took it periodically over the Middle East, where the clear atmosphere afforded perfect vision for the cameras. The Soviets went on to launch five more spy satellites over the period of the war, bringing them back at intervals of a few days to recover the films. As will be seen, President Sadat was to become incensed when the Russians failed to pass on the information to him; clearly, it was intended for their own use.

It must be admitted, however, that the United States also had two satellites that passed above the area and that also collected information, including the 14-ton "Big Bird," which sent its pictures back by radio. They almost certainly passed information to Israel, although it seems probable they did not do so until the war turned very much against the Israelis.

By the end of the second week of September, while the Arab and Eastern Bloc radio stations blasted forth, most Israeli families were preparing for the approaching high holy days of the Jewish New Year and several days' holiday. Not everyone looked forward to a rest, though, and the troops of the 4th Battalion on the Golan Heights became resigned to spending the holidays in a high state of readiness in case the Syrians attacked.

On September 24, General Hofi, who succeeded Yitzhak Rabin as commander of the Northern Command, left his headquarters at the Israeli-occupied city of Kuneitra for a General Staff meeting at Tel Aviv, taking with him that morning's air reconnaissance photographs, which revealed that the Syrians had deployed three infantry divisions in emergency dispositions, each with two infantry brigades forward, supported by a tank and mechanized brigade. In all, the Syrian force had risen to 670 tanks and 100 artillery batteries. At the General Staff meeting, the chief of intelligence and his aides presented an evaluation of the border situation, at which Hofi pointed out that there seemed to be no chance his command would receive a warning in the event of an attack. This viewpoint clearly disturbed Defense Minister Dayan, who asked Chief of Staff Gen. David Elazar for details of what was being done about that situation. Dayan stressed the importance of constructing an artificial obstacle, whereupon Hofi described the extensive minefields his command was already laying along the antitank ditch.

The following day, Dayan and Elazar went to see for themselves what was being done along the parched Golan Heights front line. The team of officers, including Hofi, surveyed the Syrian dispositions stretching away beneath them, and saw that around Kudne, 2 miles from the border and within range of Israeli 80mm mortars, the Syrians had concentrated medium artillery, which they took as a clear indication of their intention to attack. This was a grave development. The General Staff's immediate response was to order elements of the 7th Armored Brigade to move up the Golan Heights into reserve positions. An emergency stand-to was ordered in the Brigade District, leaves were canceled, and on its own accord Brigade Headquarters manned the mobilization centers ten days before it was actually ordered to do so.

Tension was rising along the northern border, and on the eve of Rosh Hashanah — the New Year — Col. Avigdor Ben-Gal, the lanky, aristocratic-looking commander of the elite 7th Armored Brigade, was told to move one of his battalions to the Golan Heights to reinforce the Barak Brigade, already holding the line. Ben-Gal was disturbed about the situation and had already reached the personal conclusion that something was about to happen, probably on Yom Kippur. He formed this opinion from past experience that whenever hostile action had occurred, they were given little time for preparation: Yom Kippur was an obvious choice, for Israel would be at her least prepared. Determined that his brigade, at least, would not be taken unawares, Ben-Gal ordered his artillerymen to reconnoiter the Heights, study the terrain and the enemy's dispositions, prepare their targets accordingly, and note the coordinates. While his gunners worked on the Heights, he meanwhile called together his battalion commanders to go over all the operational planning they had previously carried out in Northern Command. Then, on his own initiative, and without his superiors' knowledge, Ben-Gal took his senior officers for a day's outing along the front line to observe every position, study the ground, and think out their plans.

The New Year celebrations went ahead on September 26 and 27 in an unprecedented heat wave that sent temperatures soaring well above 100 degrees F. Many people stayed home, trying to keep cool in shuttered or curtained rooms, but still tens of thousands braved the blazing heat to speed along the hot-smelling tarmacadam road across Sinai to the southern resorts of Eilat and Sharm el-Sheikh, seeking in vain a respite from the debilitating heat. On Rosh Hashanah, September 26, the sun-baked Golan Heights were thronged with tourists eager to spend a few hours gazing with shaded eyes across the dried and shriveled grasses and briar-strewn slopes. Thousands of picnickers with their cars crowded the roads, holding up the big, three-axled army trucks that jerked and revved their way up hairpin bends, their tightly laced canvas hoods hiding war stores.

Ruth Salmon, an American Jewish tourist, recalls that her hosts from Haifa drove her north to see the Golan Heights that day. As they climbed the steeply winding roads, "We had to pull over while giant tank-transporter trucks roared upward carrying enormous sand-colored tanks, their exhausts pouring out thick black smoke so that we stifled in the car with the windows closed. No one said anything, but my hosts exchanged knowing glances, and I don't think anyone really doubted that trouble was brewing."

Families were reunited during the holiday. Eytan Gissen, who had returned to Israel from Syracuse University, New York, to do his military service, was on a few days' leave from his crack reconnaissance unit. He told his father "there was going to be another war — but, Arieh, his father, didn't believe it and joked and laughed at him before he left." His family was never to see him again.

For the next ten days, between Rosh Hashanah and the holiest of Jewish days, Yom Kippur, the 4th Battalion's troops joined with other forces in the line of fortifications, laying hundreds of mines, improving their weapons pits and emplacements, and extending the great antitank ditch along the Heights. In the most forward positions, artillerymen and observers crouched in sandbagged dugouts clutching radio handsets on which they reported the massing of Syrian forces. At their troop headquarters, coordinates and distances were carefully marked on maps, and batteries lined up on possible targets. The entire system, which had proved so effective in past conflagrations, moved smoothly into action.

After the holiday, Israeli newspapers reported that during the four days things were absolutely calm. Not one incident or a single case of suspected activity was reported in Israel, either along her borders or in the administered zones (the Israeli term for the occupied territories). But, as the superheated air was slowly but surely piling up the thunderclouds, so politically this was the silence before the storm.

In Cairo, Sadat took the opportunity of the anniversary of Nasser's death, September 28, to make a speech at the end of which he referred to the confrontation with Israel. "I have deliberately not broached the subject of the battle," he said, "because there has been enough talk." He was promising nothing, nor was he willing to discuss any details. All they should know was that the liberation of the land was the first, main task facing Egypt, and, God willing, they would achieve this aim. Such restrained language was unusual and might have aroused Israeli suspicion, except that in Israel it was thought to be just another stage in Sadat's retreat from his promises to go to war. For some days

Egyptian troops had been seen playing about on the Canal in rubber dinghies and other small craft, and although the Israelis were puzzled by this, little was apparently thought of it. In retrospect it is easy to collect such evidence indicating an attack, and it must be said that many soldiers believed one to be imminent; but the majority of Israelis were quite unaware of what was happening along their borders, and to them the situation seemed very quiet indeed. The Syrian troop movements did, it is true, give cause for alarm, and a state of emergency was declared in some of the new settlements in the north of Israel. But this, too, had happened many times before and was taken for a sensible precaution, nothing more.

Nevertheless, in both Cairo and Damascus the propaganda war was heating up in preparation for the attack, and toward the end of the month the Arab media published news items about "heavy Israeli troop concentrations," including tanks and heavy artillery. According to the Syrian press, Israel was preparing for a new military adventure; the Iraqis reported Israeli violations of Lebanese airspace; other Arab sources announced that 1,800 members of the Moroccan expeditionary force had now taken position on the Golan Heights. "Israel will not frighten us," said the Arab press. The alarms sounded in the Arab capitals were not unusual. The Israeli press merely noted in passing the fact that the Egyptians declared a state of alert on October 2 in the northern and central sectors of the Canal, "due to Israeli concentrations," having been advised by military spokesmen not to give it undue publicity.

All the same, among the military in Israel many were increasingly aware of the growing danger. Lt. Benjamin Siman Tov, Southern Command's order of battle officer, sent his intelligence superior, Lt. Col. David Gedaliah, an analysis of the Egyptian deployment. He stressed that this clearly indicated war preparations, but nothing happened because Gedaliah did not distribute Tov's analysis.

Early on Tuesday, October 2, Israeli Phantoms roared across the Golan Heights to sweep low over the Syrian lines, their high-speed cameras whirring. They dodged the desultory Syrian flak and hurtled back to their bases, where teams rushed to retrieve the films and develop the vital pictures. These showed unmistakably that Syrian forces had grown to 800 tanks and 108 batteries of artillery. For the first time, too, all the Syrian infantry brigades were in their emergency positions in full force, and their entire surface-to-air missile system was manned, stretching roughly parallel to the Damascus-to-Sheikh Meskin road.

In the south, the commencement of extensive Egyptian maneuvers along the Canal was observed by Israeli forces, and a growing stream of information about these activities flowed back to headquarters almost hourly. Lt. David Abu Dirham, commanding *Orkal B*, one of the most southerly fortifications, 5 miles south of Port Fuad, reported that a ship was unloading artillery equipment and ammunition. Reports came in, too, of artillery being moved into forward positions, and of unoccupied surface-to-air and surface-to-surface missile positions that were now being occupied. Minefields were being cleared along the Canal to facilitate troop movements and Egyptian soldiers were diving into the water to blow up submerged mines. Still more reports described improvement work going on to the various descents to the water, earth-moving activity, preparation of areas for crossings and for bridges and pontoons. It was all so obvious ... yet they also reported Egyptian troops in casual clothes fishing and wandering the banks.

But the maneuvers worried Maj. Gen. Avraham (Albert) Mandler, who commanded the armored division at the southern end of the Canal. He placed his 280 tanks on alert. Southern Command headquarters ensured that all standing orders for an alert were carried out, mobilization systems were checked, and leaves canceled. Despite the reluctance of the politicians, the soldiers were growing itchy.

It was on Tuesday, too, that Maj. Gen. Shmuel Gonen, recently appointed commander of Southern Command, visited the Canal and afterwards ordered a higher state of alert. Gonen sought permission from his High Command to initiate a number of precautionary steps, but the political leadership was already anxious to avoid giving the Arabs an opportunity to blame their own actions on Israeli aggression, and limited Gonen's preparations. He was allowed to increase the guards and security around the Sinai bases, and to check that Operation *Shovach Yonim*, the Israeli counteroperation plan in the event of an Arab attack, was familiar to their forces. It was at this point, four days before the outbreak of war, that instructions were given to assemble a pre-constructed bridge in preparation for a possible Israeli Canal crossing, significant in view of subsequent Israeli strategy.

By this time, however, at Southern Command headquarters, Siman Tov was far from sanguine at what he clearly saw as the growing Egyptian threat. He submitted another report to Gedaliah, but again to no avail. In fact, Gedaliah omitted Tov's findings altogether from the Southern Command intelligence summaries, and these important warnings only came to light in March 1977, when an Israeli commission investigated their near disaster in the Yom Kippur War. It was not until around midnight on Thursday, October 4, that Gedaliah seems to have finally realized the danger, and at 1:00 A.M. on Friday, he went to his commander, General Gonen. Gonen was at Haifa, following a staff meeting in Tel Aviv the previous day, when Gedaliah hurried in with the information that the Egyptians had been working on their ramparts until 10 P.M. the previous evening. This, he warned, indicated imminent action, but he still did not disclose Tov's analyses.

When dawn lit the monotony of water, sand, and concrete along the Canal that morning—the eve of Yom Kippur—the Egyptians had further increased their offensive readiness. An additional 56 artillery batteries had been towed in, bringing the total to a powerful 194 batteries. All five infantry divisions were fully deployed. Five concentration areas were ready for bridging and Canal-crossing equipment. They had completed tank ramps on which T-55s menaced the entire length of the Canal with their 100mm guns, while Soviet-supplied PT-76 amphibious tanks and armored personnel carriers were drawn up along demarcated lines. Mobile GSP pontoon units could be rapidly swung into use.

It was obvious to the Israeli staff officers by Friday that an attack was imminent from Syria too. Reconnaissance showed that their tank force had increased to over 900, while the artillery force reached 140 batteries, including heavy groups equipped with great 130mm and 150mm guns—an overwhelming advantage over the Israelis. An additional armored brigade was identified along the southern sector of the Golan front. But to Northern Command the most ominous indications of the Syrian intention to attack was that in all the phases of this massive buildup they had not occupied their second line of defense—a clear and unquestionable indication of an assault. On the instruction of General Elazar, the Israeli chief of staff, the Israeli general headquarters ordered the highest state of alert for their standing army. By late that same day, the Israeli force on the crucial Golan had increased to 177 tanks and 11 batteries of artillery—not much in the face of the Syrian might. Northern Command also advanced its headquarters up to the Golan Heights in readiness.

Like many Israelis, reserve officer Maj. Gen. Dan Laner was getting ready for the Yom Kippur holiday at Neot Mordechai Kibbutz, near the Golan Heights. General Hofi telephoned him there from Nafekh to advise that trouble was expected. After confirming that he would be at the kibbutz, Laner rang off, only to ponder why Hofi was in Nafekh. He rang back and offered him a meal at the kibbutz, but it was declined. Now thoroughly convinced that something was about to happen, Laner called his divisional operations officer and told him to report on Saturday morning.

As Dayan recalled it, "At the weekly meeting of the General Staff on Friday, October 5, we decided to order 'C' alert, the highest alert for the army, and a full alert for the air force. I asked for direct telephone lines to my senior ministry officials, and they were to spend Yom Kippur at home." At 9:45 A.M. Dayan met the prime minister, Mrs. Golda Meir, taking with him Elazar and Maj. Gen. Eliahu Zeira, the head of intelligence. They explained to Mrs. Meir the steps already taken. Between them, Zeira and Elazar gave details of the situation at the fronts, that both Egyptian and Syrians were at emergency stations, but admitting that they "seemed well for defense and equally well for launching an invasion." Their conclusion, however, was that an attack was not likely, basing this upon a belief that if war was imminent, there would be further indications and intelligence reports. Only then, they affirmed, would additional measures, including mobilization of reserves, become necessary. Intelligence thought it "most improbable that the Egyptians would cross the Canal in large forces, though they might open fire and attempt raids." Both men pointed out that American Intelligence had concluded neither Syria nor Egypt intended to attack in the near future.

This left Dayan less than happy. He stressed that, political intentions apart, the military deployment of both Arab countries enabled them to start a war within hours, and he requested that Mrs. Meir give authority for mobilization of reserves the next day if she should be asked to do so. She agreed to this. At the end of the cabinet meeting, Dayan also obtained her agreement to call a cabinet meeting at 11:30 A.M. on the following day, Yom Kippur. Mrs. Meir nodded, confirming that she would be spending the day in Tel Aviv anyway.

And so, as Friday wore on, the Israelis cautiously prepared for the onslaught. All reserve units received advanced warning to be prepared for mobilization, and all regular mobilization staffs were confined to camp ready to mobilize; key personnel were returned from leave. Danny Stein had only been married a few days when a message was relayed from his family to his honeymoon hotel at Eilat that he was to return immediately. He and his new wife drove back, he recalls, in near silence. Soon he was changed into uniform and taking leave of his recent bride.

All mobilized women and civilians in the army were removed from the Brigade District in the Golan, as was invariably the case when heavy artillery exchanges were expected. The military

government staff in occupied Kuneitra was cut down and a reinforcement of doctors and medical personnel moved into the forward areas. Meanwhile, forward elements of the brigade on the
gentle northern slopes of the Heights reported the movement of
giant convoys toward the border, but they received no clear
indications from intelligence as to the overall picture.

Nevertheless, Israeli reinforcements were trickling through to
the Golan Heights; artillery batteries arrived, increasing the
Israeli presence. At about noon, Lieutenant Colonel Yair, the 4th
Battalion commander, received orders at Kuneitra canceling all
leaves for his forces. The 4th Battalion, which with the 5th
formed the Barak Armored Brigade, was responsible for holding
the front south to Tel Hazeika, some 4 miles from Kuneitra;
with an additional company from the 5th Battalion under command, this force amounted to thirty-two tanks. The further
southern extension from Tel Hazeika was held by forty tanks,
including another 5th Battalion company. The remainder of the
5th Battalion held the rest of the line from its headquarters at
Juhader, 4 miles southwest of the key Rafid opening. All that
day, Yair's men had been occupied improving the fortifications,
while volunteers from the *Habad* movement, an orthodox Has-
sidic sect, mingled with them to organize prayers and fasting for
the following holiest day of the Jewish year, the Day of
Atonement.

At the same time, Ben-Gal's 7th Brigade headquarters also
received orders putting them on the highest state of readiness.
This was a relief to Ben-Gal who, in anticipation of the move,
had already dispatched part of his advance headquarters to the
Golan. His intuition was vindicated, for something very serious
was about to happen and his brigade was already racing against
time. Furthermore, conditions on the dusty roads northward to
the Golan and the "Purple Line" were already difficult, with tremendous amounts of traffic congesting the winding hill routes as
personnel, vehicles, and ammunition all moved north. In the forward areas, the battalions that had arrived began preparing the
tanks received from reserve forces, checking them over and

ammunitioning them. The 2nd Battalion moved off that night to take up positions at Sindiana, just forward of the main Israeli headquarters at Nafekh Camp and a mile beyond the Tapline (*T*rans-*A*rabian *P*ipeline), the oil pipeline that crosses Israel. On Saturday morning 1st Battalion was to move to avoid confusion. By noon it would be in position on the Wasset crossroads, north of Nafekh and a few miles behind the line at Kuneitra, from where it could be deployed in several directions as needed.

Meanwhile, in Cairo, the final preparations were being made, and Sadat again saw Soviet Ambassador Vinogradov, to report on the latest details for the Arab onslaught against Israel. The Russians had already nearly completed the evacuation of the families of Soviet advisers. Since the previous day, great Antonov AN-12 transports had been airlifting families from what would be a war zone within hours. Ominously, too, they launched more of their satellites in the final hours before the attack.

So, as night fell, warm and dusty from the heat wave, quiet descended upon the land of Israel as its people prepared for the one day in the year when the majority of Jews the world over unite in fast and prayer. All work ceased; buses, private cars, and trucks were driven into garages or parked, for they would not be needed the following day — the most solemn for the Jewish people, their Day of Atonement.

CHAPTER

4

The Day of Atonement

It was 4:00 A.M. on Saturday, October 6, still dark and very quiet in the hours just before dawn. In the Israeli countryside even the nightjars had ceased their whirring and the cicadas were silenced. At his home in Zahala, near Tel Aviv, Defense Minister Moshe Dayan slept with his second wife of only four months. Then the telephone rang, its note sudden and urgent, disturbing the warm darkness. It kept ringing until Dayan stretched out an arm and answered it, speaking quietly so as not to disturb his wife.

There was nothing unusual in his being awakened, for he often took two or three calls a night. But this time, after listening for only a few moments, he was intensely alert and rapped out several sharp questions. The caller from Military Intelligence repeated that according to information just received, "before sundown on this very day Egypt and Syria would launch a new war," as Dayan recalled the message.

He made sure that the dramatic news had been relayed to the prime minister, then arranged for Gen. David Elazar, the chief of staff, to meet him in his office at the Defense Ministry at 6:00 A.M. There was, he reflected as he swung from his bed, a lot to do in the next two hours. There would be a lot more to do before sundown and the predicted Arab assault, which they assumed would begin at around 6:00 P.M.

While the senior defense chiefs were hastening to their offices and alerting subordinates, the diplomatic scene was active, too. By around 6:00 A.M., diplomatic representatives in Israel were informed of the expected attack, beginning with the envoy of the United States, which had sponsored the cease-fire. The ambassador was informed that Israel did not intend a preemptive strike and would, therefore, bear the sacrifice which that renunciation implied. It was a dangerous decision, but with world opinion likely to be divided between outright opposition to Israel and fear of losing Arab oil, it was necessary to avoid any implication of being the aggressor, as had happened in 1967. The options then, too, had been to make the first strike or be obliterated; Israel had chosen survival and been condemned roundly as the aggressor. On this occasion the greater risk was to be taken—a risk, however, partly offset, at least in Israeli opinion, by the much stronger borders she possessed in 1973. The U.S. government, and later other governments, were invited to inform Cairo and Damascus accordingly, while similar exchanges were taking place in New York at foreign ministerial level.

In New York, a telegram had by then been received by the Israeli foreign minister, Abba Eban, who was there for the United Nations General Assembly. "At 4:00 A.M., Israeli time, 10:00 P.M. in New York," he declared in a later statement, "six hours before the outbreak, a telegram reached me from Jerusalem telling me that authentic information, as well as evidence on the ground, indicated that there was going to be a joint Egyptian and Syrian attack later in the day, with the aim of crossing the cease-fire line at the Suez Canal and the cease-fire line at Golan."

In the meantime, Dayan had quickly readied himself, snatched a cup of coffee, and arranged with his aide-de-camp for his senior staff to be alerted at his ministry. Then he drove to his office. A light breeze was blowing from the Mediterranean that morning, bringing a clean salt tang to the dawn. The sun was rising in the east in an aura of red and gold. There lay the arid desert, stretching interminably into bareness and strangeness, the lands of date and barley, of camels, the land of Islam. This narrow coastal strip of Asia, on the other hand, faced the Mediterranean and the lands of vine and olive, of patient oxen and cultivated fields aglow with oranges.

Jack Zeiklin also left his home at dawn that morning. It was Yom Kippur, the most sacred day in the Jewish calendar, and for nearly everyone it was a public holiday. Jack, an immigrant from Britain ten years before, was still an enthusiastic angler; not being especially religious, he looked forward to a quiet morning's fishing. Stella, his wife, he had left asleep, along with the children. He knew they would be happier staying at home during the heat wave. He drove his small second-hand Fiat away from his home near Haifa and headed for the coast at Kefar Gallim, just to the south. In his fishing basket Jack carried sandwiches, two cans of beer, and a small Japanese transistor radio, which he later thought of as a mixed blessing, for it gave him important though bad news. By the time he had left the city and was winding his way through orange and lemon groves, the sun was rising on a silent and tranquil day of peace when not even the birds sang.

Dayan knew the information from Military Intelligence was reliable; not just a report on Arab field activity but an assessment from the intelligence service concerning the Arab decision to go to war. In the past, similar messages had warned of forthcoming attacks that had then not occurred and were explained away later as Sadat's changes of mind. On this occasion, though, intelligence suggested that if Sadat came to know the Israelis were aware of the forthcoming attack, so obviating the element of surprise, it was possible he would again cancel it. Hence the intense diplomatic activity already set in motion to ensure everyone knew Israel's position. But unknown to Israel and undetected by her intelligence forces, the Arabs had made a last-minute decision to advance their H-hour from 6:00 P.M. to 2:00 P.M. The Israelis had even less time than they realized.

Dawn in Cairo was only a few minutes later than in Tel Aviv. President Anwar Sadat awoke refreshed, having, as he recalled, "slept better on the eve of battle than I had on most nights before." He carried out his usual morning exercises and was relaxed, his mind sharply focused on his special responsibilities on this, his own D-Day.

Egypt's Second Army was by then arrayed in full battle order along the northern half of the Suez Canal: the 18th Infantry Division held the line from Port Said through Kantara to the railway halt at El Balah, just north of the Firdan Bridge, from where the 2nd Infantry Division took over the line south to the important town of Ismailia. From there, the 16th Infantry Division held the line to the northern end of the Great Bitter Lake. South of that position, where the Great Bitter Lake and Canal belly eastward in a great salient, the front was held by the Egyptian Third Army, with two infantry divisions under command; the 7th, responsible for half the remaining section of the Canal, terminating near the Egyptian fortification at Mina; and the 19th, deployed from there south to Port Suez.

These five assaulting infantry divisions each had attached for close support a battalion of 120 tanks, but backing these forces were 3 mechanized and 2 powerful armored divisions. The difference between a mechanized and an armored division lay in the number of tanks deployed—a mechanized brigade having forty-four tanks and an armored brigade ninety-eight. The mechanized divisions each had 2 mechanized brigades and a single armored brigade, totaling 186 tanks, whereas the armored division had 2 armored and only 1 mechanized brigades, giving them 240 tanks. In addition, though, the mechanized divisions had extra artillery and heavy mortars. Altogether, the Egyptians had massed over 1,500 tanks; added to these forces were independent tank brigades, two parachute brigades, twenty-eight battalions of commandos, and a marine brigade.

Facing this massive Egyptian Army along 110 miles of hot and sandy Canal bank were just 436 Israeli soldiers in a series of isolated fortifications, with only 3 tanks actually on the waterline. This meager force was supported by only seven batteries of artillery, although a further seventy guns were due to move in.

Admittedly, the light screening force was supported by an armored division, under General Mandler, with three brigades. But of the tanks planned to be holding the line, only 277 were actually forward in Sinai by lunchtime on the 6th.

Shortly after dawn, General Hofi had been summoned from Northern Command to general headquarters in Tel Aviv, where the commanding officers of all the commands were informed that war would break out that day and that mobilization orders were pending until a meeting with the prime minister. In the meantime, all steps were to be taken to ensure a maximum degree of preparedness and alertness to deal with the threat. The air force was in the final stages of readiness, and the chief of staff had asked for permission to carry out a preemptive strike against Syria. After the meeting, the commanding officers called their respective headquarters urgently to issue preliminary orders. Hofi drove rapidly through the quiet streets of Tel Aviv to the airfield and flew north.

The entire Golan front was placed on a high state of alert; the fortifications were strengthened by an increase of manpower, bringing them up to an average of twenty men per fortification. The 7th Brigade, which had moved up to the Golan Heights, was concentrated in the general area of Nefekh. Orders were issued for the evacuation of civilian villages, but many villagers refused to be moved. With the Syrian Army poised to attack, the general officer commanding the Northern Command became involved in an acrimonious debate with representatives of the villages that would not be evacuated. By midday, however, they did begin to leave, and by evening all the women and children had gone.

At 9:30 A.M., Dan Laner was still at the kibbutz, in attendance at the swimming pool, when General Hofi telephoned to say that the situation was looking serious and he was to go to his divisional headquarters forthwith. Laner left promptly, and not long afterwards learned from Hofi the full extent of the Syrian concentrations. At that time on Saturday morning, Hofi still thought a preemptive strike would be authorized. At midday, Hofi was called away to general headquarters and Laner departed for his own headquarters, having activated his mobilization earlier that morning. Laner was still skeptical that all-out war would begin, having experienced numerous alerts during his time in Sinai. He actually stopped at his kibbutz to collect his bathing suit to occupy his time during the mobilization period.

General Hofi reached general headquarters in Tel Aviv just as General Gonen, commander-in-chief of the Southern Command, was leaving the chief of staff. Hofi reported on the preparations in his command and the progress in mobilization, presenting his plans to hold the Syrian attack. When he took his leave to coordinate several points with the staff, word suddenly came in that the war had begun. Hurrying back to his command with the good wishes of his colleagues ringing in his ears, Hofi took with him General Hod, the former commander of the Israeli Air Force, as his air adviser. He also asked for General Eytan to be instructed to meet him.

Roughly a year before, Eytan had been given command of the division on the Golan Heights. He and Hofi had fought together in many battles in the ranks as parachutists and he was already a legend in Israel. Small, wiry, and determined, with sharp, square features, Eytan was every inch a soldier. He had headed a battalion in the 1956 campaign that had been parachuted to the Mitla Pass in the middle of Sinai, and in the 1967 War had led his brigade in the Northern Divisional Group in Sinai to the Suez Canal. He knew no fear and inspired the men he led. This intrepid veteran had trained with the U.S. Marine Corps in Quantico, Virginia.

At 10:00 A.M. on Saturday, Ben-Gal had met his brigade commanders in Nafekh at the conference with General Hofi, who confirmed intelligence predictions that the Syrians would, indeed, attack that day, probably at around 6:00 P.M. Hofi had assigned to Ben-Gal's 7th Brigade the task of reserve force in the Nafekh area, prepared to counterattack in the northern or southern sectors, or divide to support both. As the conference concluded, Ben-Gal hurriedly drove across the arid track to Sindiana, where he addressed his senior officers, advising them that war was imminent. He then explained in detail the various tasks his forces had been allocated. Thanks to his foresight at the time of Rosh Hashanah, his brigade was ready. Nevertheless, he called a final orders group for 2:00 P.M., which, he assumed, would give the newly arrived 1st Battalion time to organize before the Syrians attacked at 6:00 P.M.

As tension mounted, the Israeli Air Force was ordered to ready its aircraft for a possible preemptive strike. This preparation meant that the aircraft had to be specifically armed for an offensive strike role. The overwhelming numerical superiority of the Arab air forces had obliged Israel to extend her resources by using aircraft in multi-mission roles. The mainstay of the Israeli Air Force is the fighter-bomber, which might be called upon for close-air support of the army or for home defense; even the Israelis' aging Skyhawks were capable of engaging Arab MIG-21s in a dogfight. The Israelis had also been able to compensate for their numerical inferiority by perfecting their maintenance and turn-around time for refueling and rearming, thus making the maximum use of their slender resources. This maintenance ability was to stand them in good stead in the coming conflict, in armor as well as aircraft.

But, following the morning Israeli cabinet meeting, at which a preemptive strike had been ruled out on political grounds, the air force was told at 2:00 P.M. to change its aircrafts' configuration from attack to defense. So, just as the Arab onslaught was about to break upon Israel, both ground and air personnel were feverishly changing aircraft stores and rebriefing aircrews for their new role.

Around noon, Jack Zeiklin recalls that he was sprawled at his chosen fishing spot, near Kefar Gallim, had his line out, and was enjoying the quiet solitude of that most holy day; if he felt any remorse for fishing while most of his relatives and friends were at the synagogue, he did not show it. As he remembered, he was lounging against a warm rock and staring at the twinkling sea. "It seemed very peaceful, and I had the radio playing quietly. It was mostly music, but suddenly the broadcast was interrupted and a voice began dictating messages, the coded recall signals ordering the reserves to mobilize immediately. I was stunned and turned up the radio, but there they were. We were about to go to war. I scrambled to repack my gear, chucked it into the car, and raced back to Haifa." As he did so, Jack saw that the road had begun to fill as reservists hastened to report, making the usually empty roads of Yom Kippur strangely busy.

Back on the Golan Heights, Yair, the commander of 4th Battalion, who was devoted to his troops, sensed that "something big was about to happen" and visited the fortifications early on Yom Kippur, only too mindful of the problems that would be posed by the ratio of forces in the event of a Syrian attack. The *Habad* visitors had been successful in their mission and to Yair's amazement he found all the troops, including the nonreligious ones, fasting and absorbed in prayer: "On Rosh Hashanah it is inscribed and on the Fast Day of Atonement it is sealed and determined how many shall pass away and how many be born; who shall live, and who shall die, whose appointed time is finished, and whose is not. ..." For a while Yair listened, too, then he called the troops together to explain the developments.

He urged them to stop fasting, pointing out that the Syrians invariably began a day of battle at two o'clock in the afternoon because that gave them adequate time to make the initial strike while minimizing the possibility of a major Israeli counterattack. Should the attack break out at two o'clock, they would have almost completed their fast, and their resulting weakness would only endanger them and their comrades. Emphasizing that he could not tell them when their next meal would be, he cajoled them into eating, and ordered them to pack their equipment ready for battle. Then he left for his headquarters. He had rightly anticipated the hour of attack; but, it seems, he was one of the very few to do so, despite past Syrian patterns.

Several hundred miles to the south, in Cairo, Marshal Ali, Egypt's chief of staff, arrived at 1:30 P.M. in an army jeep to collect President Sadat, and together they drove to the operations room. Sadat was resplendent and martial in his military uniform.

Paradoxically, it was for the Arabs, too, a religious period, that of Ramadan, when devout Muslims fast from dawn until nightfall. But Sadat had already taken religious advice on Islamic law and been assured that in the circumstances, fasting could be set aside. Nevertheless, as Sadat took his place with the commander-in-chief seated alongside him, he was disturbed to note an air of abstemious tension. For a moment he looked around, then asked the assembled staff: "Why aren't you smoking? Why isn't anybody having a drink of some kind? This operation requires your utmost attention and concentration." They were all, as Sadat recalls, embarrassed, so he promptly ordered tea for himself and settled back in his armchair to light his own habitual cob pipe; soon he was puffing contentedly. Immediately the tension eased, and with smiles of relief, his staff, too, ordered tea and took out their cigarettes.

However, by 2:00 P.M., despite the smoking and tea-drinking, tension had inevitably risen. Most of the staff were anxiously looking ahead to the coming forty-eight hours, during which the world would either see a resurgent Egyptian Army confidently driving into Sinai, or another débâcle as their army disintegrated amid the sand and stones. Sadat had no such doubts. He was supremely confident that, this time, the training and the equipment would suffice and Israel would be decisively driven back, if not actually defeated.

In the operations room at a few minutes before 2:00 P.M., all eyes were focused upon the clock as it slowly ticked away to H-hour. Then, at the stroke of two, the loudspeakers crackled that the Egyptian aircraft had taken off. Flying low, 222 Egyptian jets streaked over the Canal, bent on wreaking havoc on Israeli command posts, aerial combat headquarters, air defense and electronic jamming centers, liaison points, Hawk missile batteries, and gun emplacements in Sinai. They were especially concerned to knock out the Israeli strongpoint known as *Budapest*, located on the sandbank east of Port Fuad, from which Israel could observe Egyptian naval movements.

It was a tremendous shock to the Israeli troops stationed along the Canal when out of the peace of midday came the shriek of jets and the roar of cannon. Many soldiers were quite unprepared for the onslaught, despite the warnings and leave cancellations; they just did not believe Egypt could do it. One Israeli soldier recalls that he was playing football with a group of friends, having spent his morning duty staring out across empty white sand. "The ball had gone high and landed about thirty meters away against the wall of a building. I trotted across to fetch it when there was a sudden scream of jet engines. Thinking it was our own aircraft going out again on a recce mission, I paid little attention at first, then the air shook with explosions, and spinning around I saw a MIG-17 tearing low across the defenses, loosing bombs and rockets. I dived for cover against the building while the jets machine-gunned before clearing off."

All along the Canal front, the Egyptian jets secured complete surprise. The Israelis took many casualties among their vital command and communications posts; the very points that were supposed to alert the static defenses further back were reeling and confused, with many radio and land links severed.

Even as the Egyptian jets ripped across the Canal and hurtled into Sinai, Arabic commands erupted and with a thunderous roar, 2,000 guns opened a devastating fire across the water. From Port Fuad to Suez, the superheated air was blown apart from the shock waves of the field, medium, and heavy artillery, and an array of medium and heavy mortars added their deep-throated grunts every time they hurled their bombs high over the Canal to pitch into the isolated Israeli positions. A devastating hail of fire and steel swept the East Bank. Over 3,000 tons of destruction were fired against the handful of fortifications, creating an inferno for fifty-three minutes. Tanks swung and ground their way up the ready-prepared ramps atop the sand ramparts, depressed their 100mm guns, and with resounding cracks sent round after round across the Canal. As if this holocaust was not enough, a brigade of FROG surface-to-surface missiles launched its weapons with a belch of fire and fumes to soar high over the water and desert before plunging at supersonic speeds onto Israeli positions, where they arrived with horrifying explosions.

The sirens began to wail while all Israel was observing Yom

Kippur. By tradition, most of the country's soldiers were home on leave. Israel broadcasting had shut down for the day and ambulances were about the only vehicles to raise white dust on the otherwise deserted roads. But, as worshipers began emerging from their synagogues at the end of the five-hour services of atonement, they were startled by a different world. After the quiet solemnity of the cool synagogues, they found the sunlit streets filled with speeding trucks, buses, and jeeps. Israeli broadcasting was back on the air, and throughout the afternoon its programs of classical music and news bulletins would be interrupted by incongruous coded messages for "meat pie," "sea wolf," "yard broom," and "wool string," calling reservists to duty. Husbands, fathers, sons, and brothers, who only hours before had been in civilian clothes, clattered downstairs or out of bedrooms in uniform, pulled on berets, kissed wives, sweethearts, and mothers, and left to fight.

News of the invasion sent Israeli civilians cleaning out their bomb shelters, filling their bathtubs with fresh water, and taping their windows for the blackout. At several synagogues, services were interrupted as the sextons stood up and called out the names of young men who were being summoned to duty. Other worshipers, on hearing the news, quickly folded their prayer shawls and departed; some returned later in uniform to bid their families goodbye. Many Israeli civilians walking home were startled when their own jets swept low over major Israel cities, rattling windows and scaring old folks. They had never flown over before on Yom Kippur and the signal was widely assumed to be a call for air force mobilization.

It was the blazing heat of early afternoon on the Golan Heights when 7th Armored Brigade's orders group met at Ben-Gal's headquarters. The men, mostly very young, were standing about awaiting the commanding officer's arrival when they all caught the sound of aircraft approaching at high speed. Despite the ominous sound, they were still unprepared for the furious onslaught that was unleashed upon them. Syrian MIGs and

Sukhois screamed in power dives, fired their missiles and bombs, and zoomed away as explosions rocked the camp. Even before the officers and men could scramble to their feet amid a rain of debris, shellfire stormed upon their camp as the Syrian guns opened fire. Buildings burst apart in flame, glass and doors flew in murderous jagged sheets, and corrugated roofs scythed through the flames and smoke.

The orders group was abandoned as battalion commanders scrambled into jeeps and raced back to their battalions, swaying and jolting on the rocky roads, dodging the hail of shrapnel and shell. Under the terrific air and artillery bombardment, Ben-Gal moved brigade advance headquarters out of the battered camp and prepared to get his forces into the front line.

Gen. Dan Laner had meanwhile been inspecting his division's mobilization. The first he came to know of the attack was from an officer, who rushed into his office saying that the Syrians had opened fire all along the front. Laner's first thoughts were that his divisional headquarters staff were without the simplest logistic capability and had no means of communication with the formations he hoped would soon be joining the battle. Quickly, he took over seven half-tracked vehicles that happened along, and sent them to a nearby camp to open communications and link the division into the commander's operational network. By then, too, his reserve officers were arriving, although they barely knew what was happening.

Colonel Ben-Gal had an obsession with building reserves and well knew the value of maintaining something in hand, however small. So, while still under the initial Syrian attack, he transferred a single company from one of his battalions and placed it under command of an armored infantry battalion, thereby creating the framework of a third battalion. As more tanks were moved up to him, the new battalion became a proper tank battalion, increasing his ability to maneuver. At that time he also took under his command the 4th Tank Battalion of Lieutenant Colonel Yair, which was already in the line with the fortifications in the northern Golan Heights. With the addition of Yair's tanks, 7th

Armored Brigade entered the battle with about 100 tanks. Ben-Gal then deployed the 1st Battalion from fortification A1 on the "Purple Line" directly east of Masadah, in the foothills of Mount Hermon, south for 4 miles to the Hermonit Hill, a pointed prominence. From there, south to the "Booster" ridge overlooking Kuneitra, he deployed the 5th Battalion.

When Yair arrived at Kuneitra, he received a telephone call from the brigade commander telling him to prepare for heavy artillery concentrations—the Syrians were removing the camouflage nets from more guns. Yair promptly ordered the tanks then in Kuneitra to disperse; it was clear the inevitable day of fighting had commenced in earnest. Judging by the preparations on the other side, they were in for several days of artillery concentrations and tank battles. He issued the code word to all units authorizing them to move up to prepared positions and fire at the advancing enemy. He also directed his own tank to the "Booster," which was a ridge just north of Kuneitra and south of the dominating Hermonit Hill. As he drove up the slopes, the Syrian shelling intensified and Syrian aircraft zoomed down on his forces, bombing and strafing. As far as he could see, the front had become one line of fire, smoke, and dust that rose from the heaviest artillery concentration he had ever seen. Low-flying aircraft sprayed machine-gun fire as they swept in over the Israeli positions, dropping bombs as they pulled away. Across the open hillsides, a wave of Syrian tanks were advancing like a horde of ants. Hurriedly, he shouted orders to his supporting artillery to move into position and open fire against the Syrian concentrations. Speaking in his usual rapid manner, but trying to subdue his voice, Yair ordered his tanks to open fire and wished all the boys good luck. Shells then began exploding around his tank, and it dawned on him that they were in for some bitter fighting.

Back in Sinai, the concentration had been roaring and popping for only fifteen minutes when the first Egyptian jets returned from their bombing missions. Along the Canal their return was the signal for the general water-borne assault to begin. Steel-helmeted troops picked up their rubber assault boats, praised and called to Allah, and charged into the water. Soon the normally placid green water that mirrored the banks was dotted with hundreds of beetle-like craft being propelled by paddles or outboard motors to the eastern bank. The Egyptian troops had little to fear during this initial assault wave from Israeli defenders, who were either dead or reeling under the appalling bombardment that numbed the senses and drove men out of their minds. Boats began nudging into the sand of the East Bank where troops scrambled ashore and struggled, slipping and sliding, to climb up the sun-dried sand to Israeli ramparts. Within minutes the red, white, and black tricolor of Egypt was being hoisted by delirious troops.

The Egyptians had rehearsed every detail of their assault, dozens, and in some cases hundreds of times, and their attack had been prepared in the minutest detail. Each infantry division crossed on a front some 4 to 5 miles wide, the first wave having the task of seizing the Israeli ramparts until the arrival of the second wave, when they were to leave them holding the ramparts, advance 200 yards inland, and dig in. Then, within an hour, third and fourth waves would reinforce the first assault troops, bringing across the support units, including mortars and light artillery, whereupon each battalion would advance inland.

The first assault wave from the Egyptian 7th Brigade landed at points not covered by the Israeli strongpoints. Once on the bank, troops were quickly grouped and they headed inland, simply bypassing any Israeli positions that remained. Their orders were to establish themselves during the day some 1 to 2 miles inland, advancing in a series of moves as the followup waves held the ground behind them; this objective was to be completed by sundown on the first day, before the Israeli Air Force could strike back. Their task, then, would be to hold off any Israeli counterattack while specially trained infantry units crossed the Canal and set about the job of eradicating the isolated Israeli strongpoints. At the same time, the commando forces were to pass through the forward Egyptian infantry positions and penetrate the Israeli lines in the night to harass their troops as they tried to deploy, and to knock out any Israeli tanks as they moved forward. For this they were well equipped, with the RPG anti-tank projectiles as well as new Soviet-supplied missiles. Each bridgehead was to be pushed out in the first stages to 5 miles wide and a depth of 3.5 miles, into which it was planned to pour the armored divisions.

The 4th Armored Division, with the 25th Armored Brigade attached, was to advance inland and seize the vital Giddi Pass in the south, then drive through Um Mahza northward to the Israeli nerve center at Refidim (formerly Bir Gafgafa). Meanwhile, the 21st Armored Division, having landed between Deversoir and Ismailia, would take the northern route through Tassa to drive south to Refidim and complete the powerful combined pincer movement, which would, ideally, eliminate the Israeli stronghold in Sinai within the first days of the war.

In one sector of the Canal, south of Ismailia, the assault forces were confronted by a single Israeli tank, one of the few on the Canal itself. For over an hour this tank confounded every Egyptian attempt to pass or overcome it. Every time the enemy scurried forward, the tank swung its cannon and fired, blowing craters and scattering the infantry, while its waving machine gun chattered. Finally, the cannon fell silent, and while the machine gun kept firing, the Egyptian infantry managed to get around its wicked gun and stormed the tank. The machine gun was silent. But the Egyptian commander himself recounted their amazement when they found that the entire crew had been killed, except for a single wounded soldier who had fought the Egyptians to a standstill; he was evacuated by an Egyptian first aid team.

The surge of Egyptian troops overwhelmed the Israeli defenders. Frantic radiomen called on the second-line defenses. "My God," one hysterical young voice yelled from a bunker, "it's like the Chinese coming across." Another voice babbled: "Hundreds, thousands of Egyptians are swimming toward our fort. We need reinforcements, quickly!"

Omar Shazli, now a student in Britain, was with a unit of the

Egyptian 18th Infantry Division due to cross just south of Kantara. "Our commanders," he recounts, "had tried to get us to relax by issuing sugarcane, which we were supposed to suck like children, but it did not fool many and we all suspected that we would soon be fighting. Many of the officers were to be seen kneeling and praying—an ominous sign."

Near Kantara, where Shazli was to cross, the eastern Canal banks are of sheer rock; even so, they had been topped by the Israelis with another 40 feet of ramparts. Against this formidable barrier, Egyptian commandos made the assault by boat, then scaled the rock walls. "Fortunately," Shazli recalls, "there was not much Israeli fire from two fortifications about three miles apart as both of them were being very heavily shelled at the time of our attack. Our commandos rigged scaling ladders, enabling the infantry to get up the rock banks, and then we crossed the Canal in boats and scrambled to the top of the ramparts. There was a terrific noise from our bombardment, which was exploding all along the Israeli lines. My unit did not stop, though, but was ordered to keep going on to seize the road that runs parallel to the Canal some three and a half miles into Sinai."

But the assaulting Egyptians didn't have it all their own way. When three Egyptian launches tried to cross the Gulf of Suez to land troops on the eastern side of the Gulf, they were intercepted by Israeli fast missile boats, which sank all three.

Once the first assault waves had seized and secured the East Bank, Egyptian engineers brought up high-pressure water pumps, which had been specially made by a West German firm. Not suspecting their true purpose, the manufacturer had jokingly asked whether any fire in the world could require such water-power. These great pumps, which Sadat claims were a "completely Egyptian device" (although the china clay and diamond-mining industries have long used them), were used to cut out passes in the Israeli earthworks, which they did very effectively. Thousands of tons of earth and sand were washed away, causing great sections of the banks to collapse into the Canal. Meanwhile, other units of the Egyptian Engineers Corps were hauling forward the pontoon bridges that would span the Canal, opening up the way for their massed armored divisions to cross over into Sinai and begin their drive on Refidim. As the early Egyptian evening drew on, the situation along the Canal was looking serious for the Israelis.

Several analysts of the October War, or the War of Yom Kippur, have suggested that the chosen date was coincidental and that there was no significance that it was the Jews' most holy day. However, Sadat's autobiography says that in April 1973, at a meeting with President Assad, General el-Gamasy, Egypt's director of operations, suggested three alternative dates in that year for an attack upon Israel: May; August and September; or October. He concluded: "The most suitable of these for several reasons was the last. An attack could coincide with Yom Kippur — the Day of Atonement — on October 6 when all public services in Israel would be suspended." In Russia, too, the official news agency, Tass, was reporting Arab successes within minutes of their happening, a clear indication that the Soviets had prior knowledge of their plans.

CHAPTER

5

The Golan Heights Erupt

Israeli troops on the northern front line along the Golan Heights were at the peak of tension when the Syrian attack burst upon them. A survivor of those first terrifying thirty-six hours related that he was in a forward observation post overlooking the Rafid Gap. "The day was particularly hot and after peering through binoculars across a parched waste of nodding grasses for over an hour, my eyes were watering badly. I remember that I stopped to wipe my eyes and when I settled to look again the country below me had come to life, there were Syrian tanks everywhere."

Reports were soon flooding back to Northern Command headquarters of Syrian tank concentrations moving forward. They were led by engineer tanks equipped with bulldozer blades to clear gaps and make ramps at the antitank ditch for the bridge-carrier tanks that followed: great unwieldy, squat vehicles with girder bridge-spans balanced before them, looking like huge insects feeling their way forward. Behind the engineer and assault tanks came the main force of gun tanks, literally hundreds of them grinding forward over the sparse vegetation and crunching on the rocky tracks. Just behind the gun tanks were hundreds more armored personnel carriers carrying the infantry.

On the windswept "Booster" ridge overlooking Kuneitra, Centurion tanks of Yair's 4th Battalion were in position, their long 105mm guns all pointing menacingly toward the oncoming Syrian armor. Lieutenant Colonel Yair himself stood in the turret of his tank, his fair hair blowing in the stiff breeze, and watched the enemy columns coming at him. Syrian heavy artillery positioned between the strange volcanic "tels" or peaks of Tel Maschara and Tel Hara were plastering his battalion's positions, and the dust and smoke of battle was making it difficult to make out the details. Nevertheless, through the grimy pall Yair could see the shadowy outlines of tank-dozers and bridging tanks rumbling slowly along ahead of the main columns, clearly heading for the antitank ditch. Their purpose was to breach the Israeli defenses, thus opening the way for the main armored mass to flood through and overrun the Israeli rear, a classical armored maneuver and one, no doubt, drilled into them endlessly by their Soviet advisers.

Yair ordered his Centurions to concentrate their fire on the engineer tanks, to destroy them before they could breach the vital antitank ditch. For the remainder of the afternoon the Israeli tanks along the commanding "Booster" ridge sent round after round crashing toward the Syrian bridging tanks, often at ranges of about 2,000 yards. One of the Centurion's exclusive and most potent weapons was its ability to fire the HESH (High Explosive Squash Head) shells—a projectile which on impact squashed against the enemy vehicle with such force that it dislodged a large scab of scalding armorplate from inside the fighting compartment, sending it whirling around with gruesome effects. Again and again the Syrians doggedly pushed their bridging tanks forward, only to be destroyed by Yair's tanks. But two from the Syrian 3rd Armored Division did succeed in reaching the antitank ditch to the north of fortification A3, on the far side of the conical Hermonit Hill, where the tanks were out of sight of Yair's battalion and opposed by less successful forces. The two tanks rumbled up to the ditch and dropped their bridges, under persistent though ineffective fire. Immediately the Syrian commander exploited the breakthrough and a company of ten tanks headed for the bridges. One by one they swung into line ahead and clattered across the antitank ditch. The Israeli defense line had been breached.

Meanwhile, from the "Booster" ridge, Yair's battalion continued to fight off a powerful assault force from one arm of the Syrian 1st Armored Division's offensive. As the T-55s closed in, they brought within range their accompanying BMD armored infantry carriers. But, excellent though these Soviet vehicles were, they were no match for the Centurions, and as they were exposed below the ridge, the Israeli tanks blasted them. Soon the plain was dotted with burning Syrian armor from which black smoke billowed into the azure sky, while men scrambled away from their shattered vehicles. The fury of the onslaught by both sides created a thick smoke pall, which, added to that already raised by the artillery bombardment, was beginning to obscure much of what was happening.

By midafternoon the first formations of Israeli Phantoms were streaking down their runways, heavily loaded with bombs and rockets to strike hard at the Syrian armor already overrunning the Golan positions. The Phantoms, in their bright green, sand, and brown camouflage, screamed low over the Sea of Galilee, ruffling its smooth surface with the blast from their powerful twin jets. The first flight thundered over Ein Gev on the northern shore of the Sea of Galilee, roared up over the rugged hills, only to drop again into the valley that led to the kibbutz of Ramat Magshimim at the extreme southern end of the Israeli defense line, near fortification A1. Below them the whole of the Golan Heights seemed to be a mass of smoke and flame.

Immediately the aircraft cleared the hills, Syrian antiaircraft fire and surface-to-air missiles rose in a terrific barrage. All four Phantoms of the first flight were hit together, exploding in sheets of flame or shooting skyward streaming smoke as their pilots strove for sufficient height to eject. Only two managed to do so. Then the next flight streaked in like sharks after a shoal, rocketing and swinging in frantic attempts to evade the flak and missiles. They plunged toward a column of Syrian tanks crashing their way through the ground defenses. Rockets swooshed from their wings and bombs tumbled onto the tanks, which exploded in stunning cascades of fire, while the Phantoms jinked and turned and swept away.

More aircraft were already hurtling over the rough hills, hugging the ground. Missiles streaked up and tore them apart; others had wings and tails ripped to shreds by withering gunfire before the survivors turned agonizingly around to limp for their home bases. They clawed for altitude so they could eject over the Israeli forces if necessary. As the last of the Phantoms fled, they left in their wake a score or more of burning, shattered Syrian tanks and carriers, but too many others simply rumbled past to press home their attack.

One Israeli observer wrote:

> It had got very confused. We could only discern vague outlines of the enemy tanks, until they got close and then, literally, burst into view. When they did, we were ready and hit them badly. This left us a bit more optimistic, but then things went bad. Around 4:00 P.M. our air force began to sweep in to pound the Syrians and we felt it would soon be over. Then, as we watched, our jets were shot down, one by one. It was fantastic and frightening; a Phantom would scream over, there was a streak of white smoke and it exploded!

The worst was happening. As the vaunted Israeli Air Force roared in to destroy the Syrian armor, as it had done so effectively in the Six Day War, it encountered the Syrians' surface-to-air missiles with disastrous results. For hours it seemed the Israelis could do nothing and their losses mounted. Not only were they operating within the range of the Syrian umbrella of SA-2 and SA-3 sites, stationed behind the front lines, but they also began to encounter new types of missiles, of which neither they nor the Americans were even aware.

During those first hours of the attack, it appeared to General

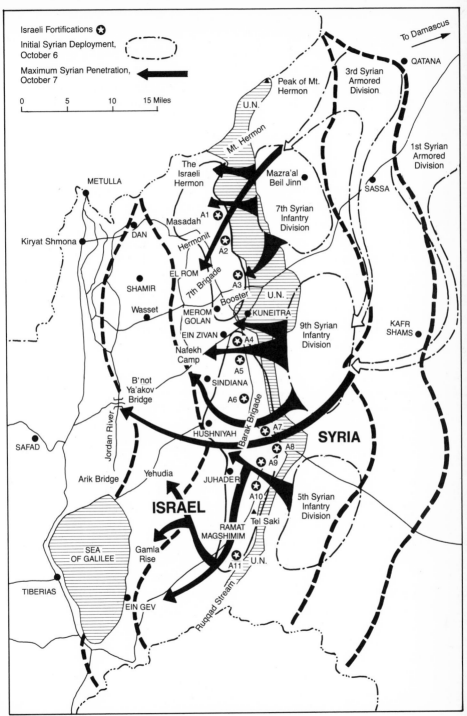

The Golan Heights Opening Action

Hofi, the commanding officer of Northern Command, that the main Syrian thrust was being directed to the north of the Kuneitra opening, between fortifications A2 and A3, and south of Jubbata el Kashab as well. Another thrust was identified along the route from Kudne in the A6 sector, with a third driving toward the Tapline route from the extreme southern flank in the A11 sector. (The Tapline is the oil pipeline that cuts across the Golan Heights from Jordan on its way to the sea in Lebanon. It was protected by high wire fences on either side and had a road running alongside.)

The Israeli Barak Brigade—which held the front from the extreme south, where A11 guarded the approach across the rugged Ruqqad stream toward the settlement of El Al, northward for some 20 miles to just south of Kuneitra—began signaling that its forces were fighting back and had already knocked out a number of Syrian tanks. There was, therefore, in the first hours, an optimism that the Syrians were only probing the defenses in large numbers, and could be held off by the light existing forces until the reserve tank brigades came up and drove them back. Reports reached Northern Command headquarters that the Israeli tanks manning their prepared ramps, hull down to protect their sides and rear, were doing well. The longer-range 105mm guns on their Centurions, in particular, were engaging the shorter-range T-55s very effectively, and knocking them out before they could close on the well-protected Israelis. An Israeli tanker who was near Tel Saki recalls:

The Syrians were moving in tightly packed formations toward us across very rough and hilly country. Our Centurion was well dug in and we could take our time, settling on each target in turn. The guns fired with a crack, and our tank rocked back with the recoil. Each time we hit a Syrian tank, once only a glancing blow on its turret, but immediately the T-55 blew up with a terrific explosion. Then, however, the battle began to hot up and we realized, with a bit of a shock, that we couldn't knock them out fast enough; there were so many they began to draw well within range before we could shoot. After several shells crashed close by, our commander decided to pull back out of their range and we withdrew, still firing.

Indeed, by 4:30 P.M. the situation was anything but rosy, and alarming reports reached General Hofi from all along the front that the Syrians were overwhelming the defenders by sheer weight of numbers, which were out of all proportion to anything they had previously deployed. All along the "Purple Line" the Syrians were breaking through. Hofi waited no longer. He ordered the elite Israeli 7th Armored Brigade to take over the northern end of the line, from fortification A5 to Tel Hazeika and northward, to include the Israeli Hermon positions.

By late afternoon the Syrian armored force driving along the Kudne route toward Tel Aksha, between A5 and A6, had massed some six hundred tanks, with which they began to over-run the mere sixty or so tanks of the Barak Brigade. The Syrian commander thereupon decided to make that the main break-through, and ordered his 9th Infantry Division to exploit the armored success. They began a three-pronged attack: the center drove for Tel Hazeika, with a northern attack aimed at the Israeli stronghold of Kuneitra, to which the Syrian 7th Infantry Division was also thrusting, while the southern attack pushed in a big left hook around A6 toward the vital Nafekh Camp, Northern Command's headquarters. At the same time, the Syrian 1st Armored Division was probing slightly south of 9th Infantry Division's southern thrust, endeavoring to push a column across the relatively unprotected area around the Tapline route toward the decisive Bnot Ya'akov Bridge. Once across at that point, they could break through into Upper Galilee.

In the failing evening light, Yair ordered one of his company commanders, Major Avner, to move forward to the Syrian breach of the antitank ditch, destroy the bridges and tanks that had so far managed to cross, and restore the situation there. By the light of fires and shellbursts, Avner's small column of Centurions rumbled away toward Hermonit Hill, while the remainder of the battalion continued the intense firefight with the massed Syrian tanks, which were pressing hard in solid phalanxes against the flimsy Israeli defense lines. Fortunately, Avner's column returned within the hour, having completed its task and strengthened the threatened Israeli line.

In the meantime, further south along the Golan front the situation was rapidly deteriorating. As had happened elsewhere on the front, the first reports of Israeli successes against the Syrian attackers had been too optimistic. The quality of the Israeli defense simply was not enough against the huge mass of armor that was flooding toward them. By 4:00 P.M. the situation at Kudne was getting desperate as a Syrian force of more than a hundred tanks had bypassed A6 on the south and was driving toward Hushniyah, a mile or so from the Tapline route. The Barak Brigade had no reserves from which to send forces to head off these Syrian breaks, and all their forces were committed. The early, enthusiastic success had expended too much ammunition. Now, as the battle intensified and the Syrian flood broadened, the Israelis found themselves desperately short of ammunition. In these circumstances the brigade commander, Turkish-born Col. Ben Shoham, a very popular young commander of thirty-eight, had no alternative but to signal Northern Command headquarters for reinforcements and request the 2nd Battalion from 7th Brigade.

Headquarters ordered the 2nd Battalion forward as Ben Shoham requested, and it drove determinedly for the line in the A7 sector, but ran into a large force of Syrian tanks and infantry. In the desperate ensuing fight, the battalion knocked out some twenty Syrian tanks and drove off the infantry with machine-gun fire. But the Syrians were equally determined, and promptly regrouped to counterattack. This time their infantry attacked the Israeli armor with "Snapper" wire-guided antitank missiles. Soon the rough ground was crisscrossed with a cobweb of fine wires trailed from the spent missiles and draped like veils from rocks and scrub. The 2nd Battalion lost many tanks before it managed to hold the enemy attack. By that time, around 5:00 P.M., dusk was beginning to shroud the frantic scene, when more trouble brewed for the desperately outnumbered Israeli defenders. The 3rd Battalion commander, Lieutenant Colonel Oded, radioed that yet another large Syrian force had driven through the line, bypassed A9, and was driving rapidly along the Tapline route.

This was bad news, for its route led directly toward Juhader and thence to Nafekh Camp, the major Israeli headquarters for the area, now threatened by several simultaneous Syrian drives. Still another Syrian force was advancing from the A10 position, also converging on Juhader. The 2nd Battalion dispatched an ill-spared company of tanks under its second-in-command to contain this latest threat by cutting across the Syrians' line of communication in the direction of Tel Saki. However, the Syrians were not to be surprised and, alert to the threat, ambushed the small Israeli force. For twenty minutes an intense fight developed amid the scrub and rocks, with opposing tanks battling like bumper cars. Guns crashed at point-blank range, their muzzle flashes searing the sand-abraded paint on one another. After this frantic duel, the Israelis managed to break out of the Syrian ambush and headed south to Ramat Magshimim, trying to ward off yet another Syrian column advancing toward Tel Saki.

The battles on the Golan Heights were hopelessly confused. The Israelis were attempting to block the increasing number of leaks in their defense system through which the Syrian flood was bursting and gaining pressure, but there were neither tanks nor time enough to stop the breaches. The most that could be done with inadequate forces was to divert or blunt the attacks, in the hope that the Israeli reserves would hold them a few miles behind the front, before the deluge of armor swept into the populated valleys beyond. Not since the Wehrmacht had swept through Belgium and France in May 1940 had there been a *Blitzkrieg* like it. The Israeli drive to the Canal in 1967 had been several thrusts strong, but this was a vast horde of armor. The Israelis might battle valiantly; but as night fell that first day, it began to look hopeless.

Back in the warm darkness of Cairo, President Sadat had good cause for satisfaction since his often maligned forces had succeeded beyond anyone's expectations. Not only had they launched a surprise attack against Israel, but they had actually established a firm foothold on the East Bank and even penetrated inland. The initial air strike had cost them, according to Egyptian sources, only five aircraft, against a Soviet estimate that they would lose some 40 percent. The infantry crossing of the Canal, too, had been relatively unopposed, thanks to the tremendous artillery bombardment, and they put their losses at around eight hundred; they had expected a much higher figure. Egypt's tactics in crossing the water barrier were strictly in accord with the lessons of the final years of World War II in Europe: huge artillery concentrations, air strikes, and rapid assaults along a long waterfront. Egypt had carried out the operation with consummate skill and determination, although, it had to be acknowledged, against very light opposition, virtually none of it armored. Israel had by any measure been dealt a severe, though not yet fatal blow.

Paradoxically, much of Israel's failure was a direct result of her rapid success in 1967. Even before the Six Day War, Russia had begun training and directing the Egyptian and Syrian armies, and the Israelis had initially been stunned by the dire possible consequences of a direct confrontation with the Soviet Union. But Israel had recovered her balance and dealt the Arabs a resounding blow in 1967. In the years since, though, despite the war of attrition, the occupied territories had become central to Israeli strategy; it was felt that they removed the danger of Arab encirclement. Instead, the Israeli occupation engendered a growing Arab determination to avenge their humiliating defeats and thereby imposed a severe burden on the Israeli defense forces. For the Israelis to hold the East Bank of the Canal against the overwhelming power of the Egyptian artillery had obliged them to construct the fortifications that over the years became shelters rather than fighting positions. Thus, by Yom Kippur, 1973, they had no effective forces in the Bar-Lev Line. Since 1969, Israeli officers had clandestinely told correspondents that they could not hope to prevent a massive attack over the Canal. They had relied on early warning by their intelligence forces to give time for them to mobilize reserves and reinforce the defenses, but misread the signs when they came.

But Sadat too was due for a reversal. At 7:40 P.M., when he had been in the operations room for five hours and forty minutes, he was informed that the Soviet ambassador wanted to see him. Sadat told Marshal Ali he was going to the al-Tahirah Palace, which had been converted into an ultra-modern communications center, and left thinking that Vinogradov had called to congratulate him on their success. But to his dismay, he heard that on October 4, the previous Thursday, Syria had asked the Soviet Union to arrange a cease-fire at the most forty-eight hours after the attack, and he was seeking now Egyptian approval. After a few minutes of acrimony, Sadat replied truculently: "Even if Syria did demand it, I won't have a cease-fire until the main targets of my battle have been achieved."

Immediately after Vinogradov left, at about 8:30 P.M., Sadat sent a cable to Assad declaring he had told the Russians he would not accept a cease-fire, and settled down to await the reply. He had to wait until the following afternoon, despite the urgency of the matter, before the Syrians replied that they had never said any such thing to the Russians.

The Arab strike had badly jolted the Israelis by its suddenness, although from the very beginning their government maintained an outward calm that belied their shaken self-confidence. Dayan gave a press conference that afternoon, opening his statement with the laconic remark: "I suppose everyone knows by this time that the Syrian and Egyptian attack started today, at ten minutes to two this afternoon." He went on to explain Israel's attitude: "We had information and we suspected that such an attack would take place; we were faced with the dilemma of whether to obtain a very important advantage, or not to do so and lose this military advantage, but make sure that the picture will be clear, the true one — and this is the start of an all-out war again.

"We decided to take the second course, taking into account the military outcome of that course, and only this morning we started mobilizing our reserves. Before that we informed other governments of what we thought was going to happen, that is to say, of the Egyptian and Syrian attacks."

In the later afternoon, while the forces on the Golan Heights were vainly struggling to hold back the Syrian invasion, Prime Minister Golda Meir broadcast to assure her people that "The enemy has suffered serious losses." But many listeners to the well-known voice with its strong American accent detected that while her voice was firm, she spoke in more sonorous and measured tones than usual. "We have no doubts as to our victory," she went on; "but it is our belief that this renewal of Egyptian and Syrian aggression is an act of madness."

Nevertheless, when Dayan addressed the nation later that same evening, he was distinctly optimistic. "The Arabs will take no advantage from this war before the cease-fire goes into effect," he said, in a clear warning that Israel would not permit them to seize territory and then shelter behind a spurious U.N. resolution that would leave them in possession. "The people of Tel Aviv will be able to sleep well tonight," he assured his audience, and even confirmed that the bridges over the Jordan River remained open and traffic between the East and West banks could flow normally. The charismatic hero of the Six Day War did admit that Israeli defense forces were stretched thin along the Canal, but he insisted that the very size of the Sinai peninsula afforded Israel's major cities ample protection. Dayan was confident that once the reservists reached the battle, the Egyptians would be expelled from Sinai. "It won't take months or weeks to wipe them out," he said; and as for the Syrians, their evident objective was to regain the Golan Heights, but he affirmed that "this they will not do."

In Tel Aviv, General Elazar, the Yugoslav-born Israeli chief of staff, appeared briefly before newsmen; his mien was stern. With his olive drab shirtsleeves rolled up in Israeli military fashion, Elazar spoke concisely. Asked if the latest conflict should be called the "Yom Kippur War," Elazar replied that it would be better termed "the war of the Day of Judgment."

But already around the world the diplomatic waters were

being muddied by a succession of statements. In London, a spokesman of the Egyptian Embassy accused Israel of launching a "premeditated attack," and said that Egypt was exercising the "legitimate right of self-defense." The Syrian Embassy, too, denied Arab responsibility. It asked all governments to support "the right of the Arab states to defend their security, and furthermore to use military action to regain Syrian territory in the Golan Heights and Egyptian territories in Sinai which had been under Israeli military occupation since June 1967."

As was to be expected, the war switched to the media as both sides used all their propaganda skills to win friends and influence people. Mr. Michael Comay, the Israeli ambassador in London, in a radio interview called on the world to condemn Arab aggression in the Middle East. It was, he said, "absolute nonsense" to suggest that Israel would start the latest fighting. "We would not sacrifice a single soldier to start aggression," he piously declared.

According to the official Egyptian and Syrian versions, the war started with Israeli attacks in the Gulf of Suez and in the Golan Heights, which were immediately rebuffed by successful Arab counterblows. Once the war had got under way, it was no longer of decisive importance to maintain this version. Indeed, the Syrian Embassy supplied this author with booklets, curiously enough, apparently of Iraqi origin, one of which states:

> In the afternoon of October 6, 1973, war broke out on both the Egyptian and Syrian fronts. Perhaps we might point out here that we have previously declared that the news of the war was conveyed to us by broadcasting networks alone. This is true from an official angle, because neither the Egyptians nor the Syrian government cared to give us prior information on the war.
>
> However, we did receive unofficial reports on the impending fight from our own sources. All available information and conclusions indicated that the said regimes sparked the war to revive the situation through a strong shock facilitating the application of the peaceful solution.

For obvious reasons the Soviet Union was not surprised by the outbreak of war; it had, after all, thousands of military advisers in key positions in Cairo and Damascus. Not a tank unit or a missile base could be moved without its knowledge, unless, of course, one assumes that Soviet officers were afflicted by both blindness and deafness. The United States, on the other hand, was no more prepared for the combined Arab attack than Israel. The spy satellites must have supplied a steady stream of pictures accounting for what happened on every square foot of ground, but apparently those who interpreted the news did not see anything ominous in the troop concentrations. Secretary of State Henry Kissinger later revealed that both U.S. and Israeli Intelligence had informed their superiors on three separate occasions during the week preceding the war that "hostilities were unlikely to the point of there being no chance of it [war] happening." They were aware of the troop concentrations, but there was miscalculation as to the intention behind them. This failure has, no doubt, been pondered long since by intelligence services and policymakers, because it showed that there is no early warning system in case of a surprise attack.

When the war began, Dr. Kissinger had been in office for a few weeks only. Quoting President Nixon as his authority, he had said in one of his first interviews that the Middle East was "perhaps the most dangerous area." There were rumors that he was to make a peace initiative soon, and the idea seems to have appealed to the Arabs. Arab diplomats in Washington said that it would be easier for Kissinger to bring pressure on the Israelis precisely because he was himself of Jewish origin and thus less exposed to attacks from his coreligionists. *The Times* (London) published an article that purported to present a plan ascribed to Kissinger for solving the Arab-Israeli dispute. It was neither better nor worse than any previous plan; but it was by no means certain that it had really emanated from Kissinger. By the evening of October 6, it had been forgotten in the wake of the hurricane of violence that swept it from view.

In Washington, nevertheless, the Arab version of the war

found some support. Early Western reactions must have convinced the Soviets that their basic assumption had been at least partly correct, namely, that it would be possible to combine aggressive actions with statesmanlike postures and calls for restraint, responsible action, and the continuation of a lasting peace. Dr. Kissinger would be assured that Soviet-American friendship would be unaffected; and meanwhile, Soviet broadcasts would declare that conditions were ripe to take advantage of the energy crisis in the capitalist world.

The unexpectedness of the war created some curious anomalies on both sides. In spite of an official blackout, in the fashionable shopping centers of Tel Aviv's Allenby Road and Dizengoff Street, the automatic lighting system blazed out at sundown, causing embarrassed shopkeepers to rush to switch it off. In Cairo, too, six minutes by air from Israel, the city lights were brightly lit for hours. One shopkeeper responded to a correspondent: "You mean we are fighting Israel with all these lights on?" People became more convinced in late evening when the government ordered that all electric lights and car lights had to be covered in blue paint.

So, as darkness fell that first night of war, most Israelis crowded around their radios and televisions for the news. Their spirit was lifted by the details of air strikes deep behind Egyptian lines and against the surface-to-air missiles between the Golan and Damascus, which were reported to be seriously damaged. By then Israel had been switched to a war footing, towns blacked out, and streets patrolled by armed guards, while stores that remained open until late were besieged by anxious housewives fearing food shortages. Only in the new settlements in northern Galilee was the pattern different; there, within range of Syrian heavy artillery, kibbutz members remained in deep shelters. The fighting was not far from those in the northern towns and villages, and the thud of gunfire carried easily across the 20 miles of Galilee. The situation was nowhere near as sanguine as was being officially claimed.

At a night meeting at Hofi's advanced command headquarters, Dayan ordered every possible means to be used to block all approaches to the Jordan Valley. At Laner's suggestion, the front was divided, with himself in charge of the southern sector and Eytan taking over everything north of the Bnot Ya'akov-to-Kuneitra road. For this task, Laner was allocated four brigades: Ben Shoham's Barak Brigade, Colonel Ran's 17th Reserve Tank Brigade, the 14th Reserve Brigade, and the 19th Reserve Brigade. But as Sunday morning approached, he surveyed his division's situation with little cause for optimism.

The Syrians were breaking through the front in numerous places, and their long armored columns were already snaking toward the plains below the Golan Heights. If the Israelis were not quick, their counterattack would have to be fought in the open agricultural land of Galilee, where the huge Syrian armored forces would run riot. Then Israel would not only have to turn the Syrian stampede, but drive it back up the Golan Heights. There were few Israeli soldiers who had forgotten the desperate battles of 1967, when they had shoved the Syrians over the hill. In Sinai, masses of Egyptian infantry were deploying along the 110 miles of front, and in the gathering darkness they too were preparing to push inland as their armor crossed the Canal in an increasing flow.

CHAPTER

6

The Syrian Onslaught

The Syrian command in the Golan had prepared for an operation based on the absence of any major physical barrier between them and Israel such as, for instance, faced the Egyptians at the Suez Canal. They planned for their greatly superior armored forces to sweep into Israel over the Golan, then through the valleys, to debouch into the low-lying populated areas in a surprise attack that would brush aside the small number of defenders in the fortifications while they were still at a low state of alert. This attack, they believed, would also forestall the arrival of Israeli reinforcements by making a deep penentration across the natural defenses of the rocky Heights—a concept directly contradicting the Israeli belief that they would always have time to organize their reserves while their regular army held the forward defense line.

It has not, so far, been revealed why the Egyptians and Syrians supposed the Israelis would not make a preemptive air strike, for the Israeli Air Force did not rely upon reserves but was always at regular strength. Had that Israeli strike been delivered, even as late as Saturday morning, it would have seriously dislocated the Syrian plan and greatly weakened their army's resolve and confidence. As it was, Arab confidence in preparing complex operations against Israel strongly indicated their correct appraisal that there would be no air strike. In the aftermath of the war, various Israeli leaders tried to explain away their failure, but without much logic or sincerity; the "facts" just did not hold up.

The prime minister provided several conflicting versions as to why no air strike was delivered. The first one was given on Sunday evening, when she explained that they did not wish to offend American sensibilities. This argument was subsequently dropped after Dr. Kissinger, on October 12 and again on the 25th, carefully put forth that the Israeli government did not expect an attack, so the issue of a preemptive strike had not arisen, and, in any case, the Americans had not been consulted. But this, too, is clearly at variance with the facts. The Israeli government had informed the Americans beforehand that they expected an attack, in the hope that they, via the Russians, could warn the Arabs that Israel expected an attack and was ready. The Israeli cabinet, too, had discussed the possibilities of an Arab attack on the eve of Yom Kippur and again on the morning of the 6th. But each time the advice of General Elazar, the chief of staff, and other leading generals, was turned down for the political reason that if Israel was seen to be the victim on this occasion, rather than the aggressor, the world would view her predicament with sympathy. It was a forlorn and misguided hope, born not of fear but of embarrassment at the previous overwhelming victories—a case of a small David grown into an embarrassing Goliath.

Night fell on the Day of Atonement over scenes of unbelievable confusion. On the Golan front, Colonel Ben-Gal checked on the position of his 7th Brigade, and took under command Yair's 4th Battalion, by then heavily engaged all along its front.

It was 10:00 P.M. when Ben-Gal's 7th Brigade as a whole engaged the invading armored elements from the Syrian 7th Infantry Division, as they began a series of attempts to break through the central sector of the brigade between "Booster" ridge and Hermonit, still held by the 5th Battalion. The Israelis deployed in brilliant moonlight, which added a final touch of unreality to the wild mountain scenery. They could see thousands of small lights, "cats'-eyes," created by the infrared fighting lights mounted on the advancing Syrian tanks. Yet another heavy Syrian artillery barrage crashed out, laying down an impenetrable curtain of steel and fire moving before the tanks; but Ben-Gal calmly ordered his brigade to hold its fire until the Syrians moved closer. The Israelis had no infrared equipment, and shortening the range would reduce the Syrian advantage.

The Syrian 78th Tank Brigade attacked *en masse*, their guns pounding the Israeli positions to cover their infantry as they worked to bridge the antitank ditch. Rapidly and efficiently the Syrians completed the bridging, then platoons raced across and deployed on the far side, covering their tanks with antitank missiles. The Syrian tanks rumbled over, and moving slowly but steadily fanned out to advance along a wide front toward the waiting Centurions of 7th Brigade. At last the Syrians ground into range at 800 yards where, by the clear moonlight, the Israelis waited, hands on firing grips, sweating as they watched waves of tanks rolling and bucking nearer. Finally Ben-Gal ordered his tanks to fire. Suddenly the darkness erupted in long jets of flame and smoke as the Centurions opened up, tearing the enemy tanks apart with their salvos, ripping out the personnel carriers that had moved behind the armor but were now fully exposed. Desperately, the Syrians returned the fire and began a fierce fight that was to last for over five hours through the night. Only after sustaining losses of over seventy tanks did the Syrians break off the attack and withdraw down the slopes. By then it was 3:00 A.M. on Sunday, October 7.

Meanwhile, at 2:00 A.M., another Syrian column had begun attacking northward along the Rafid-to-Kuneitra road, within the 1967 cease-fire lines, driving to outflank the Israeli positions along the "Booster" and Hermonit ridges. When reports of this move reached Ben-Gal, he immediately realized that his ammunition supply route was about to be severed, and sent to intercept the Syrians a force of tanks under twenty-six-year-old Captain Meir. Meir, a practical joker whose effervescent nature had run foul of his commander so many times that he had already decided to return to civilian life, led his force out toward the fortifications south of Kuneitra with the intention of ambushing the Syrians as they advanced in the darkness.

Near the fortifications, Meir ordered his tanks to position themselves at intervals in the rocky scrub alongside the main road, while his second-in-command, Mayer, was instructed to continue for another mile parallel to the Syrian advance, from where he would signal their approach and lay another ambush for the Syrians when they retreated again. Two of the tanks already protecting A4 were told to pull back off the road and cover any possible Syrian break northward. Meir, who was nick-named "Tiger," had his force positioned in time, and before long a signal from Mayer warned: "They're coming, from the south. About forty of them." The Syrian column ground unsuspect-ingly past Mayer's group drawn up in the darkness amid trees and scrub alongside the road, and headed in perfect formation toward the main Israeli force.

Meir waited until the Syrians were about 1,300 yards away, then ordered: "All stations Tiger, fire!" Instantly, a powerful searchlight lit the Syrian column, and simultaneously both Meir's main force and Mayer's force in the Syrian rear opened fire. The five rear Syrian tanks were quickly set alight, blocking the column's retreat, while the main Israeli force pumped shells into the tanks as they careened and smashed into one another while jostling to get off the road. Caught between the two fires, and unable to identify the enemy positions, the Syrians panicked, causing pandemonium as they maneuvered to get away, while the Israelis methodically picked them off. Finally the Syrians withdrew after forty-five minutes, leaving some twenty tanks abandoned in various damaged states.

In the cold clearness of dawn, "Tiger" Meir's force again moved south through a drifting haze of battle smoke, past the still-blazing Syrian tanks, until it reached Tel el-Hariyen, where it moved amid the scrub and trees and took cover. With the ros-iness of dawn silhouetting the dark hills, the Syrians regrouped and drove back again, fruitlessly seeking out the Israeli force. Then, assuming that it too had withdrawn, they pushed on toward the main road once more, straight into ambush. Mayer's tanks and the main force had them in their jaws and destroyed five T-55s in their opening salvos. Meir now ordered his force out in pursuit and his tanks moved onto the road, behind the remnants of the Syrian column. It became a killing ground. Ten more T-55s seeking shelter in abandoned artillery positions were trapped and knocked out; at this point, to the Israeli's delight, the Syrians' supply column was observed moving along the road in their wake, quite unaware that their tanks had been virtually eliminated. It, too, was savaged before what was left extricated itself from ambush and fled back toward Rafid.

At the Nafekh headquarters of the Barak Brigade, the commander, Col. Ben Shoham, was studying reports flooding back from his battalion commanders of the size of the Syrian attack. While he was deciding the next moves, he was approached by Lt. Zvi Greengold, from Lochamei Hagetaot Kibbutz. Zvi, usually known as "Zwicka," a cheeky-looking young boy with blond hair and freckles, had been assigned to a company commander's course and sent on two weeks leave to prepare. Like so many of his fellows, he had immediately hitchhiked back to his base on hearing the mobilization signals. He had been helping with the wounded in the camp when he learned that four tanks, three of which had been battle-damaged, were about to arrive. Having already asked if he could be given command, Zwicka was delighted to hear he was to have the tanks. According to Maj. Gen. Chaim Herzog, Zwicka reported to headquarters, where the second-in-command, Lieutenant Colonel Yisraeli, said to him: "Take them. You will be known as Force Zwicka. Get moving along the Tapline route."

Zwicka promptly helped remove two bodies from the tanks and got them ready for action. Soon he was leading his small force out toward the Tapline route.

Colonel Shoham was by that time greatly concerned at the threatening Syrian advances to the south, where large forces had broken through and were bypassing the Israeli fortifications. Bitter nighttime firefights were taking place across the southern Heights, and Israeli troops were cut off in the front-line fortifications. Frenzied signals to their headquarters at Nafekh finally produced authorization to withdraw, but this was easier said than done, with Syrians massed in their rear. At Kudne a relieving tank force broke through to A6, despite a strong Syrian buildup in the immediate area, and succeeded in evacuating all the men safely to Tel Zohar. Along the southern flank, where the battle was then heaviest, it was more difficult. Again Israeli tanks fought through and relieved A8 and A9, but A10 was completely surrounded, and its commander, a young lieutenant, was already badly wounded. Unable to get out, the Israelis sat tight in their defenses and called for artillery support. All that was available was a single battery of 155mm guns, and these were ordered to concentrate on A10's position. In the darkness the immensely long barrels swung on target and opened fire, deluging the Syrian besiegers with a storm of explosive, and giving temporary relief to the troops inside.

Because of this situation, Ben Shoham moved the forward headquarters of his brigade from Nafekh, intent on reaching Juhader, from where, he believed, he could better control the battle. His half-track trundled carefully along in the dark, avoiding Syrian positions near the Tapline route, and all aboard were relieved when at last they reached Juhader. By then, though, they were under constant heavy shelling, as the Syrians were getting radio fixes every time the half-track's signaler tried to contact Lieutenant Colonel Oded's 3rd Battalion headquarters, supposed to be in the area. Ben Shoham tried to interpret the action, but it was terribly disordered and there was no firm line anywhere. The Syrians and Israelis were hopelessly entangled.

On their trip from Nafekh, Ben Shoham's small unit had encountered several Israeli units pulling back, critically short of ammunition, while Syrian tanks and personnel carriers continued to pour in a seemingly endless stream across the frontier. Shoham radioed to his rear headquarters, still in Nafekh, asking for artillery support and flares in the hope they would reveal the Syrians. But, to his disgust, fewer and fewer flares were fired each time they were called for. By then the half-track's signalman had made contact with Oded, who was still in position near Juhader. Although Ben Shoham repeatedly asked Oded to join him, he and his men were heavily engaged with surrounding Syrians and could not break out.

Despite the turmoil, Brigade District was still trying to get supplies through to the encumbered positions. Captain Giora, the operations officer of the district, arrived at Shoham's position leading an ammunition column along the Tapline route. Shoham, who was then waiting for his personal tank to be brought up from Hushniyah, intercepted the ammunition column and advised Giora not to continue further. Instead, he radioed Oded and told him to try to send individual 3rd Battalion tanks to infiltrate through to the Tapline route, so they could replenish their ammunition and return to their positions. This, Oded agreed through the crackling radio link, was a possibility.

No sooner had the radio conversation concluded than the officers waiting around the half-track and the ammunition column were surprised to see a tank rumbling out of the almost unfathomable smoke and gloom. Thinking it must be a retreating Israeli tank, Ben Shoham sent a radio call to Oded asking for confirmation that his tanks were withdrawing. Oded replied that none of his tanks had managed to leave the battalion area. Thereupon Shoham yelled to Giora to go forward in person, contact the commander, and, if all was well, send him back to the line.

Bending low against the hail of shell fragments still cascading on the area, Giora ran across to the tank — by then only some 30 feet from the colonel's half-track — bawling above the cacophony of battle. Suddenly the tank crew slammed shut the hatches, there was a roar and a puff of sooty exhaust, and the tank reversed violently away into the night. Giora fled back to the half-track, his face white as he panted: "A Syrian tank!" Everyone heaved a relieved sigh, for had the tank decided to fire, it would have had at its mercy the brigade commander, his forward headquar-

ters, and an entire ammunition convoy. Ben Shoham tersely
ordered Giora to get his ammunition back to Nafekh straightaway, and watched his column jerk and rev away into the
darkness.

Giora had not been gone long, however, before he radioed
back to Ben Shoham that at the Hushniyah crossroads on the
Tapline route he had spotted some fifty tanks with supporting
vehicles. His column had slipped past in the darkness without
trouble, but he was sure they weren't Israelis. What Giora had
seen was an entire Syrian brigade from 9th Division, which had
been deflected from A6 by a platoon of three Israeli tanks fighting recklessly to defend the fortification—those three all that
remained of the original Israeli company, whose commander had
been killed and second-in-command badly wounded and evacuated. It was later learned that the tank crews had run out of
ammunition but survived by venturing out into the holocaust of
machine- and tank-gun fire and shelling to collect ammunition
from knocked-out tanks. This had enabled them to keep fighting.
Their predicament reflected the Barak Brigade's dire straits
which, after the Syrian invasion along the entire front, had been
reduced to just 15 tanks against an estimated 450 Syrian.

Having seen off Giora and the ammunition convoy, Ben Shoham set about trying to work his way back toward Nafekh. In
the meantime, however, Force Zwicka—which had left Nafekh
several hours before—was nosing its way cautiously along the
Tapline route. In that area, the Tapline route was separated from
the actual Tapline by two tall wire fences. Zwicka had been
intent on joining Ben Shoham, but instead had run into the Syrian brigade that had been reported by Giora. Zwicka promptly
advised his commander by radio that he was engaging the enemy.
But rather than advance into an obvious head-on collision with
the huge Syrian force, he sensibly decided to site his tanks in
good, hull-down positions and let the enemy come to him. They
had been waiting only a short while when the commander of
one of his tanks signaled that the Syrian column, mostly new T-
62s, was approaching. Zwicka peered into the gloom and saw

them by the faint glow of their dimmed sidelights. It was 9:20 P.M.

Anxiously, Zwicka held his fire until the Syrians rumbled closer, then, when the first T-62 was only a score or so yards away, commanded his gunner to fire. The words were barely spoken when the tank rocked back from the slam of its powerful gun and the leading enemy tank burst instantly into flames. Zwicka signaled his nearest tank to change places with him and follow his maneuvers as he worked his way into a position from which they could shoot up the entire Syrian column. For 100 yards or more the two tanks clattered forward, slewing and accelerating over the stony terrain, but by then Zwicka realized that he was alone, the other tank having lost its position in the dark. Roaring over the crest of a hillock, they were confronted by three Syrian tanks moving athwart them with lights on. Three rapid shots from the Centurion's quick-firing gun left all the enemy tanks blazing brightly, illuminating the area with a fierce yellow light that greatly aided Zwicka's movements. He again withdrew into cover and waited for the enemy to come forward.

Thirty heart-thumping minutes slowly passed, until they were alerted by a deep growl of heavy engines. A long column of T-62s appeared out of the flickering night, supported by a procession of trucks, all moving in parade-ground fashion. Again he held his fire until the lead tank was a mere 20 yards away when he blasted it. Zwicka was up against terrible odds, but he "boxed" them, withdrawing into the darkness, dodging and weaving under cover of scrub and rocky outcrops, only to pop out and hit them before disappearing again. He kept this uneven match going for over an hour, and the sole warning the Syrians got was a crash and a long jet of white flame lancing through the night to pulverize another of their vehicles. Finally, believing that they were up against a sizable Israeli force, the Syrians withdrew, leaving ten blazing vehicles on the ridge.

By then, Zwicka had been in action along the Tapline route until the early hours of the morning, and from his radio signals most of the brigade knew what he was up to. But the signals did not reveal that this very young man was pitting himself and his few men in an incredible personal battle against truly over-whelming odds (one estimate put them at 50 to 1) as they tried to stop a major thrust by the Syrian Army to win command of the Golan Heights.

Several miles further along the Tapline route, Ben Shoham realized he was surrounded. Dov, his brigade intelligence officer, suggested that as it was impossible to get back to the Nafekh headquarters by the Tapline route, they had better cut across country. So Shoham directed his tank and the headquarters half-track to head west toward the escarpment of the Golan Heights near Ramat Magshimim. They reached the Gamla Rise, on the road leading up from Ein Gev on the shores of the Sea of Gali-lee — one of the main breakthrough objectives of the invaders — at about 7:00 A.M. on the 7th, Sunday morning. But there they were dismayed to observe new Syrian T-62 tanks not far away along the escarpment, and in full view of Galilee. At that rate they would soon be down the hills into Israel proper. The Israeli tank and its accompanying half-track continued to move cau-tiously along in dim moonlight, keeping among the boulders on the slopes to screen them from the large Syrian force that was moving generally parallel to them; the heavy thud of their engines echoed across the rocks and drowned out the clatter of the Israeli vehicles.

From his position, Ben Shoham tried to clarify what had hap-pened, and the state of his brigade. So far as he could tell, all that remained was a single platoon of three tanks at fortification A6, which had no ammunition left, while between the Tapline and fortification A9 Oded had two platoons, six tanks in all, to block another major Syrian thrust. Apart from these remnants, there were individual tanks and some odd groups in various isolated positions. The company patrolling to the north of A6 to Hush-niyah had also run out of ammunition, but was, incredibly, nevertheless trying to head off Syrian forces attempting to reach their own city of Kuneitra, then occupied by the Israelis. The

Israeli force was shepherding them along and gradually deflecting them off course, hoping the enemy would not call their bluff and fire. Quite isolated from his surviving troops, Ben Shoham, whom Herzog later described as "a born leader and a good administrator, quietly firm, personally brave and very much a self-made man," spoke to his men by radio, promising help would soon arrive and urging them to hold on although the remnants had few illusions.

Back in Nafekh, meanwhile, Lieutenant Colonel Uzi, the second-in-command of the Barak Brigade, had got permission from the commander-in-chief of Northern Command to leave the base and take over the tanks fighting the desperate delaying action along the Tapline route, before the Syrians smashed through and reached the vital Nafekh Camp. This force comprised only Zwicka's small force and another seven, newly arrived, tanks of Ran's 17th Reserve Brigade, which were Israeli-modified Super-Shermans of World War II vintage reequipped with the British 105mm gun. Ran had performed miracles of logistics to get his force into action by 10:00 P.M. on the first day of battle.

Still in his secluded position on the Gamla Rise, Ben Shoham instructed Uzi to push the Syrians back. So, on the basis of Zwicka's reports, Uzi advanced south along the Tapline route parallel to Zwicka's three tanks driving along on the far side of the wire fence. However, Zwicka had only known of a small part of the overall scene. Before Uzi realized what was happening, they were being fiercely attacked on all sides by a considerable Syrian tank force, backed by infantry equipped with anti-tank missiles. Uzi's force slogged it out blow for blow for three horrendous hours, but by 1:00 A.M. they had been wiped out. Uzi himself was severely wounded when his tank was hit by a rocket projectile, which blew him clean out of his shattered tank, leaving him blinded and with only one leg.

On the other side of the fence, Zwicka had once again evaded the Syrian ambush and was nosing his way up to the fence, while the remaining two tanks were ordered to move carefully up the road in the hope they could entrap the Syrian force yet again. This time, though, his luck ran out. Without warning, all three Israeli tanks exploded in sheets of roaring flame. Instinctively, Zwicka and his crew scrambled from their blazing Centurion, falling to the ground in flames and yelling from the excrutiating pain as the flames seared their faces and hands. Zwicka's shirt and trousers were burning but he rolled into the ditch and somehow smothered the flames, fearful that at any moment his tank, which was still carrying fuel and ammunition, would blow up. In near panic, he stumbled across the rough tussocks and rocks to the fence, struggled to clamber over, and fell headlong to the other side. There he saw several Centurions still shunting back and forth.

The indomitable Zwicka scrambled for the nearest one, which he commandeered before its startled commander knew what was happening, leaving him amid the lurid glow of the burning tanks, searing flames, and whirling debris to scramble for another tank. Zwicka then tugged on the former commander's helmet and, gasping for breath, called up the brigade commander to announce that "Force Zwicka" was still operational. Even as Ben Shoham's relieved acknowledgment faded on the radio, young Zwicka realized how badly he was wounded as the terrible burns on his face and hands began to throb and blister. The scene wavered and he couldn't focus his eyes properly as waves of dizziness flowed over him. Only Ben Shoham's calm but insistent voice calling on the radio brought him back to the awful reality of the war. Charging straight for him were two huge Syrian tanks, bearing down with their guns firing. Zwicka fired and screamed for his driver to reverse. The tank shuddered as its tracks tore around on the bare rocks, then rattled backward into the inferno of the night, its gun still crashing defiance against the hopeless odds.

CHAPTER

7

The Breakthrough

At nightfall on the first day, it had seemed possible that the Israeli defenders were going to hold the Syrians long enough for the reserve tank brigades to get into position. Because of this optimistic view, the Israeli Air Force, which had suffered unexpectedly high losses during the day, was preparing to switch to the offensive on Sunday, October 7, and smash the Syrian air defense system, both missiles and antiaircraft guns. However, during the night the Syrians mounted massive attacks with several armored divisions. By morning, the situation was critical enough for it to be reluctantly agreed to alter the aircrafts' role to halting the armored offensive, before the Syrians broke into Galilee and rampaged across northern Israel. The Israeli Air Force was given a twofold task. Its fighter-bombers would strike at the concentrations of tanks, while its other aircraft would go for the air defenses and keep them occupied.

Meanwhile, Ben Shoham, although still isolated on the Gamla Rise, had received a signal during the night from General Hofi confirming that he was to assume command of the remaining forces on the southern Golan Heights—albeit they were then cut off by hordes of Syrian tanks and infantry. So, in the early dawn, Ben Shoham signaled to all the remaining troops that they were to concentrate upon his position on the Rise overlooking Galilee. By 8:00 A.M. news began to reach him that yet another Syrian thrust had broken through toward the Tapline route and was thrusting north to Nafekh and Kuneitra, finally severing any connection between his troops and the command post.

It was a situation fraught with menace for the Israelis at the southern end of the Golan Heights. In the darkness, the Syrian 5th Infantry Division's 49th Tank Brigade had crashed through Israeli positions in the vital Rafid area and was heading along the Tapline. Its 132nd Brigade of mechanized infantry had then wheeled left and was moving along the Ruqqad ridge, bypassing A10 and 11. It was maneuvering in three directions to mop up outlying Israeli positions at Juhader and Ramat Magshimim, before bearing down along the El Al route for the Gamla Rise (where Ben Shoham was stationed), whence their path was clear into Galilee. The Syrians had shown tremendous *élan*, and their overwhelming numbers no more detracted from their success than did the weight of the German *Panzers* in May 1940; besides, the Syrian soldiers had shown both determination and courage in the way they had faced the continual Israeli counterattacks. In fact, for the first time in many years the Israelis were in great trouble and barely able to stem the tide. Ben Shoham could hear through crackling headphones the strained voice of Oded, 3rd Battalion's commander, advising that their position was hopeless and asking permission to withdraw from Juhader, toward Tel Faris and away from Ben Shoham before they were quite over-run. He had only twelve tanks left, virtually the entire surviving Barak Brigade. Shoham had no alternative but reluctantly to agree to his withdrawal.

The airborne pounding began at dawn, with successive waves of Skyhawks and Phantoms swooping across the Heights in rocket and bomb attacks against the enemy's columns. The missiles and dense antiaircraft fire wreaked havoc, despite the simultaneous strikes against their emplacements. The remnants of Oded's battalion in beleaguered Juhader were still fighting at that

time, before breaking out. Their remaining ammunition was
dwindling, and they had desperately appealed for an air strike at
first light in the forlorn hope that it would relieve their position,
at least temporarily. The sun was still bouncing on the horizon
over the desolate Heights, its rays silhouetting the blackened
remains of hundreds of Syrian and Israeli tanks where they lay
mangled and smoking, when the first four Skyhawks screamed
in from Galilee.

They wheeled in low toward the Syrian positions, but as the
battle-weary Israeli soldiers rubbed their eyes and stubbly chins,
gazing hopefully up into the pale dawn, the unmistakable trails
of missiles laced the blue. The men groaned despairingly as all
four Skyhawks exploded in midair, falling as fireballs on the
hills. A second flight followed, dodging and weaving, but again
the missiles were loosed like coursers to a hare, and despite the
airplanes' jinking, the unerring missiles intercepted them. Two
crashed in flames while the other pair somehow evaded the missiles, let go their bombs, and raced away at ground level. Ten
seconds had passed and six Israeli aircraft had gone for precious
little relief. Already the Syrian tanks were rumbling relentlessly
forward like an army of ants, indestructible and blind to their
losses.

Even as Oded's dazed troops were withdrawing, the Syrian
command directed its 47th Tank Brigade to race on across the
Heights, and within an hour its troops were looking with amazement at the glittering waters of Galilee, and, there on the far side,
the sunlit city of Tiberias. Their excitement overflowed as they
set off confident of victory and within an ace of breaking into
Israel proper. There was, it seemed, nothing to bar their way to
the plunder.

In Damascus, people crowded around radios and cheered
jubilantly when news told of Arab successes in the fighting. Correspondents reported the Syrian capital quiet but expectant, adding: "The war seems very close." In truth, the thudding of artillery had been heard all Saturday night from the direction of
Kuneitra. A student, Mohammed Mustafa Rehzan, recalled:

"People stopped in the streets on Sunday morning to watch a dogfight in the sky about ten miles south of Damascus. One jet was seen to crash into a field not far away. When my friends and I got there, it was still burning, but the Israeli markings were visible. The pilot had disappeared, and although we searched the surrounding country we couldn't find him."

Israeli aircraft losses were beginning to mount alarmingly, and for the first time in twenty years doubts were expressed about the air force's ability to play a decisive role.

Lebanese villagers near the Syrian border and the disputed Mount Hermon positions had a distant view of the fighting. Correspondents standing on the hills, where the altitude tempered the fierce heat of the plains, wrote of the pall of smoke rising from the Golan Heights as formations of planes began bombing the area soon after dawn. Villagers told of seeing an Israeli aircraft trailing smoke as it plunged to the ground. Within an hour three Israeli helicopters, escorted by a Phantom, clattered in to search for the pilot. At midday they reported another Phantom seen to explode in midair as it wheeled away after bombing, and again helicopters flew in to rescue the crew. Throughout Sunday morning, the villagers watched and listened apprehensively as the artillery's thunder grew louder.

When the Syrian Air Force took to the air, a series of whirling, high-speed dogfights resulted as Israeli Mirages rose to fend them off. Formations of MIG-17s and -21s roared across the Golan Heights on their way to strafe Israeli positions and troop concentrations. At Kiryat Shimona in Upper Galilee, villagers stood in the open, hands shading their eyes from the glare, to watch a heavy dogfight between Phantoms and MIG-21s. For seconds only the planes whirled a cat's cradle of trails before they all broke off, leaving a lone Syrian aircraft spinning to the fields while spent shells pattered down. In most of these encounters the Israelis' greater skill and experience paid off, and they took a heavy toll of Syrian MIGs—later claims that North Vietnamese pilots were flying some of the Syrian fighters notwithstanding.

On both sides of the border, civilians were inevitably caught up in the violence. Mary Malka sat on a suitcase outside what used to be her three-bedroom house in Migdal Ha'emer, an Israeli village just below the Golan battlefront. With one eye blackened and her arms covered in bandages, she recounted what had happened. "We didn't hear anything," she said of the bomber that destroyed a neighboring school and ripped apart her home. Two such sudden explosions occurred during the night, the first one blowing out five apartments in a seven-story block. Mrs. Malka, aged thirty-seven, told how she and her husband, mother, three sons, and two daughters were having tea on the front porch when, "all of a sudden, we were thrown onto the floor. Everything is gone from the kitchen—all the food, everything. I never expected this. Even during the Six Day War we didn't feel it here." Their red stone house was ruined, the inside torn out and the roof caved in. Nearby, on the third floor of a shattered apartment block, a Moroccan woman, her back bent with age and her head covered with a tattered kerchief, looked at her ruined home, threw up her hands, and wept. Both explosions were probably caused by **FROG** surface-to-surface missiles fired by Syrians, since both occurred with no warning of their supersonic approach.

Throughout northern Israel, the sounds of war were clearly audible from the embattled Golan area, and the cloudless sky was filled with Phantoms and Mirages heading toward the battle. Teenagers let out of school because of the fighting watched the parade of armor heading toward their staging area. Near Tiberias on the Sea of Galilee, where Jesus is said to have walked on the water, flights of fighter-bombers ruffled the same waters as they streaked in to engage the Syrians. All the while residents of Tiberias watched the action from their balconies, which gave them a clear view of the Heights. Like spectators at a sports ground, they watched aircraft speeding into the war zone, heard the explosions, and saw smoke rising from the distant, ancient hills.

Even at this early stage, Israeli pilots who had survived the first unexpected missile onslaught devised tricks to combat them. Returning to what one correspondent called the "days of goggle and scarf flying" they learned to spot the telltale white puff signaling a missile firing, then turned violently and too sharply for the missile's guidance system to follow. Nevertheless, this new technique and the air strikes against the missile sites produced only temporary relief for the hard-pressed Israelis, for when their fighter-bombers attacked the SA-2 and SA-3 sites later that day, they were still subject to heavy opposition. For the first time, too, the Syrians activated their new SA-6 missiles, which were mounted on tracked vehicles giving them total battlefield mobility, unlike the SA-2s and SA-3s, which could be located and destroyed.

These SA-6 missiles had never before been used, and they took the entire West, as well as the Israelis, by surprise. British military analyst Edward Luttwack believed that even the Soviet Army had only limited numbers of the new missile, soon codenamed "Gainful," which was proving more accurate than the American Hawk, its nearest counterpart. It could hit a plane flying from ground level to 7 miles up, using its own radar to focus on the incoming plane, launching its rocket at the right moment, and directing it to the target. Their immediate effect was to provide a new dimension to the armored offensive to which the conventional, post–World War II answer had been the tactical air strike. Syria also had a second novel weapon, the SA-7 — "Strela" — a missile fired from a bazooka-type launcher against low-flying aircraft (known as the SA-7 "Grail" in NATO nomenclature). Both these weapons suddenly provided mobile cover for the vulnerable armored formations and radically altered conventional Western battlefield tactics.

Although Ben-Gal's 7th Brigade was managing to hold back the Syrian offensive on the northern sector of the Golan Heights, despite several localized penetrations, powerful and well-coordinated Syrian attacks had virtually destroyed Ben Shoham's Barak Brigade in the southern Golan. It was therefore inevitable to the Syrian command staff, poring over the battlefield maps and noting the movement of the colored flags, that they should switch their main offensive to the south to exploit the breakthrough there. A signal was sent to the commander of the elite Syrian 1st Armored Division, which had been assembled at Kiswe, some 20 miles behind the front, ordering him to direct his force toward the Rafid opening with the intention of reaching the Bnot Ya'akov Bridge.

The powerful armored division, which had brigades equipped with the newest Soviet T-62 main battle tank—hitherto unseen in the West—moved off in long, dust-raising columns that divided at Sanamin. There, one brigade headed for Rafid, while the other swung more sharply for the Golan through El Hara to reinforce the 9th Infantry Division's attack toward Kuneitra and the key Israeli installations at Nafekh. The attack was further intensified by sending the mechanized brigade of the 3rd Armored Division as well. That division was even further north, near Katan, but with the stalemate in the northern sector it was a sound tactic to deploy part of its strength at the breakthrough, and the brigade moved south across the desolate lava flows to join in the attack at El Hara. A force of some six hundred Syrian tanks was engaged in the southern Golan; against them were pitted the twelve remaining tanks from Oded's savaged 3rd Battalion and scant individual units cut off in the fortifications. However, there was the faintest gleam of hope in the first slow trickle of Israeli reserves, whose tanks were starting to mount the steep tracks onto the Heights. The race to hold the escarpment was clearly on.

The massive Syrian armored force was first spotted by the defenders of A10, still sheltering in their fortifications under barrage and counterbarrage. They signaled headquarters that this strong force was advancing northward along the Tapline route, and east toward Ramat Magshimim. This news was received by Ben Shoham at his Gamla Rise location, at which he turned his field glasses in the direction indicated and could clearly see the massive dust cloud they raised. But there was nothing he could do, cut off from his forces; his single tank and the half-track might as well have thrown handfuls of peas for all the effect they could have against the hundreds of tanks advancing toward them. It was still early in the morning, so the two vehicles trundled out of the boulders where they had sheltered and headed down the Rise toward the Arik Bridge, across the Jordan at the point where the river enters the Sea of Galilee. They encountered settlers fleeing in the face of the Syrians, and these were picked up; they also met the second-in-command of the 7th Brigade's 2nd Battalion, which had been placed under his command, and of which this officer was the sole survivor. The heavily laden vehicles finally rolled down the Buteiha Valley, turned north past the Arik Bridge, and eventually reached Nafekh headquarters at 9:00 A.M.

Back at his base, Ben Shoham was far from happy. His depleted forces were trying to stem the Syrian main thrust and every tank was needed to aid them. So, not long after his arrival, Shoham set off again toward the Tapline route to catch up with Colonel Yisraeli's force, which had been fighting there most of the night. No sooner had his tank rumbled from sight, however, than more Centurion tanks began to reach Nafekh. These tanks from the 79th Reserve Brigade, under Colonel Ori, were organized into groups of three as they arrived, netted into the communications system, and told to follow the brigade commander's tracks toward the Tapline route. The 2nd Battalion's second-in-command, who had been picked up that morning, was given another small force and told to advance along a route parallel to the Tapline route toward Hushniyah, to forestall a Syrian thrust to outflank the Tapline. A company of tanks was soon on its way along both routes. In the meantime, Major Dov, the brigade intelligence officer left behind by Ben Shoham, reorganized the Barak Brigade's headquarters in Nafekh.

For a while optimism rose as it looked as though matters were improving, and everyone was cheered by radio signals from the commander indicating that he had knocked out eight tanks so far. But once again hope was short-lived, for at midday the new

2nd Battalion's commander was frantically signaling that he was under intense attack by about eighty tanks advancing from the Rafid opening and Hushniyah. This was the advance force of the 1st Armored Division. The 2nd Battalion's six tanks left to stem the attack were hopelessly outnumbered and requested permission to withdraw. Ben Shoham, though, radioed that at all costs they must hang on to prevent the Syrians' bypassing the Tapline route and reaching Nafekh. He called several times, requesting confirmation of the situation, but the radio went dead; these six were not heard from again.

At 12:30 P.M., the radio crackled once more. Syrian tanks had reached Tel Abu Hanzir, after breaking through the 2nd Battalion, and had thereby outflanked Nafekh. The situation was suddenly very grim. Brig. Gen. Raful Eytan ordered Shoham and his force immediately back to Nafekh to prepare for its defense, while Yisraeli, the deputy brigade commander, confirmed their withdrawal too. Ben Shoham's tank led his pitifully small force back along the Tapline route, constantly harried by the Syrians. Several times the two forces met in headlong clashes. Five T-62s, as well as numerous trucks and personnel carriers, fell to the Centurions' guns as slowly but surely the force fought its way back toward Nafekh.

Behind them, Yisraeli was bringing up the rear and keeping off the enemy tanks that snapped like jackals at the heels of the Israeli column. Still the Syrians attacked in increasing numbers, and Yisraeli's four tanks were hard put to maintain their fire fast enough. The long barrels traversed right and left in turn, hitting at the harassing forces, then yet more Syrians crossed their path. Yisraeli's gun swung to cover them, then the dread words "Sir, no more ammunition!" came from the loader. For a brief moment Yisraeli was stunned; then, having no option, he ordered his tank to charge the enemy, and opened fire with the coaxial machine gun. The Syrians halted, unsure what was about to happen, awaiting the fearful crack of the wicked 105mm gun and the flash that would immolate them in its fireball—but they never came. Instead, the leading Syrian tank fired its shell straight into Yisraeli's tank. Smoke shot from the turret and the 40-ton machine stopped dead.

Ben Shoham didn't know that his deputy had been killed, and he pressed on for Nafekh, anxious to get there before the Syrians overran it. On all sides, Syrian tanks were thundering past them, firing on the move. The Israelis shot back, filling the valley with thunder and flashes. Then, when it seemed the race was lost, the Syrians faltered, slowed down, and unbelievably began to reverse. They pulled back before the tiny Israeli force whose guns pulverized one after another, turning them from sleek monsters into smoking, disjointed hulks. Panic set in, and for the first time in the battle Syrian troops began to abandon their tanks in their anxiety to escape the Israeli force. Ben Shoham saw his chance and signaled to headquarters for an air strike immediately to finish off the disintegrating force. Eager to avenge his decimated brigade, he hauled himself into the turret and tugged the pintle-mounted machine gun around to spray the fleeing enemy troops. They raced on until, only 300 yards from Nafekh, they passed yet another disabled and smoking Syrian tank. Ben Shoham and Katzin, his operations officer, barely glanced at the hulk as they scanned the surrounding brown hills for the enemy. Without warning the machine gun on the enemy tank swung round and opened fire, its single dying burst tearing both Ben Shoham and Katzin to pieces. Within minutes the three senior officers of the Barak Brigade had gone, like so many of its men.

All civilians had been evacuated from the Nafekh district by early Sunday morning. The camp was by then free from intensive shelling because, it was later learned, the Syrians believed that their own forces were further advanced than they really were; in consequence, their heavy artillery was firing out over the camp. Still, it was anything but quiet as the hills echoed and rumbled with gunfire.

At about 11:00 A.M., General Eytan instructed Lieutenant Colonel Pinie, the deputy commander of the Brigade District, to prepare antitank defenses around the camp's perimeter. Pinie immediately went in person to the southern perimeter fence to check it. At the fence he stopped and swore bitterly, for there, not 2,000 yards away, was massed Syrian armor even then positioning for immediate attack. Pinie stumbled back to Eytan with the news that the Syrians were within small arms range of the headquarters. How they had not been spotted moving forward has never been explained, but considering that the Israelis had been fighting desperately all night and that Ben Shoham's column had retreated before and sometimes alongside the Syrians, their arrival should have been expected.

Mark Shimon was with a team sent to man the defenses with a bazooka. "We set off at the double, never expecting the Arabs would be there before us, but as we sited the bazooka, one of the fellows yelled that the place was live with tanks. There were at least twenty bearing down on us, backed by heavy mortar fire from infantry. The camp began to erupt as shells and mortar bombs smacked down in quick succession. We managed to align our bazooka on a Syrian T-55, but caught it only a glancing blow and the shell shot off and exploded harmlessly. Our next round hit another tank in its track, which splintered and unreeled. But the tank turned its gun on us, although fortunately it missed by about twenty feet. After that, though, we ran back toward the camp headquarters while machine guns raked the ground behind us."

Colonel Ori's reserve brigade had joined the front line earlier that morning, to the right of 7th Brigade. One of his battalions, however, was still traveling north through Nafekh when it was halted by Eytan, who had already perceived that they were soon going to be under heavy attack. He then broadcast an SOS ordering Ori's entire brigade to withdraw back to Nafekh. It was doing so when it saw, moving parallel, the battalion of T-62s that had destroyed Ben Shoham's force along the Tapline route. The camp was under heavy attack by the time Ori's tanks reached Nafekh. Syrian forces had overrun the outer defenses, and were firing systematically into each building, reducing the place to a blazing inferno. For the reserves, who twenty-four hours previously had been with their families and friends, the sight of blazing tanks and scores of dead was totally unnerving. Nevertheless, they rolled forward under a ceaseless enemy barrage and engaged the greatly superior forces at close range. Meanwhile, at 1:15 P.M., Eytan ordered his advanced headquarters out of the camp, north along the Tapline route for some 3 miles.

Dodging intense machine-gun fire and heavy mortaring, Pinie instructed two infantrymen with a bazooka and six shells to follow him, and yelled over the noise of battle for his operations officer and the assistant intelligence officer as well to join his group in a slight hollow near the fence. Most of the perimeter fence had been smashed flat by the Syrian tanks, which were roaming the camp like elephants among the corn, crushing buildings and sweeping aside puny defenses; anything more solid was blown to bits by point-blank shelling. Pinie's team hugged the ground as another hut exploded in a red flash that whirled a thousand flying fragments of glass and timber as lethal as shrapnel. Pinie acted as loader while the operations officer, who had never fired a bazooka in his life, lined up the unwieldy weapon on the nearest tank, about 200 yards away. To Pinie's fury, both the first two shots missed and he screamed at the officer: "If you don't hit the bastard with the next shell, you lose your job as number one on the bazooka!" Breathlessly, they waited as he lined up another shot. There was a whoosh, and the projectile streaked away to smash into the tank's driving aperture. It shuddered to a stop astride the crushed fence while the crew bailed out, falling to the ground and scurrying away as the Israelis plastered them with submachine-gun fire. Two days later the tank's engine was still ticking over.

Other T-62s and T-55s were grinding relentlessly into the blazing and shattered camp, their guns crashing as shells ripped away every vestige of order. With only a few bazooka shells remaining, things looked black for Pinie's group, caught directly in the path of another two oncoming tanks. They hurried to get in a further shot, but thirty-six tons of camouflaged steel was bearing down. Suddenly the lead tank shook with a terrific explosion and clanked to a stop, smoke pouring from it; a second roar, and the other tank exploded in a frightening sheet of flame. From behind Pinie's group came the distinctive "cracks" of 105mm guns, and whirling around they saw the familiar low shapes of the Centurions. Ori's 79th Reserve Brigade, equipped with new tanks, was arriving and fanning out across the southeast corner of the sprawling camp.

Grabbing their bazooka, Pinie's team suicidally raced toward the battle raging around the workshops, where T-62s and some of the reserve brigade's Shermans were slamming away at each other. Flinging themselves into slender cover, they quickly hit a T-62 with their fifth projectile, but immediately another rounded monster clanked from behind the blazing building. Their last shell streaked away and missed. To their horror, the tank's 115mm gun swung toward them; then there was a great slam of shell on steel and the T-62 erupted in a sheet of flame. A single Centurion thundered out from the workshops. There was no mistaking the cheery but blackened and scorched face of the commander who leaned out of the turret. It was Zwicka.

Unknown to them, Zwicka had met up with Colonel Yisraeli's force at dawn and fought in the battle that delayed the Syrian 51st Tank Brigade's attack along the Tapline route. Then, just when Zwicka had thought they were gaining the upper hand, Yisraeli had frantically ordered his force back to Nafekh to escape the Syrians' outflanking movement. Following the death of both Yisraeli and Ben Shoham, Zwicka had used his initiative and ordered his battered Centurion off the road (thereby missing a Syrian ambush) and rocked and bucked his way across the wild terrain to reach the Nafekh camp just as the Syrians were breaking in. He had joined forces with a reserve tank then arriving, and with more enthusiasm than sense his exhausted crew had attacked the Syrians. According to General Herzog, "Zwicka fired wildly at everything in sight—at the hills and the fences and at the Syrian tanks that had already flattened the perimeter fence." The truth was that his tank driver was in the shock of exhaustion and could no longer react to orders after twenty hours of continuous, nerve-twisting battle. During the pandemonium Zwicka attached himself to Ori's brigade and with them drove off the Syrians, back over the shambles of the camp onto the Tapline route once more. The Syrian advance had been stopped at Nafekh and the blackened, smoking wreckage of their tanks, personnel carriers, and trucks lay everywhere, in the camp and on the dun-colored hills. Over twenty hours after leaving Nafekh the night before, "Force Zwicka" returned to be met by Major Dov, who stood and watched silently as the young man painfully lowered himself from the tank. He was wounded and bloody, his clothes burned and his blond hair blackened and scorched. Apologetically, he looked at Dov: "I can't any more," he whispered.

The late afternoon sun slanted across the smoke pall that hung over the Golan Heights and shrouded scenes of unparalleled confusion. For the first time the Israeli Army was falling back in disorder. Colonel Pinie realized that the sights he saw that evening brought back all the horrors of his childhood in war-torn Europe. A ravaged army straggled back in defeat. Major Dov and one other were the only survivors of the Barak Brigade's headquarters staff. Dov was appalled by the scenes on the road south from the Heights. Shorn of their commanders, remnants of Israeli units trailed along, mixed up with trucks, administrative vehicles, artillery pieces, and even tanks; they were, Dov concluded, motivated only by panic. Angered at the sight, he ordered his half-track to block the road, and his driver slewed the vehicle around to clatter across the path of the fleeing army. According to General Herzog, Dov said: "Now, this is where we stop running. Nobody is going to pass us here." From then on, each unit that reached them was halted and the senior officer or NCO was ordered to turn about. Inspired by his unique position, Dov resolutely set about creating a local defense to block the Syrians' path southward.

The shock of the onslaught was, perhaps, beginning to pass, and out of the confusion a handful of senior officers began to reorganize. Colonel Men, Eytan's second-in-command, was back at the division's main headquarters in the Jordan Valley when he learned that his chief was cut off in Nafekh. He immediately decided to rescue him, and with five damaged tanks moved up the road toward the fighting. When his small force reached Dov's roadblock, he gave his support to the effort, and soon they had some twenty damaged tanks at Aleika, about 3 miles from Nafekh. Meanwhile, urgent requests sent to support units in the Jordan Valley speeded ammunition, fuel, and repair units up to aid them. They would retreat no further.

The battle on the northern sector of the Golan front had also continued relentlessly throughout Saturday night. When dawn at last lit the slopes of the ridges, it revealed the full magnitude of the carnage. The valley between Hermonit and the "Booster" was littered with burning vehicles, both Israeli and Syrian; many had their turrets blown off, and others had simply run off their broken tracks and been abandoned by their crews. The ground was to become known to the Israeli Defense Force as "The Valley of Tears," and a great many more men from both sides would die there yet.

The 78th Tank Brigade of the Syrian 7th Division attacked again at 8:00 A.M., their assault preceded by another massive artillery bombardment that drove the Israeli tankers to slam shut their hatches and sit tight while the shells rained down. The Syrians advanced across a 2.5-mile front between the two ridges, intent on pushing a tank force up the dried watercourse below Hermonit to seize the important Wasset crossroads. Ben-Gal conserved his battalion as they sought to stop the full brigade attack, carefully mustering reserves, however small, so that there would always be one last barrier to the enemy. The 5th Battalion on the right and the 1st Battalion on the left fought grimly, and by 1:00 P.M., had driven off the Syrian attack, which left another trail of wreckage.

During the lull in the fighting, the 7th Battalion moved from positions south of Kuneitra to reinforce the central sector at Hermonit. That afternoon the Syrians mounted another attack against the single company the 7th Battalion had left behind, but it too was repulsed.

The main attack began at 10:00 P.M., for the Syrians had realized that their infrared equipment gave them a definite tactical advantage over the Israelis, forcing them to fight at close quarters where their better training was negated by the Syrians' vast numbers. The attack was a powerful one. Throwing all they could into an effort to punch through to Wasset and thence the Jordan Valley, the Syrian 7th Infantry Division was joined by their 3rd Armored Division, in turn reinforced by the crack 81st Brigade, all with the latest T-62 tanks. This great mass of some five hundred tanks was faced by the remaining forty or so tanks of Ben-Gal's brigade, which had to let the enemy get close while they suffered a massive artillery bombardment. This time the Syrians did not attempt to smash the Israeli force, but to bypass it, leaving their accompanying infantry to insinuate themselves amongst the Israelis and attack the tanks with RPG antitank missiles.

For three hours it was a desperate mêlée, in which coaxial machine guns went for the Syrian infantry, while the main guns blasted the tanks at close range. An Israeli tanker wrote: "It was madness. We just bumped into one another as we tried to maneuver, and on one occasion our driver got so close to the enemy tank at which our commander was trying to shoot, he yelled at the driver, 'Reverse, you fool, reverse or we'll run him down!' The tank jerked backward straight into another tank, hitting it with a terrific clang, just like a blow from a sledgehammer. Whether it was a Syrian or ours we never knew." It was hair-raising for the Syrian infantry, too, as they raced between the battling monsters, and many were crushed beneath tons of steel.

The battle reached a horrific pitch until the night was just a lurid red haze, shot through by gushes of yellow flame; then, equally suddenly, it was over. The Syrians began withdrawing after heavy losses. The Israelis too withdrew to their ramps and listened to the sounds of the enemy in the darkness trying to recover their wrecked armor, while others wearily rearmed and refueled.

To their south, Major Dov and his survivors stared northward where the dark edge of the rocky outcrops was aglow with the flames of battle. Dov made it clear to all the men grouped that night in the windswept darkness that no armor remained between them and the Jordan. Should the Syrians break through their roadblock, there was nothing to prevent them from rolling into Galilee.

CHAPTER

8

"Allah Is with Us!"

At the headquarters of General Mandler, in the southern sector of the Sinai front, the state of battle after twenty-four hours was no more clear than of that raging in the north. At the onset of the Egyptian amphibious assault, Mandler had directed his armored forces to advance to the Canal; but by late afternoon on Saturday, he was frankly unsure of their exact progress. Since he believed the main Egyptian attack would be in the northern sector of the front, he had directed the brigade of Col. Gavriel (Gabi) Amir there, while Col. Amnon Reshef's brigade moved directly west to defend the central sector, and Col. Dan Shomron's brigade passed through the rocky Mitla Pass to cover the Canal just south of the Great Bitter Lake. Mandler's force of about three hundred tanks was divided between the three brigades, and by early evening it was assumed at headquarters that the armor had made contact with the fortifications along the Canal. The only exception were the four fortifications located along the narrow dyke through the salt marsh north of Kantara and *Hizayon*, at the Firdan Bridge. Five tanks at the extreme end of the Canal had tried to reach fortification *Nissan* on the quayside at Port Tewfik, but found it already cut off.

Brigadier General Pino, Mandler's second-in-command, felt the fighting was so incoherent that he flew by helicopter along the artillery road as far south as the Mitla Pass. Several times during the flight his pilot had had to drop low into folds in the desert to avoid the attention of patrolling Egyptian MIGs and MIG-18 helicopters. But when he returned, it was with a comparatively concise picture of the situation to present to Mandler.

Overoptimism again perverted the Israeli view of the battle. Just as in the Golan, where the first impressions had been gained from reports of Israeli armor destroying large numbers of Syrians, so in the south, tactics were initially bedeviled by wrong impressions. In the belief that the armor had reached the fortifications, in accordance with the plan for Operation *Shovach Yonim*, no attempt was made to evacuate them in the face of the powerful Egyptian assault—although when General Elazar, the chief of staff, spoke to General Gonen of the Southern Command at 6:00 P.M. on Saturday, he did in fact counsel evacuating any fortification that imperiled his men without barring the enemy's progress.

Elazar's strategy was to impede the Egyptian assault rather than hang on to the Canal, and at that early stage, he realized that his forces were going to be hard put to hold the Egyptians for the next forty-eight hours, for already he was thinking in terms of counterattacking on Monday. For his part, Gonen ensured that his communications network was functioning efficiently from his forward headquarters in Sinai, and then, at midnight, he moved his own staff forward into Sinai to better control the front. During the next hours he received constant but erroneous confirmation that his tanks were patrolling between the fortifications and were in contact with them. It was this initial miscalculation about the ability of the Israeli armor to reach and protect the fortifications that was to hamstring much of their effort during the following week of bitter fighting.

But while the Israeli Command was rather complacently preparing to throw back the Egyptian cross-Canal invasion, the Egyptians worked furiously through Saturday night and into the early hours of Sunday to establish bridges. They had carried out the first stage of their plan, and their infantry were dug in some 2 to 3 miles inside Sinai, awaiting any Israeli attempt to drive their armor through to the Canal. Behind this screen, largely armed with antitank missiles, their engineering battalions were constructing ten bridges—three around Kantara, three between Ismailia and Deversoir, just north of the Bitter Lakes, and four in the sector Geneifa-Suez, on the shortest route to the strategic Mitla Pass.

During the opening phase of the crossing, the Egyptians had landed commandos along the entire length of the Canal, and had sent helicopters loaded with commandos across the southern Sinai Desert to seize the Israeli installations at Sharm el-Sheikh, controlling the Gulf of Aqaba. It will be recalled that in the 1968 war games, Israeli Major General Mordechai Gur had predicted this possibility, and, perhaps because the Israelis assumed the Egyptians would try this venture, they forestalled the commando raid. The Israeli Air Force had pounced on the helicopters and sent fourteen of them crashing to the sand and rocks. Reports from Israeli units sent into Sinai to deal with these incursions declared that operations were progressing satisfactorily.

Mandler's brigade commanders had been at his divisional orders group on Saturday morning when a phone call from Gonen warned Mandler that 6:00 P.M. was the likely enemy H-hour. Mandler had promptly passed on this information and advised his commanders to deploy in accordance with the *Shovach Yonim* plan by no later than 5:00 P.M., but, he stressed, on no account before 4:00 P.M. in case the forward movement of the Israeli force might prompt the Egyptians to open fire. At that point the Israeli deployment was still in the straitjacket of avoiding provocation in the hope of preventing a conflict—the kind of ostrich-inspired attitude that has motivated much of the West's responses to Soviet encroachments.

Col. Gavriel Amir's brigade was already on the move when the Egyptians began their bombing. Soon after that, however, part of his brigade was detached by Mandler, who ordered him to take the rest of the brigade toward Baluza on the main road from Sinai, skirting the southern edge of the salt marshes. Amir had not even reached that town before he was redirected to make contact with the brigade holding the northern sector of the Canal, and link up with the *Mifreket* fortification at the northern end of El Balah Island. But by the time they arrived, the armored battalion defending that area had been virtually wiped out. While Amir was meeting with the battalion commander in the line, he was contacted by Brig. Gen. Kalman Magen, who advised that he was commanding the sector north of Kantara, and instructed Amir to further divide his force. Two companies were to continue to *Mifreket*, while the remainder under Amir was moved to East Kantara to join up with the *Milano* fortification. At *Milano* the force was again divided, with units moving north and south of the position as well as giving close support. So, in the face of a powerful Egyptian offensive, the Israelis were committing their armor in penny-packets just as they were doing in the Golan, with the same disastrous results. Their pious optimism that the world would not seek to blame Israel for the latest outbreak of war if they maintained a state of low readiness, coupled with a fatal belief that their fortifications could hold up the Arabs long enough for their reserves to mobilize, was ensuring that the Israelis fought against overwhelming numbers with the very minimum of resources.

Through the night, Amir's force at *Milano* moved to and fro along the Canal under constant fire from Egyptian infantry armed with RPG bazookas, while from atop the embankments on the far side of the Canal, antitank missiles whizzed erratically across the water, destroying many of the tanks that had somehow evaded the masses of mines laid by the first waves of invading infantry. In the battle to their north, the other companies actually succeeded in knocking out a bridge. But to their amazement the Egyptians had it repaired in a matter of hours and their forces were moving across it soon after midnight.

Conditions in the marshy ground at the northern end of the Canal were extremely difficult. Among the five tanks in Amir's

(ABOVE) *Egyptian commandos crossing the Great Bitter Lake north of* Botzer. Photo by H. el Konayessi. (BELOW) *Egyptian crossing equipment.* Photo by H. el Konayessi

(ABOVE) *Egyptian 18th Infantry Division streaming into Sinai.* Photo by H. el Konayessi. (BELOW) *Egyptian troops storm through Bar-Lev Line.* Photo by H. el Konayessi

Egyptian flag hoisted over East Bank of the Suez Canal. Photo by H. el Konayessi

Israeli tank commander hit by shell splinter. Photo by Terry Fincher, courtesy of Photographers International

Surrender of the last Israeli fortification, Nissan. Photo by H. el Konayessi

Wreckage of Israeli Phantom, downed by a missile. Photo by H. el Konayessi

Egyptian troops explore tunnel in Bar-Lev Line. Photo by H. el Konayessi

battalion that had reached the Canal was one commanded by a young, up-and-coming artist named Ovida. The gunner of the same tank was one Yadin Tannenbaum, an accomplished and internationally recognized flautist. Neither they nor the rest of the crew really had much idea of what was going on, but generally believed they would soon mop up the invaders. Their company commander had simply told them that an Egyptian infantry force had crossed the Canal and they were to eradicate it. They moved into an area that was quite unknown to them and for which they had no maps; nevertheless, they progressed along the Canal, although continually harried by the Egyptian infantry, of which they took a heavy toll with their machine guns. All the while they were under constant enemy artillery bombardment from across the Canal.

At 11:00 P.M., Ovida's tank was approaching *Mifreket* when it slithered off the track and became bogged down. As all their efforts to drive out only bogged them more deeply, they had no alternative but to stay with the tank. After about an hour they saw an Egyptian bulldozer slowly climbing from the river, breaking a way through the ramparts as it moved. Tannenbaum hit this bulldozer with his first shot, and when a tank followed a few minutes later, they destroyed that too. But, to their horror, the burning tank clearly illuminated the whole area, leaving them nakedly obvious under the bright glare and totally revealed to the enemy. Within minutes the enemy had their range and two missiles struck them in quick succession, setting the bogged tank on fire. The driver and signalman promptly scrambled out and away into the darkness of the desert, but neither Tannenbaum nor Ovida escaped the inferno. (Later on, the world-famous composer Leonard Bernstein wrote a flute piece in memory of Tannebaum.)

By 3:30 A.M. Sunday morning, Amir was concentrating what remained of his brigade in the northern marshes, mostly by the light of Egyptian searchlights which, while marking for their own artillery, also proved valuable beacons for the Israeli tanks lost in the dark marshes. Tanks continued to reach his position after extricating themselves from the marshes, and as the night wore on they made endless attempts to stop the crossing Egyptians. Then, to Amir's relief, at eight o'clock Sunday morning he heard that Maj. Gen. "Bren" Adan had arrived at the Canal and that his armored division was not far behind. This meant that the reserve forces were moving forward, and it then seemed that the unequal battle might soon end. Tired and confused, Amir called Adan by radio to ask: "What have you arrived with?" To which Adan impatiently snapped: "One hundred divisions!" By then Amir's brigade of tanks was reduced to a quarter of their number.

When Gonen's meeting had ended, Col. Amnon Reshef, too, had hurried back to his brigade headquarters and issued orders for *Shovach Yonim.* But at 1:30 P.M., fresh intelligence reports warned that the Egyptians were preparing to open fire, and accordingly Reshef put his own artillery at alert. The attack began at two o'clock precisely, a deluge of fire descending onto the forward positions at an estimated incredible 175 shells a second, 10,500 in the first minute. Reports then followed that the Egyptians were crossing the Canal. Immediately Reshef ordered his brigade into the battle, and within minutes columns of tanks were moving forward to their allotted positions on the ramps from where they could cover the Canal. But as they roared in, Egyptian tank-hunting groups that had already seized the positions opened fire with hundreds of RPG bazooka shells, while from the far side of the Canal T-62 tanks and Sagger antitank missiles joined in, repelling the Israeli counterattack.

The slaughter was ferocious as tanks slammed away at one another with high-explosive shells and machine guns swept the enemy infantry. The Egyptian soldiers fought stubbornly, although hundreds were cut down in that first savage encounter, and they kept attacking. A Pentagon tank expert commented in *Newsweek* that "The reason the Israelis ran into trouble this time is technology. The Israelis believe that a tank is the best weapon against another tank, but they didn't count on the advances made in sophisticated antitank weaponry."

Meanwhile, Reshef had identified two major Egyptian crossing sites, at Ismailia, to which he sent a company of tanks, and
at Firdan, to which he directed a second company. Firdan was
a particularly dangerous spot, for the troops holding the *Hizayon*
fortification there were in dire trouble and had suffered heavy
casualties from the shelling. The patrol Reshef sent to contact
the garrison soon ran into an Egyptian force and contact was
lost; it eventually reported back after losing most of its officers.
While this was going on, most of the remaining battalion's tank
strength was being destroyed by missiles and enemy tank guns.

The third brigade in Mandler's division, that of Col. Dan
Shomron, had just completed its training cycle and was preparing
to relieve Reshef's brigade in the line when the assault began.
Like the other brigade commanders, Shomron had raced back to
his headquarters after Mandler's briefing, and his force was moving off when the Egyptian air strike raided his camp. Nevertheless, he got his forces away, sending a battalion each through the
Giddi and Mitla passes, and a third battalion between the two in
case either of the passes was already blocked by the enemy.
Shomron's intention was to launch a counterattack against the
Egyptian bridgeheads in the southern sector, which directly
menaced the passes and his route south through Sinai to Sharm
el-Sheikh. But to his annoyance he received a signal from Mandler directing him instead to attack in the central sector, in support of Reshef's brigade. Shomron protested that indications predicted a major crossing would take place in the south, and he
argued that he should continue in that direction. Mandler reluctantly compromised, sending only one battalion north while the
others continued their advance directly toward Suez.

By 4:15 P.M. Shomron's battalions were through the passes,
when yet another signal from Mandler stressed how serious the
situation was becoming with Egypt's forces across the entire
length of the Canal. Shomron would therefore take command of
the southern sector, a 35-mile-wide front from the Bitter Lakes
to 12 miles south of Suez. Already intelligence had identified
along that front the Egyptian 19th and 7th Infantry divisions, the
6th Mechanized Division, and the 4th Armored Division behind,

ready to pass through once a bridgehead was secure. In addition
to this considerable force, the Egyptian 130th Independent
Marine Brigade was grouped at the Bitter Lakes ready to cross
in PT-76 amphibious tanks and BTR-50 personnel carriers.
Their task was to break out of the bridgehead promptly and drive
inland to block the passes through which Israeli reinforcements
would arrive.

The battalion that advanced along the Giddi route intercepted
the Egyptian 130th Marine Brigade, already 10 miles east of the
Canal and moving for the pass with all speed. Shmuel Michaelson, who was driving an M-60 Patton tank, recalls: "We
emerged from the pass and began to descend the stony route
toward the Canal. A great dust cloud coming toward us was
clearly an Egyptian tank force and I wondered how we could
possibly deal with such a force. But when we got close enough,
we were delighted to find it was not tanks, but amphibious personnel carriers. Our gunners set to and within minutes the open
ground was ablaze with destroyed carriers."

No matter how many Egyptian tanks and carriers there were,
the thin-skinned amphibious vehicles were no match for the battle tanks, and dozens were knocked out. Egyptian Sgt.
Mohammed Mahmoud Nada, a naval frogman attached to 130th
Marine Brigade, wrote in his diary about those first hours in the
advance across Sinai:

we crossed at 2:30. . . . We await the order to advance and attack.
There are losses, tanks have blown up. The first tank which blew
up is mine. . . . On Saturday our advance was blocked and some
ten amphibious tanks went up in flames. Enemy tanks were
advancing and shelling us. We took up positions to block them
. . . dug slit trenches for protection. We are concerned about the
Israeli air force, which could surprise us tomorrow morning. We
are being shelled. . . . This is the cruellest night we have ever
known in which we faced death, hunger, thirst, fear and cold. . . .

It was eight o'clock on Saturday evening by the time Shomron's forces reached the fortifications in the southern sector,

although they failed to reach *Nissan* because all the approaches had been mined and were swarming with Egyptian infantry. The evening was alive with the roar of battle as the Third Army persisted in its attempts to secure a foothold along the Canal banks.

In general, it is not the actual assault on a river crossing that causes casualties, because normally the assault relies upon surprise. The casualties begin later, when the defenders mount their inevitable counterattacks. Along the Canal, however, curious conditions prevailed. The Egyptians surprised the Israelis not so much by their timing of the invasion but, rather, by the size of it. Thus, although their crossings were being violently opposed, it was by forces of insufficient size to withstand the massive assault without equally substantial reinforcements. Those reinforcements had been deliberately restrained in an attempt not to provoke the very invasion they alone could have stopped.

Defense Minister Dayan later claimed that on the Syrian front Israeli forces were properly deployed, although as the battles rapidly developed this became less apparent. He admitted, however, that until the reserves had been mobilized they must expect losses, but added: "Then we can conduct the war as we want." Along the Canal it was certain that the defense system was incapable of obstructing the Egyptian landing. But, of course, the isolated fortifications had never been intended as a "Westwall," merely as a system of observation points from which the twenty or thirty soldiers manning them could, if required, oppose a localized commando action. It was intended that their strength should lie in the armored units, which would immediately move to link them up and would patrol the banks in between the fortifications. However, when the test came and efficient Egyptian forces landed on an unprecedented scale, the Israeli armor arrived too late and in too small groups to resist the landings effectively.

In particular, Israeli defensive plans had not envisioned the large-scale use of infantry antitank weapons such as the wire-guided missiles that were deployed in huge numbers to redress the balance between infantry and armor. The battles were, in

Dayan's words, "tough, heroic, and depressing." The sixteen strongholds that collectively constituted the Bar-Lev Line fought individual battles for survival, each "a solitary, isolated isle, conducting a bitter and desperate struggle, a struggle of life or death, of surrender or breaking free." From the very onset, the Egyptian artillery concentrated on pounding the fortifications, forcing the small garrisons to keep their heads well down and subjecting them to a stupefying torrent of shells, while Egyptian tanks and infantry were sent across by boat, raft, and bridge.

On Sunday, an Egyptian military communiqué announced: "Our forces are still crossing the Suez Canal in massive numbers and forging eastward amid raging air and tank battles on the East Bank of the Canal." Indeed, as Egypt's offensive got into full swing, they fought desperately to strengthen the Canal bridgeheads won in their surprise attack. At the same time, Israel was claiming that her air force had destroyed most of the ten bridges the Egyptians had put across the Canal, having conceded that about four hundred tanks had already crossed. But with their bridges gone, the Israeli spokesman gleefully told correspondents, their situation would be "not a pleasant one." The truth was, of course, that as fast as any bridge was damaged, the Egyptians replaced it within hours.

Newsweek editor Arnaud de Borchgrave described the action on the Canal front with the Egyptians:

> Suddenly, our Soviet-made jeeps veered sharp right through a hole in the roadside embankment. We found ourselves bumper to bumper with hundreds of other military vehicles, all waiting to cross the Canal via pontoon bridges. But there was no confusion, no disorder. One by one, the army trucks eased their way down the small hill. As each one inched onto the pontoon, the troops aboard — clad in light parkas and hoods against the wind-whipped sand — broke into wild cheering. "Allah is great," they shouted, and they waved their weapons in the air. Climbing the opposite bank they surged into Sinai, moving in long columns that stretched to the horizon, all covered with camouflage netting.

Soon after we had made our Canal crossing, Israeli artillery fire began to explode around us. At the first sound of the telltale whistle, a fraction of a second before impact, my companions and I ducked and ran for cover. But we soon realized that the Egyptian Army was going about the business of war practically oblivious to the shells kicking up clouds of sand nearby. Several soldiers yelled: "Don't worry, *Allah maana* (Allah is with us)!" During four hours in the Sinai, I didn't see a single shell hit anything. Nor did I see a single casualty or even an ambulance.

The correspondents were taken to see a captured Israeli fortification, *Gabasat.* "Mangled and twisted steel girders, partially collapsed sandbagged walls and scorched bunkers bore testimony to heavy fighting. And everywhere there was abandoned equipment — helmets, machine guns, bazookas, antitank ammunition and first aid kits, all with Hebrew marking. . . ."

With the evidence before them, many correspondents were taken aback by the optimism of the Israeli statements that were being put out, after a tense day in which it was manifest that the ground troops had received a heavy pounding and the Israeli counterattack was taking longer to materialize than had been expected. There was, therefore, a tense atmosphere when the Israeli cabinet met at 10:00 P.M., and listened to the commanding officers of the Northern and Southern commands present their reports on the day's fighting. Both commanders estimated they were containing the invasion; in fact, Israeli field commanders were confidently advising the press that when they had repulsed the Egyptian and Syrian attacks, their troops would carry the war into enemy territory. Maj. Gen. Shmuel Gonen, of the Southern Command, had said that the Egyptians had failed to achieve their aim along the entire Suez Canal front and Israel could feel confident there would be a successful outcome. At the cabinet meeting, this was reinforced by Chief of Staff Elazar's confident report that the Syrian attacks had been stopped and had registered no significant success. There were, however, reports claiming that the Syrians had captured the important Mount

Hermon position, although, according to Dayan, Elazar stubbornly insisted that the troops holding that position were still in communication with Northern Command. Nevertheless it was very clear from his report that in the south, too, conditions were far from as hopeful as the first information had suggested, although it was admitted that only one stronghold had fallen into Egyptian hands.

That the fighting was confused is certain. What is less clear is why the army chiefs were stubbornly maintaining to their government that the situation was less menacing than it really was. On the Golan, by that time, an entire brigade had been wiped out. Formations reduced to battalion and even company strength were trying to stem attacks by whole divisions that were poised to roll down into Galilee, which would place them within easy reach of Tel Aviv and Haifa.

These reports also implied that the situation in the south was graver than that on the Golan front, the Egyptians having crossed the Canal in force; it seems the military chiefs were claiming that the Syrians had not actually broken through the defense lines. Reinforcements were expected to begin arriving in the north soon, so that by noon of the 7th the Israeli tank force would be greatly strengthened, and by that evening, it was predicted, several hundred would be engaging the enemy. In Sinai, however, the much greater distances involved meant that no substantial Israeli armored forces could be expected to reach the Canal front until Monday at the earliest. Paradoxically, then, the Sinai Desert, which was believed to provide Israel with defenses in depth, had become a barrier to the rapid reinforcement by reserves that was the keystone of Israeli strategy.

Of course, no one had really foreseen a situation in which the Egyptians would be permitted to mobilize and deploy in such force without a punitive Israeli response, nor—and this was the most important point—that they would cross the Canal with such speed. The first day's fighting had placed the Israelis on the defensive for the first time since 1948, while they belatedly mobilized their reserves. (According to the London Institute of

Strategic Studies, this meant that 330,000 reservists had to be mobilized in seventy-two hours to support the standing army of 30,000. Egypt had an army of some 260,000 regulars backed by half a million reserves, and Syria's 120,000 regulars were reinforced by another 200,000 or so reserves. To this could be added approximately another 428,000 should both Jordan and Iraq decide to join in the battle.)

The Egyptians had given a textbook example of a water-borne attack: overwhelming force delivered at the point of assault, followed by an infantry deployment in depth to secure the bridgehead into which the armored forces were poured, until sufficient strength was achieved for a powerful breakout into the interior. The danger point of such an operation lies in the buildup, when the bridgeheads are gorged with supplies and troops, and it is then that the defenders could be expected to strike with air and armored power. But Egypt's latest Soviet equipment covered all these eventualities. Sagger and RPG missiles were deployed far enough forward to prevent an immediate counterattack by the available Israeli forces, and extremely heavy concentrations of artillery dealt with the limited Israeli counterbattery actions, while the SAMs created a veritable *cordon sanitaire* through which the Israelis could barely penetrate.

After the war of 1948, Israeli military strategy had rested on the concept of training, surprise, and deterrence; but in 1973, they failed to apply any of these three elements. According to the retired Gen. Matityahu Peled, his country's signficant error in 1973 was not to put into practice its two military doctrines of transferring the war into enemy territory and fighting on one front only until a decisive victory had been won. After the success of the Six Day War, the attitude of Israel's leading strategists, Moshe Dayan and his chief of staff, Chaim Bar-Lev, had changed from the basic theory of deterrence that had served for nineteen years. Convinced that Israel's borders were secure along the Jordan River, the Golan Heights, and the Suez Canal, the "greatest antitank ditch in the world," as it had been described — although that label had also been applied to Belgium's Albert

Canal prior to 1940—they had constructed the Bar-Lev Line.
That had been a fundamental modification of Israel's previous
offensive concept of the strike into enemy territory. But the fact
was that Israel could no longer risk an offensive into either Egypt
or Syria for fear of provoking the Russians, and so could no
longer use her favorite political threat, the preemptive strike.

In the years following the war of attrition, Israel should have
kept most of her army on the borders, strengthening her limited
forces on the Suez and Golan fronts. A deployment scheme
should have been originated and, in spite of the high cost, a large
army should have been maintained on the borders to instill into
the enemy a feeling of insecurity, to discourage them from
believing they could successfully attack Israel. Israel's existing
offensive strategy did not match her defensive tactics, which considered territory more important than genuine security. The
strategy of territorial depth was founded upon a small force
being able to hold the front line under the protection of air
superiority while reserves were quickly mobilized. Not only did
air superiority fail to deter in the Yom Kippur War, in the face
of sophisticated missiles, but the consequent failure to mobilize
immediately once the Arab threat was recognized denied the
armored divisions the resources they needed to reach and hold
the fortified line. The Israeli High Command dithered between
two concepts, that of immediately transferring the war into the
enemy's territory and a belief that the option was redundant.
Gen. Arik Sharon admittedly had no such doubts. He was convinced that the depth strategy was disastrous for their forces
because it denied them the initiative and essential mobility of an
immediate offensive, which could have thrown the the Egyptians
right off-balance by its force and surprise. Therefore, in the Yom
Kippur War, Israel did not immediately transfer the war into the
enemy's territory, but waited for them to take the offensive,
which they did. For the first time, Israel failed to use her military
strategy to make it absolutely clear to the Arabs that if they went
to war, she could defeat them. The Arabs had in consequence
launched their attack and were pounding on Israel's frontiers.

At the cabinet meeting, Dayan, as he reveals in his memoirs, had not intended to express his own views; after all, it was a military situation in which the task of reporting was that of the chief of staff. But, after hearing the military summaries, Dayan felt obliged to tell the government his views of the situation "in all its stark severity. . . ." In Dayan's view, there were three difficult factors facing the Israelis. The first, he said, was the very size of the enemy forces lavishly equipped with the latest Soviet weaponry. In addition, the Arab forces, he pointed out, were of a very different caliber from those who had fought in 1967; they were "good troops using good equipment and fighting with determination." Second, the enemy's antiaircraft missile system was presenting grave problems for the Israeli Air Force; so long as their planes could not overcome it, they could not give adequate support to the Israeli armor or help annihilate the enemy armor. The third factor was the necessity of holding the frontier lines with very small forces, so as to avoid mobilizing Israel's population, and the high risk that course of action entailed in terms of the time taken to mobilize reserves.

In Dayan's view, then, it was doubtful whether they could seriously interrupt the Canal crossings for twenty-four to thirty-six hours, which gave the Egyptians two nights in which to erect more bridges and rush their forces into Sinai. Unlike the northern front, where reserves would soon be available to check the Syrian advance, the Canal was the critical battlefield. The air force, he believed, would face a grim task when it attacked the Egyptians the following day, since it would have to deal not only with the Egyptian Air Force but with the formidable antiaircraft system, too. He concluded optimistically, nonetheless, that if on the following day they had a good deal of luck and managed to end the day's battle favorably, by Monday and Tuesday the Israeli armor would have arrived and could begin to engage the enemy in tank warfare, which although it would be difficult had good prospects. Dayan proposed, therefore, that the Israeli forces in the south should withdraw to a second line of defense and contain the Egyptians within a belt 12 miles from the Canal.

As the cabinet meeting ended, the mood was tense and those present were far from happy. Dayan, in particular, sensed his isolation from his colleagues, who had disliked his views and especially the suggestion of withdrawing to a second line, although that would enable the Israeli forces to create a defensible line out of range of the static SA-2 and SA-3 missiles. It would not eradicate the mobile SA-6 missiles, but these were only now appearing on the battlefield, and, in any case, facing that system alone greatly lessened the number of missiles. Against just the SA-6s, the Israeli Air Force should have been able to operate with much less danger. But the cabinet ministers were, according to Dayan, "seized by the optimism in the chief of staff's survey and above all by their own wishful thinking."

All Saturday night the Canal was dotted with pontoons loaded with tractors and equipment that the Egyptians tried to float across the shell-torn water. Israeli tanks poured shells and machine-gun fire into the cauldron, while themselves under constant sniping from Egyptian infantrymen deployed among them with antitank weapons. After several hours of this bloody combat, Dan Shomron realized that this was no renewal of the war of attrition, but a full-scale war, in which the fortifications were contributing nothing to opposing the crossings. Indeed, along the Canal, as in the Golan, they were impediments to the Israeli armor, which was being held back to defend them. The fortifications also had perpetual call on Israel's artillery, which should have been plastering the bridges and ferries. Shomron asked Mandler for permission to evacuate all the fortifications so that his armored forces could fight the mobile battle for which they had trained, but he was refused. He sent another imperative message: Could fresh infantry be sent to reinforce the fortifications, then? The answer was simple—there were none available. Desperately, Shomron spoke directly with Mandler. "Either we defend the fortifications," he said, "or we block the Egyptian attack. We can't do both." But Mandler replied that there was no alternative, and since he did not himself have the authority to evacuate the fortifications, Shomron would indeed have to do both.

There followed a night of sheer frustration and exhaustion for the Israeli tankers as they attacked the Egyptian crossing points, only to have to break off when the fortifications appealed for help. Then as they lumbered across the desert between Canal and fortification, they ran into countless ambushes from Egyptian infantry deployed in the darkness with their antitank missiles; in places the ground was webbed with the thin control wires from spent missiles. Once the fortifications were relieved and the attackers had fled into the night, the weary tankers drove their machines back through more ambushes to shell and machine-gun the crossings once again. Of the one hundred tanks that had rumbled through the passes on Saturday afternoon, seventy-seven were smoking hulks by early Sunday morning. Two thirds of the brigade's total losses in the war were incurred during that terrible first night.

At the northern end of the Canal line, Colonel Amir's brigade reported that it had destroyed a bridge, but against that he was left by morning with only ten tanks. The others had fallen to infantry-fired antitank missiles, and enemy tanks from longer range. Mandler reported to Gonen on Sunday that his division was reduced to a third of the tanks he had set out with.

At nine o'clock Sunday morning the first Egyptian armored units moved slowly and warily across the bridges and deployed into Sinai, whereupon Dan Shomron used his reconnaissance unit to establish long-range observation points to feed his own intelligence network. Then, when the Egyptian armor began to move out from the crossings, their long guns looking like rats cautiously coming out of their holes, Shomron brought to bear all his small remaining forces. He concentrated them where their combined firepower would do most good and destroyed many enemy tanks at long range. But the fortifications were still demanding aid, and at 11:00 A.M., Shomron had no alternative but to contact Mandler and insist on a decision: Either the tanks would remain with the fortifications and fight to the end, or he would leave the fortifications and concentrate on holding up the Egyptian advance. Reluctantly, it seems, he was ordered to deal with the crossings, but advised also that there were no reserves yet available or air support since the air force was operating in the Golan.

Shomron's three artillery batteries concentrated then on the crossings, firing across the sand dunes from 2 miles east of the Lateral Road, opposing an Egyptian force of seventy-five batteries. An hour or so later, at 1:00 P.M., the *Lituf* fortification, just south of the Bitter Lakes, fell to the Egyptian 7th Division, and all its survivors were taken prisoner; later evidence showed that the Israelis who were taken prisoner had, for the most part, an extremely hard time.

For the remainder of Sunday, Shomron's brigade opposed the strength of the entire Egyptian Third Army. He had his tank battalions, each with no more than ten tanks, in positions west of the Artillery Road, although one battalion was re-forming to the rear of the Mitla Pass after its beating on Saturday. All his armored infantry had been taken from him, and from observers in the remaining fortifications he knew that the Egyptians were massing for a powerful advance. He therefore decided not to deploy his forces piecemeal any longer and watch them being ground up, but to use them as a true armored fist with which to launch a preemptive punch into the Egyptian armor as it massed for the attack.

One battalion made a feint toward the captured *Lituf* fortification, which drew some of the Egyptian armor away northward. Then his other two armored battalions drove for the *Mafzeah* fortifications, midway between the Bitter Lakes and Port Suez at the southern end of the Canal. Gaining momentum, his armor crossed the Lexicon Road in a fierce running battle with the armored supporting units of the Egyptian 19th Division. It was a bitter fight, with both sides stubbornly resisting, but the Egyptians had already moved forward a great number of ammunition trucks, ready to support the advance into Sinai once their 25th Armored Brigade had crossed. These trucks were easy targets for the Israeli tanks and exploded with great force. Shomron's brigade fought a classic armored battle of movement, keeping the Egyptians off-balance and unable to regroup to mount a systematic counterattack. By late Sunday night, the Egyptian force was in disarray and its planned attack thrown completely out of gear.

President Sadat had stayed away from the command headquarters all Sunday, confident that operations were going according to plan and believing that his presence would only create nervous tension. He relied, instead, on Marshal Ali, the army commander, to keep him informed. In the evening, however, Vinogradov, the Soviet ambassador, called again. According to Sadat, he greeted Vinogradov with the words: "Well, I received President al-Assad's reply only half an hour ago. He denies your story altogether—the official message you conveyed to me from the Soviet leaders, yesterday." The Soviet ambassador's face went white, but he nevertheless informed Sadat of another message from his government, claiming Syria had made another request for a cease-fire.

Sadat responded angrily: "Now listen, this subject is closed." He went on to make it clear that he would not have a cease-fire "until the objectives of the battle have been achieved." These objectives, Sadat emphasized, were to control the East Bank of the Canal—by then virtually achieved—and advance to the strategic passes, for which Egyptian armor was massing preparatory to its breakout from the bridgeheads. Sadat obviously realized what cost he would have to pay for these objectives, for he told Vinogradov: "I'd like you to tell the Moscow leadership to send me some tanks at once. This will be the biggest tank battle in history." At that time Egypt had an estimated 300 tanks already in Sinai out of the 2,200 deployed on the Canal-Sinai front. As their losses in crossing the Canal had been, according to Egypt, "remarkably light," Sadat clearly expected a fierce and costly battle.

It was then, on the evening of Sunday, October 7 according

to Sadat, that the Soviets confirmed their intention of establishing an air bridge, by which their long-overdue ammunition and equipment would be airlifted to Egypt immediately. Nevertheless, in spite of Soviet protestations that Syria was already asking for a cease-fire, and announcing only then their intention to begin an airlift, there is evidence that the Russians had prepared to involve themselves not just from the outset of the battle, but well in advance. The freighters that began arriving in Alexandria during the first week of the war had left their Black Sea ports before the war started, and must have been loaded well before that. In all this there is an echo of the Soviet invasion of Hungary in 1956, for that invasion force had begun moving toward Budapest from Russia and Romania before the crisis began.

In October 1973, Soviet diplomats were busy elsewhere in the Arab world, exhorting Morocco, Algeria, Libya, Jordan, and others to go to the aid of Egypt and Syria. They were obviously intent on stoking the conflagration into a major Middle East war, which only superpower intervention would be able to extinguish; and, in the context of the Arab world, that had to be the Soviet Union. Already, then, within hours of the war's beginning, the hand of the Soviet Union could be seen manipulating the situation, until after the war had dragged bitterly through two weeks, its covert preparations culminated in a major flashpoint in superpower relations.

CHAPTER

9

"Why Are You Withdrawing?"

On the third day of the Yom Kippur War, Gen. David ("Dado") Elazar, the soft-spoken but tough chief of staff, addressed correspondents again, with the self-assurance of a man accustomed to quick victories. "Gentlemen, we have begun the destruction of the Egyptian Army." His words were almost drowned by Phantoms screaming over to begin hammering the Egyptian bridges.

Elazar's words stemmed from important decisions made the previous day. But unfortunately for Israel, things did not work out as planned.

Defense Minister Dayan had left Tel Aviv to arrive at Gonen's Southern Command headquarters at 11:40 Sunday morning, intent on having a first-hand look at the way the battle was developing. On hearing that Dayan was on his way by helicopter, Gonen advised that he should turn back as there were Egyptian commandos occupying the hills that overlooked Southern Command headquarters, who might shoot down Dayan's helicopter. The balding defense minister with the characteristic black eye patch nevertheless arrived on time and immediately asked for the latest report on the critical Canal front situation. Dayan recalled drinking a great deal of black coffee, listening contemplatively to Gonen's appraisal, then reacting decisively. "This is war," he said, according to General Herzog. "Withdraw to the high ground," and his finger traced a line across the map east of Refidim (Bir Gafgafa), through the Jebel Ma'ara and Jebel Yalek mountains, to Abu Rudeis on the Gulf of Suez. "Leave the fortifications," Dayan suggested, "let whoever can evacuate. The wounded will have to remain prisoners."

This was ruthless decisionmaking, but the circumstances demanded quick decisions. Dayan was quick to see the Arab superiority in numbers and equipment as the most serious problem, and the fact that with aid from Russia and especially Libya, they could continue fighting despite heavy losses. As Shomron had already made plain, the fortifications were a dead weight around the necks of field commanders, who could fight only so far before rushing back to defend them. Nevertheless, Dayan's proposed new line would have abandoned the Mitla and Giddi passes, the former Egyptian base of Refidim, and the Ras Sudar area, and that is hard to understand since the passes had always figured so highly in Israel's Sinai strategy. It can be seen only in the light of a permanent abandonment of a Canal front line, since the passes were in the nature of valves: It was difficult to push a force through them, but comparatively easy to restrict a flow of force from them. Retention of a strong Israeli line along the hills would have left the Egyptians in possession of the passes, thereby barring further Israeli excursions to the Canal, except after bitter fighting, but it would also have enabled the Israeli Army to contain its enemy within a defensible area while giving political satisfaction. Perhaps it was a panic reaction to a very critical situation; perhaps it was true statesmanship. In any event, had the suggestion been followed, the outcome of the Yom Kippur War would have been very different. Who knows what political effects may have resulted? Whether Egypt's President Sadat would have been more, or less, amenable to a settlement with Israel once given back the East Bank of the Canal, the passes, and the oil fields, is still imponderable.

In the face of Dayan's arguments, Gonen agreed to abandon the fortifications, but argued against the withdrawal to the mountains. Already the growing Arab confidence after their successes was rapidly becoming akin to a resurgent Islamic belief in a holy war and was attracting contingents from Morocco, Tunisia, Algeria, Jordan, the Gulf States, and Saudi Arabia. A major Israeli withdrawal at that time would have been interpreted as a sign of defeat and could have fired Arab confidence to catastrophic proportions. It was essential in those first hours and days for the Israelis to give the Arabs no inkling of how near collapse they were.

Dayan deferred the decision on withdrawal to Southern Command, and Gonen resolved to maintain his forward positions on the lateral artillery road, roughly 5 miles back from the Canal, with his main forces along the Lateral Road a further 10 miles back. Thus, his advance forces were in contact with the forward Egyptian troops and able to react to any signs of their breaking out, while his main forces were outside immediate missile and artillery range. To break out, the Egyptians would have to venture outside the protection of their SA-2 and SA-3 missiles, which the Israelis thought would give their aircraft a chance to stop the armor. At that time the southern front had not yet encountered the formidable SA-6 mobile tracked missile, nor the SA-7 shoulder-fired infantry weapon, both of which would move forward with the advancing armor. By the evening, Gonen had most of his newly arrived reserves deployed and was managing to contain the Egyptian advance, although under great pressure. According to General Herzog, the situation on Sunday, October 7, had revealed the basic misconception of the *Shovach Yonim* plan, which had presumed that three hundred Israeli tanks would be sufficient to stop a full-scale Egpytian attack, whereas it was becoming obvious that three divisions would be barely able to do so.

At midday on Sunday, Gonen divided the Sinai front, with Adan's division taking over the northern sector, Sharon's division the central sector, and Mandler's the southern sector. Therefore, by the afternoon, divisions were taking over responsibility for the brigades that had themselves taken over from the battalions holding the front at the outbreak of war.

Gen. Ariel ("Arik") Sharon had been a larger-than-life figure in Israel for more than half of his forty-five years, ever since the first Arab-Israeli War in 1948, when he had led a charge into strong Jordanian positions with the cry, "Follow me!" thus coining the Israeli Army's battle cry. But Sharon had resigned from the army two months before, following a distinguished career in the 1967 War and the war of attrition, after becoming convinced that he would never be made chief of staff. His characteristic bluntness, flamboyant personality, and charismatic leadership had led to his being dubbed the "Israeli Patton," after the American commander of World War II, who had displayed the same characteristics. With his usual boldness Sharon was already proposing that they launch an immediate counterattack, employing all the available divisions. Gonen, however, refused, in the belief that it was necessary to consolidate his forces and straighten his defense line. His available forces were still meager compared to the powerful Egyptian Army opposing him, and had he committed one or two of his divisions, he feared that it would invite a strong Egyptian counterattack in another sector. Between Gonen and Sharon there existed a relationship curiously parallel to that between Patton and the British Field Marshal Montgomery in World War II; the dash of the one conflicted with the caution of the other. Perhaps that is why neither Patton nor Sharon reached the very highest command posts.

During Sunday afternoon Gonen had also made several other adjustments to his command to strengthen his resistance to any Egyptian attack. At 3:30 P.M. he had transferred an armored brigade to Mandler, to secure the passes, and placed Reshef's brigade under Sharon's command in the central sector; it was these sectors that offered the most direct route for the Egyptians into Sinai by way of the passes. By ten o'clock that evening, commandos had entered the Ras Sudar oil fields area in the south Sinai. These, too, came under Gonen's Southern Command, and thereby narrowed Mandler's area of responsibility to the south of the Canal line, enabling him to concentrate on blocking any Egyptian drive for the passes.

Dayan had got back to the general headquarters, which he termed "the Pit," by early afternoon, and he further pressed his suggestion that the army should withdraw, only now it was just to the line of the passes. Pessimistically, he insisted that to defend the country the Gulf of Suez would have to be abandoned, retaining only a token force at Sharm el-Sheikh. Along the Golan Heights, he said, a line should be established before the escarpment overlooking the Jordan River. But General Elazar also differed, firmly adhering to his own view that in Sinai the line had to be held before Ras Sudar, commanding the Gulf. Still Dayan persisted, and went to the prime minister with his proposals for a general withdrawal. According to Herzog, Dayan told the prime minister: "Golda, I was wrong in everything. We are heading toward a catastrophe. We shall have to withdraw on the Golan Heights to the edge of the escarpment overlooking the valley and in the south in Sinai to the passes, and hold on to the last bullet."

At 4:00 P.M., Elazar was summoned to the prime minister's office for an urgent meeting and found himself defending two positions: First, he maintained that a withdrawal to the passes would cost too much in lost facilities; and, second, he vetoed Sharon's scheme for an immediate attack and a Canal crossing, although he did favor a counterattack to break up the enemy's main concentrations. The prime minister, according to Dayan, was shocked at Dayan's own opinion that the Egyptians could not immediately be thrown back, Dayan says in his memoirs: "It was clear from their critical cross-questioning after my realistic remarks that they thought the weakness lay not in our current military situation but in my personal character, that I had lost my confidence, and that my evaluation was incorrect." The prime minister listened to both sides, and approved Elazar's request to go straight to Southern Command and investigate in person.

After the defense minister and the chief of staff had left her office, the prime minister must have gone through a traumatic period of assessment of her country's position, faced as she was with so many conflicting views and strategies. Israel was, after all, in a unique situation. For the first time since 1948, the country was on the defensive, had lost the initiative upon which her comparatively small forces relied to beat the numerically superior Arab armies, and was obviously struggling to find the correct response. Mrs. Meir fell back on a well-tried and proven formula—the former chief of staff and brilliant orchestrator of the 1967 victory, Lt. Gen. Chaim Bar-Lev.

On that hot Sunday afternoon, the silver-haired former chief of staff who was currently minister of trade and industry was trying to maintain a semblance of normality by visiting supermarkets and stores. From these mundane duties he had moved on to visit an emergency organization when he received a message that he was to go to the prime minister's office without delay. He arrived at five o'clock and went from the scorching sunshine into the cool of her office to find the seventy-five-year-old prime minister sitting disconsolately with her head in her hands, utterly distraught at the events of the previous twenty-four hours. When Bar-Lev was seated, she told him about Dayan's visit and his gloomy predictions. After making sure he understood the critical situation, she asked him whether he would leave what he was doing, go up to the northern front, and advise her on what she should do. To this proposal Bar-Lev gladly agreed, but he suggested that both Dayan and Elazar should first be consulted. Mrs. Meir promptly did so, and found both in ready agreement, even to the point of authorizing him to give orders on the spot if he considered it necessary. Bar-Lev left soon after, having only broken his journey very briefly to call on Dayan, who gave him a military shirt to wear.

While Bar-Lev was heading north, Elazar was on his way south. Both men, the incumbent chief of staff and his predecessor, were bent on creating order out of the improvisation and confusion then reigning. It was seven o'clock that same evening when Elazar arrived at Southern Command headquarters, accompanied by reserve general Yitzhak Rabin (who would eventually succeed Mrs. Meir as prime minister), for a meeting with Gonen, Mandler, Adan, and Magen. The last had been about to replace Mandler just prior to the outbreak of the war. Sharon was to have been there, too, but was unable to make the meeting because of helicopter failure, although he did arrive just in time to see Elazar briefly as he was leaving. Elazar put before the meeting his plan for a counterattack on the following day.

Maj. Gen. "Bren" Adan's division was to attack the Egyptian Second Army's positions from the Kantara area, while Sharon's division remained in reserve near Tassa, on the Lateral Road about 20 miles east of the Canal at Lake Timsah. Adan would launch a concentrated divisional attack from north to south, across the Egyptian front, the objective being to blunt any possible Egyptian offensive. Then, should Adan's attack look successful, Sharon's division, which would be in reserve near Tassa, would launch an immediate attack against the Egyptian Third Army, driving from the Bitter Lakes southward toward Mandler's forces. But if Adan's attack was held, Elazar warned, then Sharon's division was to reinforce it. Whatever happened, Elazar insisted, his forces must stay away from the Canal bank and keep out of range of the formidable array of Egyptian infantry antitank weapons ranged along the embankments by both their 18th and 2nd Infantry divisions.

However, despite Elazar's emphasis on the dangers of encroaching too close to the Canal, Gonen still asked for permission for his forces to cross to the West Bank if their attack was successful. Elazar grudgingly gave his approval to a scheme for crossing at the southern point of each divisional sector, *provided that* Egyptian bridges were captured, and only then with his express approval. Similarly, Elazar retained overall control by insisting that Sharon's division was essentially a reserve for Adan's northern sector attack and its movement would only be at his personal approval. Mandler's division, meanwhile, was to hold its position ready to support Sharon if he attacked southward.

Just as Elazar was hastening away to his helicopter at the end of the meeting, Sharon arrived. The pugnacious, tousle-haired divisional commander had his own well-analyzed ideas which he, too, wanted to put to the chief of staff. He wanted to relieve the fortifications; but Gonen didn't like the idea of a night attack, especially after Saturday night's experiences. He therefore ordered Sharon to revise the plan for the following day, when he would decide after reviewing the situation. But, Sharon insisted, the wisest step would be to seize a foothold on the Canal, cross it, and confuse the enemy with the boldness of their tactics. He knew he was alone in advocating an immediate counteroffensive in Sinai, basing his ideas on the assumption that their forces were unlikely to be reinforced from the Golan front. It would, he argued, be senseless to wait, as this would permit the Egyptians to fortify their positions and install missiles on the East Bank, which would be certain to make a later Israeli counterattack even more difficult and hazardous. That most of the Egyptian armor was still on the West Bank was seen as a great advantage, since it would not be able to intervene effectively. An immediate Israeli attack would exploit one of the Arabs' traditional weaknesses, their inability to improvise once their plans were upset. Sharon wanted to shock the Egyptians with an immediate attack, which they would not expect, and then keep them off-balance. Such an initiative would also eradicate the missile sites, thereby allowing the Israeli fighter-bombers to begin destroying Egypt's armored forces.

This was a daring concept, but Gonen in particular preferred to exercise caution. There was, he pointed out, the danger that if substantial forces were moved from the north to reinforce such an action, it would invite another massive Syrian attack. Also, it was stressed, if the Israelis suffered heavy losses in forcing a Canal crossing, their offensive would be ended, and with it perhaps any hope of reaching a decision on the southern front. It was better, Gonen argued, to wait until the Egyptians had transferred most of their armored forces to the East Bank and launched their inevitable attack into Sinai, by which time the superior Israeli armor would be in a better position to destroy them. Only then, Gonen and Elazar said, should Israeli units cross the Canal to seize the West Bank under the best possible circumstances, as there would be no major Egyptian armored units remaining. Neither would there be any danger of the Egyptians withdrawing their armor back to the West Bank again, because by then their missile umbrella would have been knocked out. Israeli aircraft would be operating freely over the Canal Zone, able to destroy the Egyptian bridges, and so cut off their armor in Sinai to wither on the vine.

On Monday morning, October 8, Elazar confidently told correspondents that they were about to begin their counterattack and saw the end of the war in sight.

Adan's division was in position along the main lateral El Baluza-to-Tassa road, which had been constructed especially to facilitate the rapid movement of armor along the Canal. Gabi Amir's brigade was ready to move off south toward the *Hizayon* and *Purkan* fortifications in a 5-mile-wide band between the Artillery Road and the Canal-side Lexicon Road, destroying the enemy as it went. At the same time, the brigade of Col. Natke Nir would move along on Amir's left flank and west of the Artillery Road toward *Purkan*, opposite Ismailia. The third brigade of Adan's division, that of Col. Aryeh Karen, meanwhile was to keep east of the Artillery Road as it moved south toward *Matzmed*, at the northern tip of the Great Bitter Lake. At that point a limited Canal crossing would be attempted, using Egyptian bridges. Following Adan's destruction of the Egyptian Second Army, Brig. Gen. Kalman Magen would launch another force from the very northern sector to mop up any resistance. At 6:15 A.M., Gonen contacted Sharon to remind him that he would not be attacking toward the fortifications, and pointedly confirmed that his role would largely depend upon Adan's success, which no doubt irritated Sharon by its biting superfluousness.

Final approval for the operation had been received just before 6:00 A.M. from general headquarters, and at 8:00 A.M. the attack began according to plan, with two brigades driving south under intense Egyptian artillery fire. Amir's brigade hardly encoun-

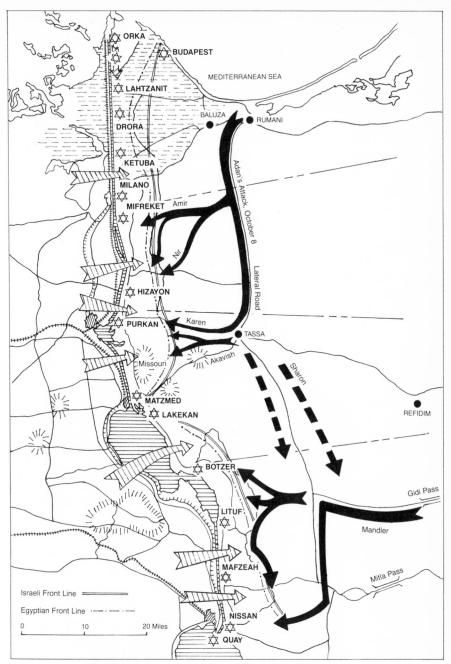

ORKA

BUDAPEST

MEDITERRANEAN SEA

LAHTZANIT

BALUZA   RUMANI

DRORA

KETUBA

MILANO

MIFREKET   Amir

Adan's Attack, October 8

Nir

Lateral Road

HIZAYON

Karen

PURKAN

TASSA

Missouri   Akavish

Sharon

MATZMED

LAKEKAN

REFIDIM

BOTZER

Gidi Pass

LITUF

Mandler

MAFZEAH

Mitla Pass

Israeli Front Line

Egyptian Front Line

NISSAN

0   10   20 Miles

QUAY

Israeli Attacks Against Egyptian Bridgeheads, October 8, 1973

tered opposition until he reached Firdan at 9:30, when they were heavily engaged by infantry missiles and rockets. Nevertheless, they dealt with these successive attacks from units of the Egyptian 2nd Infantry Division, one member of which recorded that "the Israeli tanks were throwing up great clouds of dust and sand, and as we could not see them clearly we fired straight into the dust, occasionally seeing a flash as a tank exploded. But at the same time the enemy tanks were shooting into our positions and when an infantry company attempted to intercept them with antitank missiles, they were badly cut up by machine-gun fire. The most strange thing, though, was that instead of driving toward us, the Israelis seemed to be going past."

By that time optimism was already growing at Southern Command headquarters that the enemy was beginning to fall back in some panic, although the battle was still raging across miles of sand, with tanks wheeling and maneuvering. Accordingly, Adan was sent orders to broaden his front and try to grab the three bridges at El Balah Island, Firdan, and Ismailia, using the minimum of force. Adan admits to having been surprised by this command, but believing it to be based on sound intelligence he ordered Amir to attack the Firdan area with air support. Since Adan's artillery had still not arrived at the front, he was to be supported by two batteries from Sharon's division. He continued to watch the progress of his division anxiously. By the late morning it was all too apparent that his brigades were moving too far to the east and away from the enemy's main forces; the effect of this error was that instead of rolling down and destroying the northern flank of the enemy's still narrow bridgehead, Adan's brigades were crossing the Egyptian front and totally exposed to their firepower. Thus, when the attack went in, it was a brutal frontal assault straight into the massed enemy positions, instead of a surprise flank attack.

Things began to get very confused around midday while Nir's brigade maintained a steady advance with very limited air support. Karen's brigade, meanwhile, was on its way toward Ismailia when it was given orders to seize bridges. Amir's force, too, was wheeling toward the Canal, and under fire from Egyptian tanks and infantry on the ramparts on the Egyptian side of Firdan. The attack was still being pressed home when suddenly hundreds of Egyptian soldiers burst from concealment among the dunes. Levi Stone, a student who had returned to his reserve battalion, recalled: "It was an amazing sight. We were concentrating on the ramparts where we could clearly see the enemy, when without warning the dunes swarmed with enemy troops, all seemingly carrying missile launchers. They simply ran in close among the tanks and let fly at us. Most times they could hardly miss!" And an Egyptian observer reported: "Our soldiers gave the enemy tanks no chance, unsupported as they were without infantry. I watched an infantryman kneeling in the dune with his antitank missile launcher at his shoulder. He did not falter in his aim when an enemy tank bore down upon him firing its machine gun. The missile swerved away and smacked into the tank, instantly setting it on fire." Within minutes the Israeli force was in great trouble. Soon the order was given to withdraw, leaving many tanks in flames.

While the battle had been developing in the north of the Canal line, at 11:00 A.M. Gonen had ordered Sharon to move south to hold his division in readiness near the Giddi Pass, aware of the time it would otherwise need to get to its starting line, and believing that the battle was developing satisfactorily. He would instruct Sharon in which direction to move as soon as the battle clarified itself. Even when reports began to reach his headquarters of the fierceness of the fighting, and although Adan indicated that he had lost six tanks, Gonen was not too alarmed and still ordered Sharon to keep going beyond the Giddi Pass. However, Gonen could get no confirmation from Sharon in response to these commands, and he felt obliged to send his chief of staff by helicopter after Sharon, only to find he still had one brigade in Tassa, one 6 miles south, and the third with Sharon's advance headquarters near the Giddi and Mitla passes.

By this time Adan, who was observing the battle from high ground, had ordered Nir, a short, blunt-spoken brigade commander, to move two battalions south to Firdan and link up with Amir in a two-brigade attack. The two brigades attacked on parallel axis about 2 miles apart, at two o'clock. Little more than two battalions strong in reality, they moved through loose-shifting sand dunes under a continual heavy artillery and mortar bombardment. Soon they were also under heavy antitank fire, and within a quarter of an hour the second-in-command of the leading battalion had been killed and a number of tanks knocked out. A new weapon engaged them when the Egyptians brought into the fight truck-mounted Katyusha multiple rocket launchers, which loosed a torrent of fire at them, the missiles flaring up like gas jets. When they were about 800 yards from the Canal, and barely able to see a few yards ahead through clouds of dust and rolling black smoke from blazing tanks, they were attacked by hundreds of Egyptian infantrymen with antitank weapons. To either side of him Nir could glimpse them through the smoke, and hear the roar of tanks exploding in sheets of flame. Suddenly the Israeli attack that was supposed to mark the nadir of the Arab forces was going very wrong. To the amazement of both the Israelis and the Egyptians, the Israeli 190th Tank Brigade was on the verge of annihilation.

Brig. Hassab Abu Saada, who commanded the Egyptian brigade opposing Nir, described the scene: "The enemy opened his attack moving forward at a speed of 40 kilometers an hour. As soon as the Israeli tanks crossed the camouflaged infantry trenches, the infantry jumped out of the trenches like devils and began to attack the 190th Brigade. Our tanks and all the antitank equipment concentrated in the area against the enemy and destroyed him. In three minutes the 190th Israeli Armored Brigade was destroyed. . . ."

Lt. Col. Asaf Yagouri, the commander of the leading battalion, was blown from his tank and taken prisoner. This event was exploited to the full by the Egyptian media, who produced him on television, although according to Israel he was not a brigade commander but a battalion commander. Whatever his rank, it was a major opportunity for the Egyptians and a humiliating defeat for Israel.

Adan was watching the raging battle from his hilltop and called Natke Nir, his brigade commander, when it was apparent that his forces were deeply in trouble, asking: "What happened, why are you withdrawing?" He got back the pithy rejoinder: "If you continue to ask me questions, there will be nobody left to answer you in a few minutes!"

The battle was later described as the biggest tank battle since El Alamein, when Montgomery's British Eighth Army destroyed Rommel. It may have been so, but it nevertheless highlighted errors in Israeli tactics comparable with the early British desert failures when they, too, committed large tank formations to battle without artillery, infantry, or air support. In the battles raging along the Canal, the Israelis began to see the fundamental fallacy of their post-1967 belief that armor alone could defeat the enemy. When a second attack went in, it too was beaten back by the jubilant Egyptian infantry, who well and truly erased their ill-starred reputation of 1967. It must be pointed out that the Israeli brigades were very much under strength, whereas they were opposed by the entire 18th Infantry Division supported by antitank reserves from the Egyption Second Army and independent tank brigades.

Sharon, of course, had been instructed by Elazar to act as reserve for Adan and only deploy on his personal instructions. Gonen, then, had jumped the gun earlier that morning when he directed Sharon's division southward to prepare for an attack against the Egyptian Third Army. His armored forces were desperately needed in the north, where, by Elazar's instructions, he should have been driving to take the pressure off Adan. Probably their combined weight could have reversed the battle's outcome. When, by early afternoon, even Gonen realized that Adan's attack was going badly wrong, it was too late to order Sharon's immediate attack, because his forces were scattered along some 36 miles of desert between Tassa and the Mitla Pass. It was also too late to loose Sharon's planned drive against the Egyptian Third Army. Gonen had no alternative but to order Sharon to reverse his southward drive and attack in the central sector, to take the Egyptian weight off Adan's brigades.

Records indicate that Adan actually heard this radio conversation, and Sharon's reply that he would answer the request in five minutes' time. Sharon's problem was that the safe ground over which he had traveled that morning was by then held by the enemy. But added to that difficulty was the sheer logistics of turning about a division, with all its armor, supply trucks, and support vehicles. It gives another curious comparison with Patton, who, in the Battle of the Bulge, did manage the incredible task of reversing divisions within just a few hours. But here, unlike the Americans in France and Belgium, the Israelis were outnumbered and the task was daunting. While Sharon was presumably deliberating, Adan straightaway informed Nir and Amir, his brigade commanders, that they could expect an Israeli counterattack within fifteen minutes—which suggests he didn't really know how far south Sharon had gone—and asked if his men could hold out that long. Both confirmed they could do so, as they were destroying large numbers of Egyptian tanks despite the continual pressure. Then Sharon signaled that he would not mount the attack.

In all fairness, Sharon was not in a position to counterattack at that time. But even by moving in the right direction, he might have diverted sufficient Egyptian strength to allow Adan's brigades to withdraw to stronger positions. There was little enough time for the brigade commanders to wonder at his refusal. Just before 3:00 P.M., the Egyptians launched a powerful counterattack of their own against Aryeh Karen's brigade, which had been pushing down the Artillery Road and was turning toward *Matzmed*.

The Egyptian force churned northeast through the soft sand from the *Machshir* and *Televizia* features—low-lying prominences just protruding above the surrounding desert—and attacked the Hamutal crossroads, to the rear of the *Purkan* fortification. Hamutal fell within the half hour. The battle was still heating up, though, and heavy Egyptian artillery began to thunder against all the identified Israeli positions, including Adan's hilltop headquarters, where several shells crashed down, killing members of his staff. By then, Adan was extremely anxious and called both Nir and Amir back for consultations.

They met upon the shell-torn hilltop, close by Adan's command half-track. Even as they talked, their own battalion commanders were frantically appealing for help amid a ferocious firefight in which tank guns were thudding at close range, and missiles whizzed like demented fireworks among the whirling, pounding tanks until they impacted with a flash. Infantrymen raced through the choking clouds of sand and dust-laden smoke, wheezing as they fought for breath in the superheated air.

By four o'clock Adan was dejectedly digesting the loss of their position at *Ziona*, adjacent to the Hamutal crossroads, when a sweating, white-faced signalman handed him a new report: another big Egyptian offensive had begun. A mechanized brigade and a tank brigade had broken out from Firdan, and were driving east in a move that would outflank Karen's brigade as it drove in toward *Matzmed*. A second great tank force was also advancing from the *Missouri* feature in a solid, mile-wide phalanx toward the Ismailia-Tassa road—a huge formation of tanks, enclosing armored infantry personnel carriers. Clearly, this was the major Egyptian breakout that had been expected.

Both Nir and Amir rushed back to command their struggling brigades, and were not long in reporting to headquarters just how critical was their position. They asked permission to withdraw to improve their situation. Reluctantly Adan had to agree. Nir soon found that as well as being heavily outnumbered, their condition was seriously worsened by the late afternoon sun, which was shining directly into their sights; obviously the Egyptians had timed their attack well. The mass of Soviet-supplied T-55s and a substantial number of T-62s rapidly approached the Israeli line, opening fire at some 2,500 yards range. For thirty minutes or so the Israeli tankers peered through blinding sights at the indistinct shapes advancing toward them. Then, just before five o'clock, the miracle happened. The sun set behind the high ground. Immediately the scene changed as the glare was replaced by the soft afterglow. Now the Israelis were in the gloom of the eastern desert, while the Egyptians were silhouetted against the still-light western horizon. Sammy Greenbaum, gunner on a Patton tank, recalled: "It was fantastic. One minute my eyes were streaming with the glare and then it was gone as the sun dipped. The Arab tanks were like black models against the skyline and we picked them off while their shots began to overshoot and disappeared into Sinai." The Israeli gunners took out the tanks and personnel carriers in rapid succession. Nir saw one of his officers destroy twenty-five tanks one after the other.

The first wave of Egyptian tanks faltered and ground to destruction. A second wave of armor passed through the smoke and fire and got to within 400 yards when they, too, were shattered by the well-placed Israeli tanks. As the Egyptians fell back, the order was signaled for the Israeli armor to attack. Across the desert the commands were drowned in the tumultuous bellow of tank engines from Pattons and Centurions grinding forward in pursuit, their cannons roaring as they chased the Egyptians back toward the Canal. As Herzog recalls, "The burning tanks created a series of bonfires across the desert." Nevertheless it had been what Wellington would have termed a "close run thing," for the Israeli brigades had barely hung on. Meanwhile, Sharon's division was trundling back toward them, but by then the Israeli line was further back in some places than it had been in the morning.

The failure of the Israeli offensive left the Egyptians exultant at their unparalleled success, although they too had been given a bloody nose. And while the Israelis retired to consider again their tactics, the Egyptians had lost the initiative for the moment. The Israeli action had severely contained their bridgehead and forced them to delay their major offensive.

That Monday night the Israeli cabinet met in sober session as it heard the depressing reports on the day's fighting. It was a stormy session, with much recrimination. Afterwards Dayan flew to Sinai for an on-the-spot meeting he had called with Elazar, Gonen, and his senior commanders. Most were bitter at the day's operation, since after the extreme difficulties of the first two days, the strong force of three armored divisions that had at last been concentrated had been frittered away. No doubt there was some acrimonious discussion between Elazar and Gonen, for the latter had not carried out the chief of staff's plan, which might have been more successful. Adan and Sharon sat in on the meeting, bleary-eyed, unshaven, and exhausted after three days of continual exertion. Neither was in his youth, and both had been jolted around inside tanks endlessly, bearing heavy responsibilities. More than anything they were angry that all their efforts to race their forces across Sinai to punch a hole in the Egyptian front had met with disaster. It had been a wasted day. They were still on the defensive, whereas they should have been dictating the battle by that evening.

Dayan recalls that Sharon was especially furious, having analyzed the battle, understood what was happening, and drawn the correct assumptions that the only way to defeat the enemy was to cross the Canal and destroy the missile system. A Canal crossing would also allow them to strike at the rear echelons of the Third and Second armies. Sharon was in a difficult situation, for until his resignation he had been Gonen's superior, and there was some friction between them. At the meeting he again propounded his views, but insisted that they couldn't expect miracles; it just wasn't feasible to hope for an intact Egyptian bridge to fall into their hands. What was needed, he urged, was bridges and rafts of their own, and there were none yet available.

Elazar summarized the plans for the following day. Sharon was to complete preparations for a Canal crossing. In the meantime, the other formations would assume defensive positions to block further Egyptian attacks while their men rested and reorganized. This was a sensible and important step, for while both sides had suffered heavy losses, the Egyptians were already on their way to replacing their lost tanks.

President Sadat had sent a personal appeal to President Tito of Yugoslavia, which was answered with the immediate dispatch of 140 tanks, ready armed and fueled so that they could go straight into battle. It has not been clarified, but the Soviets claimed they were Soviet tanks sent via Yugoslavia. Algeria, too, was shipping tanks and weapons to Egypt. Israel was not so fortunate, for she could rely only upon the United States, and replenishment of her resources would take longer. Nevertheless, Israel had a particular strength over her Arab opponents—her ability to maintain and repair her equipment. As former Royal Navy officer Norman Jopling, an expert on logistics, commented: "Israel could recover and put back into operation a large proportion of her damaged armor," something the less sophisticated Arab armies could not do.

During Monday night, while the leaders argued, the Israeli garrison broke out of *Purkan* opposite Ismailia, which had been cut off by the Egyptian counterattack directed at the Hamutal crossroads. The men straggled all night across the starlit sands, only to become stranded in the midst of a fierce tank battle. Sharon sent a force of just three tanks, an armored personnel carrier, and four lightly manned armored cars, under Col. Amnon Reshef, to retrieve the garrison. As it approached where the *Purkan* garrison was believed to be, the force commander saw that the brigade of Col. Raviv Tuvia, also from Sharon's division, was being heavily engaged by a larger Egyptian force on high ground near Hamutal. In the confusion of the fight, Reshef's rescue force drove into an Egyptian infantry ambush in which a number of its vehicles were knocked out and most of the officers wounded. By then, however, the garrison had been found.

In the middle of a ferocious armored battle in the darkness, Reshef recalls seeing a huge, ungainly object moving toward them. As it came closer and emerged from the smoke and darkness, it could be seen to be a tank carrying the thirty-three survivors. It was an action that typified the bravado of the Israeli officers in looking after their men. But it must be said that to risk a brigade commander, a brigade artillery commander, and a battalion commander, all of whom were with the small rescue force, was a reckless act in Israel's imperiled circumstances.

CHAPTER
10

"No Elegant Victories"

When the Arabs began the war, it was early morning in New York City, where Dr. Henry Kissinger, the U.S. Secretary of State, was asleep at the Waldorf Astoria Hotel, while President Richard M. Nixon was staying at Key Biscayne in Florida. In Europe, Chancellor Willi Brandt of West Germany was visiting British Prime Minister Edward Heath and, so far as is known, the Soviet leaders were in Moscow. The news produced an immediate flurry of activity. After the Anglo-German meeting at Chequers, the prime minister's official country home, a combined Anglo-German initiative was announced at the United Nations by a British official spokesman. Curiously, this was flatly denied by Brandt upon his return to Bonn. He claimed that the situation in the Middle East had been discussed but no common initiative decided upon. Bonn, nevertheless, did announce its deep concern about the military conflict in the Middle East, which had already assumed such proportions. Unofficially it was confirmed that West Germany's policy would be strictly neutral.

In Paris, President Pompidou's advisers said that he would wait and see, while in Sarrebourg, the minister of defense, Pierre

Messmer, said that an attacking army always had some advantages in the beginning. This inoffensive comment was interpreted by other French politicians as unnecessarily pro-Israeli, and shortly afterward Colonel Qadafi of Libya sent a letter to Paris complaining about France's "reserved attitude." This was hardly fair in view of France's pro-Arab policy since 1967 and her huge arms deliveries to Libya in particular. In all the eastern European capitals except Bucharest, as well as in most African and Asian capitals, Israel was sharply condemned for having launched a surprise attack against Egypt and Syria. This was despite a statement the Egyptian foreign minister made on American television, admitting that his country had struck first. This admission was simply ignored. In western European capitals there was a good deal of hand-wringing, but little else.

The only action was taking place in New York and Washington, where Joseph Sisco, Assistant Secretary of State for Near-Eastern Affairs, called Kissinger at his New York hotel at 6:00 A.M. with the disturbing news of military action on Israel's borders. At 6:30 A.M. Kissinger telephoned President Nixon, who gravely told him to "make a major diplomatic effort" to restrain fighting from breaking out. Kissinger informed the U.N. Secretary-General Kurt Waldheim and also the Soviet ambassador. Then cables were hurriedly sent to King Faisal of Saudi Arabia and King Hussein of Jordan, asking them to use their influence to restrain Egypt and Syria.

Kissinger had been extremely surprised by these developments, for only the day before he had seen Egyptian Foreign Minister Mohammed Hassan Zayat, who had given no indication whatsoever that Egypt was about to go to war. Just a week before, in fact, the Egyptian government had signed a contract worth hundreds of millions of dollars with the American Bechtel Corporation for the construction of a major oil pipeline in Egypt, even though Cairo and Washington had had no diplomatic relations since 1967. Kissinger had also met Mr. Abba Eban, the prestigious Israeli foreign minister, two days before, when they had agreed to seek new peace talks following the Israeli elections in November. After the fighting began, a state department spokesman said: "We never had any indications there was a military action intended. . . ."

On that Saturday morning, however, whatever Mr. Zayat told Kissinger gave him little comfort, and Abba Eban merely reaffirmed that Israel would defend herself against attack. The Syrian foreign minister was not available for talks. Two hours later, news reached Washington that the Arab attack had actually started, and American policy became one of urging restraint and a return to the cease-fire lines as soon as possible.

During this time, President Nixon, in Key Biscayne, was being kept informed of developments by telephone calls from Kissinger as he worked to get the shooting to stop. Presidential aides issued a statement saying that Mr. Nixon was "very, very concerned." After trying in vain to determine a peace formula with the Arab and Israeli foreign ministers in New York, Kissinger flew back to Washington, where in a bustle of telephone calls he spoke to every permanent member of the Security Council. Then in the evening he convened a meeting of the Washington Special Action Group, which included William E. Simon, chairman of the President's Oil Policy Committee; Kenneth Rush, the Deputy Secretary of State; Admiral Thomas H. Moorer, chairman of the Joint Chiefs of Staff; Defense Secretary James R. Schlesinger; CIA Director William E. Colby; and Joseph Sisco.

Meanwhile, the contact already established with the Kremlin produced only equivocation from Mr. Brezhnev, who said he was very sorry, claimed the news had just reached him, and he could do nothing. Of course, he declared sonorously, there would have to be concerted American-Soviet action, but he added that perhaps they should wait a little until the dust settled. The Russian view was that one should consider one's course of action very carefully, and this could not be done in a hurry. Mr. Brezhnev did not agree with President Nixon's suggestion that the Security Council should be convened, unless one knew what one wanted it to do. Such a reaction, he well knew, would enable his Arab clients to continue their spectacular actions before the United States managed to intervene diplomatically.

In the meantime, the Egyptians announced their own intention to call a special meeting of the U.N. General Assembly "to make an informative statement." The Arabs were confident that they could rely on an overwhelming majority in the General Assembly, where, moreover, there was no veto. This was a shrewd move, as quite a long time was needed to convene the General Assembly's 135 members. While this was happening, the Egyptian and Syrian forces would be able to seize territory before any cease-fire was imposed. Sir Laurance McIntyre of Australia, president of the Security Council, wanted to issue a personal appeal for a cease-fire. But to do so he needed the agreement of the permanent members as to the contents of such an appeal, and this he was unable to obtain.

So, by Sunday afternoon, twenty-four hours after the outbreak of war, there had been no progress at all. President Nixon thereupon directed Kissinger to call for a special meeting of the Security Council. But as a security measure, Nixon also decided to dispatch a carrier task force from the American Sixth Fleet to take up a holding position half a day's sailing from the Suez Canal. This force, headed by the 60,000-ton aircraft carrier *Independence*, with three supporting destroyers, had been stationed in Greece. It immediately left for an area southeast of Crete, a few hundred miles from the Egyptian coast.

While politicians wrangled and the Big Powers kept careful watch on each other and matched each other's weaponry, the Israelis were planning the next steps in their campaign.

With massive Israeli ground forces turning the Syrians back at the very edge of the Golan Heights, the Israeli Air Force was at last able to switch to deeper penetration raids into Syria. Its task was twofold: interdiction missions, and the systematic destruction of Syria's military infrastructure. After the deep raids into Egypt had led to the war of attrition, no doubt the Israelis thought hard before turning their bombers loose in Syria. But it was necessary to knock out the supply basis to equalize to some degree the odds against Israel, even though there existed the very real threat of a collision with the Soviet Union. On October 8,

Israeli Phantoms raided the Dmer, Halhul, Nasseriya, and Seikal air bases around Damascus, while others together with Sky-hawks strafed and rocketed armored columns and concentrations behind the front. But they still had to endure horrifying antiaircraft and missile fire, as well as Syrian interceptors. Exaggerated claims were made by both sides as the dogfights became a part of the propaganda war.

So long as the surface-to-air missiles dominated the Golan airspace, Israeli ground strikes would remain costly, and at the current rate of attrition it was obvious they could not continue for long. Already Israel had appealed to the United States for deliveries of weapons, including aircraft that had been ordered long before the war. But the American replies were evasive, and at one point President Nixon hesitantly agreed to deliver just two more Phantoms to Israel, while Israel was losing more than that in each strike! Clearly, the key to Israel's strategy on the northern front was the Syrian air defense system. So, on October 9, the air force commander authorized an audacious air strike on the Syrian general headquarters in Damascus, which, it was believed, was also controlling that system.

The operation required very careful planning, and aircrews were given the latest intelligence reports. The general headquarters complex, they were told, was unfortunately located in a heavily populated, predominantly residential area of the Syrian capital. The entire area was ringed with SAM sites, and there were numerous light antiaircraft guns in positions covering all possible approaches. It was not possible, air force planners explained, to make a surprise raid by circling to the north of Damascus, since the high peaks of the rugged mountains to the north were riddled with concealed antiaircraft and missile emplacements, as well as radar networks. Only one opportunity existed—a low-level precision raid to take out specific buildings, similar to the RAF's wartime Mosquito raids when Gestapo buildings in Copenhagen and Oslo were singled out. This time, however, no one doubted that the defenses were infinitely more sophisticated.

Careful attention was paid to the selection of crews for this

(ABOVE) *Israeli M-48 Pattons, with British 105mm gun.* Photo by Terry Fincher, courtesy of Photographers International. (BELOW) *Israeli Super-Shermans moving forward in Sinai.* Photo by Terry Fincher, courtesy of Photographers International

Gen. Chaim Bar-Lep. Photo courtesy of Britain/Israel Public Affairs Committee

(ABOVE) *Centurion tanks moving off the road in Golan Heights.* Photo by Terry Fincher, courtesy of Photographers International. (BELOW) *Israeli howitzers firing upon targets in Golan Heights.* Photo by Terry Fincher, courtesy of Photographers International

Gen. Ariel ("Arik") Sharon.
Photo courtesy of Britain/
Israel Public Affairs
Committee

*Gen. David Elazar, the Israeli
chief of staff.* Photo courtesy
of Britain/Israel Public
Affairs Committee

(ABOVE) *Egyptian infantry with Sagger missile launcher following T-62 tank, October 14.* Photo by H. el Konayessi. (BELOW) *Egyptian armor advancing in Sinai.* Photo courtesy of Britain/Israel Public Affairs Committee

highly dangerous mission, and a young colonel who was already a distinguished veteran of the Six Day War was chosen to lead the attack. More detailed briefings explained how vital was the success of the mission to the forthcoming Israeli armored counterattack, for if the Syrian air defense system remained intact, close air support of the armor would be impossible. Fully apprised of both the danger and the importance of their mission, youthful crews trooped out to their waiting Phantoms, their faces set with the grimness of their task and the realization of the slim chances of survival.

The Phantoms had been expertly serviced, fueled, and armed with a variety of specially selected weapons; they would each have only one shot at the target. At exactly Zero Hour, engines whined, spluttered, and bellowed into life, blasting away clouds of scorched cement dust and sand. Then the Phantoms were rolled out in turn, lined up in position, each one rocking on its spindly undercarriage as bellowing engines strained against the brakes. The next second they arrowed along the runway, nose-wheels lifted, and they were off, wheels already retracted before they had cleared the airfield. Watchers on the ground shaded their eyes against the glare as the Phantoms rapidly faded out of sight. A young woman in oil-stained overalls, her long fair hair pulled into a ponytail, waved briefly, then they were gone.

The Phantoms' high speed soon took them over the Heights, where their embattled comrades glanced up from their own grim fight. Then they flew into excessively bad weather, with high winds that buffeted them so that they rocked perilously along on their ground-hugging flight path through the hills. But they had no alternative. Had they climbed, the Syrians' radar would have immediately picked them up, and seconds later the missiles would be swinging on their launchers. The pilots just gritted their teeth and tightened their grip on the controls as the heavily laden planes jinked in the wind. Low, squally clouds lay across their path and for agonizing minutes the pilots flew by instruments alone. Conditions were so bad that the mission was within seconds of being aborted when they suddenly flashed into the sun once more and there below were clearly identifiable navigation points. The flight commander headed for Damascus.

Damascus was on a war footing, with martial music and news being broadcast from public address loudspeakers. But the sudden appearance of the Israeli Phantoms took the citizens and defenders completely by surprise. The Israeli formation was tearing across the rooftops even before the air-raid sirens started to wail. People rushed for cover, snatching children off the sunny streets as the antiaircraft guns began to crackle. By then, however, the Phantoms were lining up their attack on the Syrian general headquarters. The flight leader identified the building and with no time for hesitation pointed the Phantom's sharkhead toward it, screaming across the dumbfounded city with a howl that broke windows, then letting its bombload tumble away. A single SA-7 Strela missile streaked from the shoulder of a quick-witted Syrian soldier, only missing the Phantom by yards. Then the other Phantoms were attacking and the air was full of flying bricks, glass, and concrete that whirled out of the smoke pall.

The planes broke away as they were raked by accurate gunfire, but one aircraft slammed down in a ball of fire. Another Phantom took a shell in the observer's seat yet still raced for home, trailing smoke. The raid was over in seconds. It left the Defense Ministry and the Damascus radio station badly damaged, but, regrettably, so were houses and buildings in the fashionable area where many embassies were located. A Norwegian United Nations observer was killed, along with his wife and young daughter. A hospital and the Soviet cultural mission were also hit.

The Phantoms headed back for their base, with the damaged aircraft protected by the rest of the formation, and all landed safely. When the results of the mission were evaluated, it emerged that the precision attack had been highly successful. Indeed, although it was not fully realized then, the Syrian air defense system had been virtually eliminated. The Russians immediately flew in more electronic equipment and missiles to replace the Syrian losses, but the system would not be nearly as effective for a long time.

Israeli bombers also attacked industrial targets in Damascus and Homs, and struck at Syrian ports, doing extensive damage to the dock facilities and sinking several ships, including a Russian one.

In New York, the Security Council met at last, although very briefly, on Monday, October 8. Abba Eban made a statement drawing the Council's attention to "the United Nations' Observers' Report (S/7930) which reports to you specifically about Egyptian encroachments across the cease-fire line, about Syrian encroachments across the cease-fire line. Where in that, or in any other documents, is there the slightest reference to any Israeli encroachment across the cease-fire line?" But Eban's words had little impact, and the Council was promptly adjourned without taking any action.

The following day the Council met once more, for a totally fruitless session. John Scalli, the U.S. representative on the Council, had not formulated a specific draft resolution but simply called for an immediate cease-fire and a return to the 1967 cease-fire lines. The Egyptian foreign minister, with the support of the Soviet and Chinese representatives and most of the other members of the Council, declared that this was totally unacceptable. Syria's foreign minister, Ismail Zakariya, declared that "Israel had formulated a plan which left Syria no option but to react, in order to protect itself." All of Israel's careful avoidance of mobilization or any other provocation in the hours before the Arab attack had been a complete waste of time.

Just before the meeting started, news had reached New York of the Israeli air raid on Damascus. Yakov Malik, the Soviet representative, seized on the news to harangue the Council about yet another Israeli aggressive act. Malik insisted that six, and maybe as many as thirty, Soviet citizens had been killed in these "bloody acts of Israeli aggression." (Later it was announced that the report had been unfounded. It was an outright falsification, comparable only to Austria-Hungary's lie about Serbia's hostile act in 1914.) He called Josef Tekoah, the chief Israeli delegate, a "representative of murderous gangsters," and ranted about the filthy hands and barbarism of the Israeli leaders. Then, when Mr. Tekoah declared that responsibility had to be put where it belonged — namely, on the Russians, with their encouragement of fanatical barbarism and hatred of Israel — Malik walked out of the assembly to the applause of the delegates.

In what Israeli delegates called the atmosphere of a lynching party, Tekoah continued his speech, saying that without the Soviet Union the Middle East could have been at peace. The Security Council then broke up in an atmosphere of jubilant malice, having achieved nothing. The initiative had passed to the superpowers, in particular to Washington and Kissinger. On September 1, the Cairo weekly, *Ahkbar al Yom*, had made a statement that summed up Arab feeling: "We are facing the chance that Kissinger will find the solution which he regards as suitable for our problem." The article condemned the United States for arming Israel, and concluded: "The solution in this case is that we should start the war before Kissinger forces it upon us," implying that a heavily armed Israel might attack the Arab world. For the moment, though, on Tuesday, October 9, the Soviet Union and its hangers-on believed that time was on the side of the Arabs.

Nevertheless, the Soviet Union and its Arab clients states really had little cause for complacency. Just as in 1942 the wheel of fortune had swung at some point in the Allies' favor, so, too, on Monday, October 8, the wheel had turned in the Israelis' favor, albeit almost imperceptibly. It was certainly not military success that gives reason for this assumption, but rather an organizational change. As we have seen, the Arab onslaught had revealed weaknesses in Israel's command structure as well as her strategy. But by Monday, both were being corrected, and in their wake was to be created the momentum of victory.

After the prime minister's briefing, General Bar-Lev had traveled north to the Golan front, which he reached at eight o'clock on Sunday night. At General Hofi's Northern Command headquarters, he was able to study the maps on which the deep Syrian salients were all too obvious from the lines of pins and flags. The atmosphere, too, was very depressing, with the jumping shadows cast by lamps jiggling on their cables to every crash and concussion of the endless barrage roaring over the Golan Heights.

The men were tired, as most had fought almost nonstop since Saturday. They were red-eyed, unshaven, and disheveled. To this dispirited group, who had so recently seen the destruction of the Barak Brigade and the deaths of many comrades, Bar-Lev brought hope as he talked in his quiet, melodic voice. He approved Hofi's dispositions for a defense along the Jordan River, for which Laner had been given overall responsibility, and the establishment of a series of antitank strongpoints. They then turned to the deployment of the division of Maj. Gen. Moshe Peled, which was just arriving in the area. It had been suggested that the division should concentrate in the Bnot Ya'akov Bridge area, but Peled didn't agree, pointing out that his tanks had already traveled many miles on their tracks, a slow and hazardous operation resulting in many breakdowns. It was agreed, instead, that he should send his division along the southern route through El Al, along the edge of the Ruqqad escarpment toward Rafid and Hushniyah. This would cut the axis of the Syrian 1st Armored Division, which was still moving through the area. In addition to his own division, Peled would take under command all the remaining Israeli forces scattered along the El Al-to-Rafid road, which included several isolated infantry garrisons still holding out in surrounded fortifications.

This offensive in the north was the result of Elazar's decision to dig in in the south and let the Egyptians crumble themselves against the Israeli armor, very much in the manner of Montgomery's pre-Alamein battle of Alam Halfa; only when the Egyptians had weakened themselves would Southern Command go over to the offensive again.

Along the Golan front the situation was still very dangerous.

The Syrians had broken through to the crest of the escarpments and were "looking down the chimneys" of the Israeli settlements. There was no more room to maneuver and Elazar wanted them driven back forthwith.

Before returning to Tel Aviv, Bar-Lev made a quick visit to Laner's advanced headquarters, beyond the Arik Bridge, where he listened to a cautiously optimistic outline of the situation. There, too, Bar-Lev gave confidence by describing the critical nature of the battle, and impressed upon the staff that it was their task now to upset the Syrian Command's plans. Israel, he said, was about to seize the initiative once more and take the war to the enemy in her customary way. Just thirty-six hours after their shattering defeats, they were about to go over to the offensive. Bar-Lev left behind him a much stronger morale and a determination to win.

When he arrived back in the blacked-out city of Tel Aviv late that same night, Bar-Lev straightaway reported to Mrs. Meir that the counterattack was to begin the following day with Peled's fresh division. He believed that with luck they would gain the upper hand, for although the situation was still fraught, it was not quite hopeless. Mrs. Meir leaned on her desk, her tired eyes fixed intently upon her old friend. When he finished she looked at him, resting her elbow on the desk and waggling her gnarled hand expressively in a typical Mediterranean expression of uncertainty. "The great Moshe Dayan," she said. "One day like this. One day like that!"

At ten o'clock on Sunday night, Peled called an orders group at his Tzemach headquarters. He explained the plan for a two-pronged attack, with the 19th Reserve Brigade making the main effort up the El Al-to-Rafid route—although this brigade had already suffered losses in fighting since early that afternoon—and the 20th Brigade following it through. Behind them, he directed the 70th Reserve Brigade to mop up any Syrian stragglers and consolidate Israeli positions; it was also to protect the right flank from Syrian forces below the Ruqqad escarpment. On the left flank the 14th Reserve Brigade would advance from the Gamla Rise through Mazrat and Kuneitra to Hushniyah.

Throughout the cold, starlit night, the division's tanks rumbled into position, and by first light the armored columns had formed up, their guns pointing toward Syria. While the artillery continued to thunder and intermittent air strikes shrieked and scratched white trails on the dawn's eggshell sky, the armor waited. Then, at 8:30 A.M., the order was given, tank engines bellowed black smoke, and the Israeli armor began to move forward.

The 19th Brigade went along the stony track toward El Al, meeting with little opposition at first, but then the Syrians began to pound it. Their troops were well concealed among the thorny scrub and rocks, from where missiles snaked across the hot ground while mortars thudded and artillery shells zoomed over from positions a mile or so back. Seven Israeli tanks exploded in sheets of flame, while the others fired back, their 105mm shells screaming into Syrian positions. The flat, open terrain permitted a heavier force, and Peled immediately loosed the 20th Brigade in support. Its tanks pounded the Syrians, while one battalion moved to outflank the Syrian positions.

For several hours the Israelis pressed home their attacks against increasingly heavy artillery concentrations, and eventually the Syrians began to fall back, still fighting stubbornly. Meanwhile, the 14th Brigade on the left had broken through to the lateral road near Ramat Magshimim, but Peled ordered it to wheel a battalion against the Syrian right flank to relieve the pressure on his other brigades. The commander of the 14th Brigade erred and directed his tanks the wrong way. Peled saw what was happening and angrily ordered the 19th and 20th brigades to drive headlong into the Syrians. Their momentum carried them forward, and the vintage American Shermans, with their British 105mm guns, defeated a force that was equipped with the latest Soviet T-62s. Before the Israelis' ferocious attack the Syrians broke and were shot to bits as they withdrew in disorder; most of their tanks were destroyed, but over sixty were simply abandoned by their panic-stricken crews. All three Israeli brigades then raced forward in a classical armored battle. By 1:00 P.M. they had reached the Tapline route and blunted the Syrian advance once and for all.

Notwithstanding the fact that they had been severely dented, the Syrians were by no means defeated. At Tel Saki—one of the conical hills some 100 yards east of the main road and midway between Israeli fortifications A11 and A10—the Syrians had constructed an extensive antitank defense system, which extended across the main road and blocked any advance toward the important positions at Juhader. It was a major position, with a considerable force of tanks, infantry, antitank missiles, and guns, supported by heavy artillery. The Syrians had pulled back their 132nd Mechanized Brigade into position before Peled's division attacked, and then further reinforced the positions with three companies of BMD-2 armored vehicles mounting Sagger antitank missiles, and two companies of 106mm recoilless anti-tank guns. A Syrian prisoner of war recounted how they watched the Israeli advance that morning and claimed that every company fired thirty antitank missiles.

As 20th Brigade advanced, its leading battalion ran into the outer defenses. An Israeli soldier wrote:

> We had been attacking for some hours along the main road and it seemed we had succeeded in pushing back the enemy. Suddenly, though, the Syrians opened up on us with antitank guns and missiles, firing from well-concealed positions in the rocky ground on both sides of the road. Several of our tanks brewed up. Our commander yelled that he could see a gun dug in behind some boulders and partly concealed by a thorn bush. Our tank gun trained onto the target, but before we fired a shell crashed off our front plate and went screaming away, shaking us badly. Then another tank pushed passed [sic] us and hid the gun from our sight. But the tank in front blew up with an awful sheet of flame. The smoke and dust were terrible and we could see very little, so our commander crashed the tank on and we found ourselves right in front of a Syrian crew with a missile launcher. We simply ran over them, and thankfully the noise of battle drowned out any other noise.

The determined Syrian opposition badly mauled the leading battalion, which was pinned down until the brigade relieved it with a major attack. But the Syrian defenses were extensive, and although the 14th Brigade, too, drove up in support on the left, it wasn't until the 19th Brigade also joined in, making it a full divisional attack, that any headway was made and the Syrian defenses began to break. The 132nd Mechanized Brigade then withdrew.

Throughout Monday, Laner's 21st Division was desperately engaged in preventing the Syrian 1st Armored Division from breaking through to the Jordan River between the Arik and Bnot Ya'akov bridges. Col. Tewfiq Jehani, the commander of the Syrian 1st Armored, was a formidable opponent who urged his division implacably onward, bypassing any Israeli strongpoints, which he left to wither rather than expend his forces eradicating them. This approach was typified by the division's leading 91st Brigade, which slipped past the Israeli strongpoints at Nefekh and raced west. Under Col. Shafiq Fiyad, the brigade's leading units reached Snobar, 12 miles inside the Golan Heights, and the furthest point the Syrians were to penetrate. As they neared the customshouse they were only ten minutes from the Bnot Ya'akov Bridge and a breakout into Galilee.

The three brigades of 21st Division fought bitterly to prevent the Syrian breakthrough, despite heavy losses in both officers and equipment. Colonel Ran's 17th Brigade was ambushed by the Syrians and lost several tanks before two of its companies managed to pull back, and, after a wide flanking movement, attack the rear of the Syrian force, destroying all thirteen tanks. Meanwhile, Ori's 79th Brigade battled against other Syrian forces that were bypassing Nafekh along the Tapline route heading for the Huleh Valley. Laner ordered 17th Brigade along the Yehudia Road east toward the Tapline route and Hushniyah, while 79th Brigade drove from the north toward Sindiana and Hushniyah, thereby squeezing the Syrian 1st Armored Division as it, too, pressed along the Tapline route. Near late afternoon Ori's reserves, reinforced by a company from 7th Brigade, outflanked the Syrians by driving on Sindiana from the north. By evening, this force had stormed Sindiana and controlled the Tapline route in the Nafekh area, from where they deployed along the Sindiana-Ramtania-Hushniyah route, ready to drive south toward Ran's 17th Brigade and Peled's brigades, which were moving north.

The capture of Sindiana had a decisive morale effect on the Israelis, who, after days of defeat, saw that given a reasonable ratio of forces they could stop the Syrians. But the Syrians still had plenty of punch left, and on Tuesday morning they counterattacked at Sindiana in an effort to relieve Hushniyah, which was their administrative center for all forces in the Golan Heights. They launched a powerful attack, supported by artillery and Katyusha rockets; but Ori's 79th Brigade held them off with long-range tank fire.

Ramtania, like Tel Saki to the south, had been heavily fortified. The terraces overlooking the Tapline bristled with tanks and antitank weapons sited to enfilade the flank of any forces using the road. Nevertheless, Ori's brigade took the position with an assault that had to fight for every yard of advance, and by nightfall Ramtania, too, had been captured by the Israelis.

While this was going on, Peled's division to the south had also been advancing after a 3:00 A.M. briefing by its commander to maintain pressure in the belief that their momentum would carry them across the "Purple Line." Rapidly increasing daylight, however, revealed that instead of the essentially infantry-based defenses of the day before, they were now opposed by strong Syrian armored formations of the 46th Tank Brigade—which had replaced the 132nd Mechanized Brigade—protecting the southern flank of the 1st Armored Division, still heavily engaged around Hushniyah.

By eleven o'clock that morning, Peled's division and Laner's 21st Division had coordinated their operations and were moving on Hushniyah in a pincer operation intended to capture or destroy the bulk of the Syrian armor in the pocket. It was no pushover, though, and when Peled ordered a battalion from Colonel Mir's 19th Brigade to move off in concert with units of 17th Brigade, it ran into a great concentration of Syrian armor and guns along the Yehudia Road and was almost annihilated. Nevertheless, on the right flank the brigade gradually crumbled the 46th Tank Brigade, and by midday it had reached Tel Faris, only 2 miles from the "Purple Line." But the Syrians were not giving way lightly. Reinforced by armor that was moving in from Syria, they stubbornly fought for every hill and hollow. By then, Peled's division was sprawled across two of the three major Syrian axis of advance, and 20th Brigade was a spearhead directly into the main Syrian position, drawing so much fire that in the fierce heat of midday its position was almost untenable.

By Tuesday afternoon, the situation of the Syrian forces was looking acutely dangerous, and at his Tel Kudne headquarters Colonel Jehani was in a dilemma. Because their attack north of Kuneitra had been held by Gen. Raful Eytan's armored forces, the Syrians had subsequently made their main effort across the southern Heights. They had therefore concentrated their divisional supply lines in the Hushniyah area, intent on building up an adequate supply of fuel, stores, and ammunition to enable their forces to push rapidly into Israel. But, as reconnaissance reports revealed at midday on Tuesday, the entire Hushniyah area was being rapidly encircled by two powerful Israeli armored thrusts — Laner's 21st Division from the west and north, and Peled's division from the south. With the missile control center in Damascus destroyed, the Israeli fighter-bombers, too, were beginning to operate freely and swept over in waves to strafe and destroy armor and supplies. Jehani pushed more and more armor southward in an endeavor to contain Peled's thrusting columns; but, as he fully realized, if they failed to stop the Israeli encirclement, he would lose an entire division. Determined to hold on despite the deteriorating situation, Jehani directed his forces in the Hushniyah pocket to counterattack Peled's armor.

Peled was so far unaware of the Syrian dilemma and had ordered the 14th Brigade to drive hard into the Syrians to achieve the maximum penetration. Supported by fighter-bombers and artillery, Shermans, Centurions, and Pattons streamed in choking dust clouds across the sun-baked plateau toward Hushniyah. After a brisk fight, they gained control of the main Hushniyah-to-Rafid road. Thus, relieved of Syrian pressure, 20th Brigade pressed forward again, and—following a short, sharp engagement in which Israeli infantry stormed Tel Faris and destroyed several PT-76 tanks by thrusting grenades inside their hatches— the important observation post was in Israeli hands. Unknown to the Israelis, though, a small Syrian detachment remained concealed on the slopes and gallantly directed Syrian artillery fire for several days until discovered. Mir's 19th Brigade again attacked Hushniyah, and after battling fiercely against the Syrian 40th Mechanized Brigade, succeeded in capturing a hill dominating the Syrian defenses and pushed on toward the town. But in the night the Syrians stubbornly infiltrated units back onto the hill to reestablish themselves in force. There followed a night-long mêlée, with Israelis and Syrians battling for control, and by morning the Syrians had been pushed off once more. Still, the Syrians were determined to hold on. They brought their 15th Mechanized Brigade south from the 3rd Armored to strengthen the southern front, which was beginning to show dangerous cracks under the continual Israeli pounding.

At midday on Tuesday, Elazar reviewed the situation at the chief of staff's conference. In Syria, he told the committee, the counterattack was going well, and he believed that if they continued to press forward they would achieve their priority of knocking Syria out of the war. That would, of course, leave Israel free to reinforce Southern Command against Egypt, the major enemy. Therefore, he told the gathered officers, policy must be to improve the ratio of forces on the southern front by allowing the Egyptians to waste themselves in attacks against a strong Israeli defense line. It was expected that the Egyptians would make their major offensive soon, as Soviet doctrine dictated a strong offensive by about the 11th or 12th, in two or three days' time. Once the Egyptian attack had been broken, Israeli counterattacks would become viable, including the possibility of a Canal crossing in the Deversoir area.

Apart from the crucial battles resounding along both fronts, however, there was also an internecine conflict developing among Israel's soldiers and politicians, most of whom had their own strongly held views on the way the war should be fought. These disputes came to a head on Tuesday, when Elazar took a leaf from Mrs. Meir's book and he, too, called General Bar-Lev to his general headquarters for a discussion. When they met, Elazar explained that he was far from happy with the situation in Southern Command, where many of the fortifications were still cut off. Most important, Elazar said that between Gonen and Sharon a relationship had evolved that threatened the efficient conduct of the campaign.

Arik Sharon has been described as a "swashbuckling, popular, back-slapping extrovert, always readily available to the press." He was the antithesis of General Gonen, his successor as commanding officer of Southern Command, who was a methodical, taciturn professional soldier and strict disciplinarian, curiously like Patton's great rival, Field Marshal Montgomery, although without his ruthless winning streak. This clash of personalities was further complicated because Gonen had formerly been Sharon's subordinate commander of a reserve division, and that relationship had been completely reversed. As General Herzog put it, "Gonen now had under command an officer who not only had been his superior a few months earlier, but one whom very senior, tried and seasoned officers found extremely difficult to control." Sharon had become Gonen's biggest headache.

In an endeavor to rectify the delicate command situation in Sinai, Elazar asked Bar-Lev if he would take over the post of commanding officer of Southern Command. Elazar reputedly told Bar-Lev that he did not believe Gonen had failed in his task, but the predicament along the Canal required strong control. How much that comment was a reflection of Gonen's handling of the attack on Monday, when he had sent Sharon's division south instead of holding it in reserve for Adan, is not clear; neither is it ever suggested that he had given in to pressure from Sharon himself, who had wanted to drive for the Canal. Nevertheless, the facts are there to draw on, and there seems little doubt that had Elazar's instructions been followed, the battle on October 8 might have had a very different outcome.

Bar-Lev replied that he would take the post provided the prime minister and the defense minister agreed, and so long as an adequate arrangement was possible with Gonen, whereupon he drove home to collect his uniform. There, he received a telephone call from the prime minister thanking him for accepting the post and asking him to attend a cabinet meeting. Dayan, who phoned just afterwards, minced no words: "Get down there and make decisions," he told him.

Bar-Lev arrived back at general headquarters at ten o'clock that night to hear from Elazar that Gonen had reacted strongly to what he saw as his dismissal, and complained that he was being held personally responsible for the condition in Sinai. At this Bar-Lev retorted that he wasn't prepared to be simply Gonen's adviser and would only go to Southern Command if his status was clearly defined. A formula to encompass the dignity of all the commanders had to be found. Tactfully it was explained to Gonen that although no one felt he justified public censure, the unfortunate circumstances made it essential for Bar-Lev to command. As Bar-Lev was snatching a brief sleep on a couch in Elazar's office, the chief of staff managed to persuade Gonen that he should accept the proposals.

While Southern Command was being put in order for the coming counteroffensive, in Tel Aviv, Defense Minister Moshe Dayan addressed a meeting of Israeli editors. To them, Dayan outlined the Israeli military strategy to give priority to the Syrian front, declaring that every effort would be made to destroy her armed forces and to hit the country strategically by bombing military and economic targets, although he promised they would avoid the civilian population. But he caused some disappointment when, turning to the Egyptian front, he admitted they didn't have the strength to push them back over the Canal, stating it wasn't possible to knock out the Syrians at the same time. He even hinted at the possibility of withdrawal to a shorter defense line, covering only Sharm el-Sheikh.

In Dayan's view, it was important to deploy along the new lines, for he believed that even the Security Council would not stop the Arabs if they believed themselves capable of continuing the war. As he put it, there was not likely to be such a decision, anyway; if there was, it would be vetoed by Russia and China; and, in any case, the Arabs would ignore it. Describing the Israeli losses, he said, "Hundreds of our tanks have been knocked out in battle. Part we can retrieve . . . part we cannot retrieve. . . . In three days we have lost fifty planes." He concluded with an announcement that he was to appear on television to explain the truth of the fall of the Bar-Lev line and to give the public a clear picture of the somber situation. To this one of the editors responded, "If you tell the public today on television what you have told us, this means an earthquake in the nation's consciousness and in that of the Jewish people and the Arab people."

The results of Israel's hastily organized and overconfident first counteroffensive in Sinai brought home to them as nothing else could that this would be no short war in which the fully mobilized Israeli Army would romp to the Canal. Indeed, Dayan's conference caused such alarm and his subsequent television appearance was speculated upon with so much apprehension that Mrs. Meir requested him not to appear. Instead, Maj. Gen. Aharon Yariv, Elazar's assistant and a former chief of intelligence, who also replaced the ebullient Elazar as spokesman, broadcast a clear and balanced review of the situation, grimly warning that "The people of Israel can expect no easy or elegant victories."

The expected Israeli *Blitzkrieg* in the Yom Kippur War was becoming the fiercest conflict in the series of Arab-Israeli wars. From the bramble-covered Golan Heights to the shifting Sinai sands, the biggest tank battles since World War II were continuing, involving hundreds of armored vehicles crammed into just a few miles of front. But more ominous than that, the two superpowers were both sending in their latest weaponry, eager not only to aid their clients but also to test the dazzling electronics and the missiles under real battlefield conditions. The Yom Kippur War was becoming what Spain had been to Russia and Germany in the 1930s, a tryout for a possible much bigger and infinitely more disastrous conflict.

By the early hours of Wednesday morning, on the Golan Heights, 20th Brigade controlled Tel Faris and the Rafid crossroads, thereby cutting an important Syrian line of communication. Peled's division had by then reached the "Purple Line" and firmly controlled the southern rim of the Heights, should Jordan contemplate an attack. The only significant Syrian force still holding out was in the Hushniyah pocket, which half a battalion from 19th Brigade was still attacking.

A 3:00 A.M., the cold atop the Golan Heights was intense, while the night air was slashed with shellfire and tracer bullets and startled by explosions. Peled issued orders for the next phase. The 70th Brigade on the extreme right flank was to press on with all speed, cross the "Purple Line" at El Hanut, and roll up the Syrian positions as it advanced to Buka'a. The 20th Brigade would simultaneously drive along the Tapline route to eradicate Syrian positions west of the Ruqqad stream; 14th Brigade was to move to the Israeli A6 fortification along the Kudne Road, where 19th Brigade would pass through and move along the Tel Fazra to Kudne Road. This was bad policy, for the Israelis were repeating their earlier mistakes of committing comparatively small task forces against very strong Syrian armored concentrations, and they paid the price. Syrian tanks, missiles, and antitank guns raked them with fire and Israeli losses were very heavy. There is another curious parallel to early British desert operations when commanders had insisted on sending so-called "Jock" columns of small tank forces against strong Axis positions with the same results. Dan Shomron's brigade in Sinai had already shown the way in the Yom Kippur War with his armored fist concept. After several of Peled's tanks blew up in a Syrian minefield, he, too, concluded that he would have to concentrate his whole division for the attack on Tel Kudne.

With the Israeli attack developing toward Tel Kudne, Colonel Jehani wisely evacuated his forward headquarters from the tel. As Peled's forces churned toward him, so, too, Laner's 21st Division launched another attack, with Ran's 17th Brigade attacking Hushniyah from the north while Ori's 79th Brigade roared along the terraced ridge to the south of Kuneitra in support. Hushniyah became to the Syrians what the Falaise pocket had been to the Germans—a killing ground. As the sun neared its zenith on Wednesday, its merciless rays burned down on scenes of unbelievable carnage. Two Syrian brigades were trapped in the Hushniyah pocket. Although they fought courageously—inflicting heavy damage when the 79th Brigade injudiciously advanced too fast—they were doomed. As noon passed, the area became a huge charnelhouse of smoking Syrian equipment; hundreds of tanks, guns, trucks, personnel carriers, Sagger missile carriers, and tons of ammunition lay in vast piles of wreckage, a sad debit for the 1,400 Syrian tanks that had roared across the cease-fire line just four days earlier. The routes back to Syria were littered with the most modern equipment the Soviet Union had ever supplied to any army.

Peled had, meanwhile, communicated his proposal for a concentrated divisional attack to General Hofi, who had already noted what was happening and was on the point of ordering General Eytan's northern force to take over the offensive and begin the drive into Syria. He accordingly instructed Peled to hold his positions, and by midafternoon what remained of his battered division was drawn up along the "Purple Line." General Eytan's brigades were ready to go and the Israeli armor was at last poised for the pursuit. Israeli emotion was expressed by the tankmen who chalked "ON TO DAMASCUS" on their Shermans and Centurions. Moshe Dayan stood on a prominence, his American-style forage cap pulled well down, and vowed: "We're going to show the Syrians that the road runs from Tel Aviv to Damascus as well as from Damascus to Tel Aviv."

CHAPTER

11

To Bridge the Suez Canal

While the battles on the Golan Heights were gradually turning in Israel's favor, along the Suez Canal front a stalemate had endured since Israel's defeated offensive on the 8th. Southern Command's formations were fighting continuous skirmishes to contain the Egyptians within their bridgeheads, where they had entrenched a formidable force of five infantry divisions. Their armor was, in the main, still on the West Bank. It comprised two armored divisions, two mechanized divisions, and two independent armored brigades, some nine hundred tanks in all. Throughout these days the Egyptians persisted in making localized forays toward the Israeli positions. For their part, the Israelis were still unable to overcome the missile umbrella and lacked sufficient heavy artillery to pound the bridgeheads from long range.

Adan's division was dug in along the northern sector of the Canal, with its three brigades deployed along different axis: Nir's brigade with some forty-six tanks on the Ma'adim Road; Gabi Amir's twenty-five tanks along the Spontani Road; and Aryeh Karen's forty-eight tanks along the Talisman Road—the Tassa-to-Ismailia route. Opposite them were elements of the Egyptian 18th Infantry Division, supported by their 15th Tank Brigade, and the greater part of the 2nd Infantry Division, with the 24th Tank Brigade.

Well before dawn on Tuesday, October 9, Adan radioed instructions to his brigades to commence a slow advance at 5:30 A.M. Accordingly, the armored brigades cautiously nosed their way west of the Artillery Road, except for Karen's brigade, which found its axis already occupied by elements of Sharon's division and had to bypass the congestion by plowing through deep, shifting sand dunes. By 7:00 A.M. the sky was light and in the soft, washed-out grayness of first light a startling sight met the Israelis' eyes: There, some 2 to 3 miles ahead, were literally thousands of Egyptian infantrymen frantically digging in along their front. Ditches were being excavated, fences hastily erected, and mines laid by the score, while trucks constantly revved back and forth with fresh supplies.

Things soon began to heat up, and from both flanks reports told of skirmishes with the Egyptians. At 8:30 A.M., a signal was received from Sharon's divisional operations officer that one of their brigades, under Colonel Haim, was attacking Hamutal. Because Sharon's division was heavily engaged, their operations officer requested that Adan's division attack Halutz to draw the Egyptian fire. In fact, Karen's brigade was already driving for Halutz but making slow progress through the trackless, shifting dunes. They had wanted to use the Talisman Road, which formed the boundary between Sharon's and Adan's divisions; if that could be cleared, they declared, they would be able to move much faster. Although in such circumstances a road is assigned specifically to one division, no such definition had been made in this instance, and two brigades had camped along the road that night so that there had been, by morning, considerable congestion. Adan radioed Gonen asking that the road-clearing be assigned to his division, but the somewhat cantankerous commander prevaricated. At first he agreed to Adan's suggestion; then, after speaking to Sharon at nine o'clock, presumably to let him know what had been decided, he changed his mind and left the entire road in Sharon's sector. In some exasperation, Adan pointedly told Gonen that whoever had the road should also have the area dominating the road, and proposed that the divisional sector boundary be moved to a ridge some 2 miles north of Talisman. Eventually Gonen agreed to this idea, but much time had been wasted.

It was already 10:00 A.M., and as neither Amir's nor Nir's brigade was yet in contact with the enemy, it was decided that they should warily advance westward while the divisional artillery took on the mass of Egyptian infantry still feverishly working on their defenses. However, before any action could begin, the Egyptian artillery opened up a heavy concentration. As Adan was forbidden to risk his limited armor in actions that would lead to its attrition, he had no alternative but to order Nir back to the Artillery Road, although the other brigades continued to support Sharon's northern flank.

At 1:00 P.M., the comparative inactivity in Adan's sector erupted into full battle when Amir signaled that tanks and infantry were advancing toward the *Zrakor* and *Havraga* features. Amir confidently asserted that he could contain them, but Adan was not so sure since he had so few tanks. To be on the safe side, he ordered Nir to move south to aid the weaker brigade, but the situation rapidly worsened. The trouble was that while Amir believed he could drive off the Egyptian force, he hadn't reckoned on the difficult terrain; there were innumerable hillocks to hide the Egyptian forces, so that as they drew closer, Amir's troops could not see them. Faced with a now overwhelming influx of enemy infantry and armor, Amir called for air and artillery support. Adan responded by directing his divisional artillery to concentrate there, even though artillery is not very effective in the desert, for anything less than a direct hit is likely to be cloaked by the soft sand. Soon the distinctive cracks drifted across the open desert, followed by the hum and zoom of shells that terminated in dull crumps as they thudded down amid the oncoming Egyptians.

Nir's brigade, meanwhile, was struggling south but was still about 7 miles away. Adan moved up in his command post half-track to a point from where he could see Amir's tanks firing at long range at the Egyptians without much effect. For an hour or so there was a serious situation as Amir's widely dispersed forces struggled to deal with an overwhelming number of Egyptian tanks, personnel carriers, and infantry. His small force holding Zrakor was badly hit and there were signs that the brigade was disintegrating. Then, at 2:30, Nir's tanks were seen plowing over the hilly country to the north. Although they advanced rapidly, the scene before them was of such confusion amid sand, dust, and smoke that Nir radioed frantically he couldn't tell the fighting tanks apart. The confusion continued a while longer as the two Israeli forces tried to link up ther radio networks, but eventually the increased weight of Israeli armor began to tell. Finally, the Egyptians broke off, and were soon in full retreat. Gonen then chose to warn Adan that his brigades were not to pursue the enemy, which Adan regarded as unnecessary as he hadn't contemplated such a move, certainly not until their own casualties and damage had been assessed. It was another example of Gonen's unfortunate and abrasive manner.

The fighting was still not over, though; half an hour later the Egyptians re-formed, and by four o'clock had started a second assault. This time they supported their attack with a heavy, hour-long artillery barrage, followed by a concerted deluge of truck-mounted Katyusha rockets, which in turn was followed by another artillery concentration that laid a heavy, rolling cloud of acrid yellow-stained phosphorus across the front. Unknown to the Israelis, the Egyptians were moving forward large numbers of infantry under cover of the smoke. These dug in among the dunes between the *Zrakor* and *Havraga* features, ready to launch another violent assault.

Yet another massive artillery and Katyusha barrage heralded the attack. Soon the dunes were alive with charging Egyptian infantrymen. They ran toward the Israeli positions, waving missile launchers, submachine guns, and rifles. The Israelis themselves were in some chaos, with tanks that had been refueling returning to the front to mingle with their own and Egyptian tanks and personnel carriers that had passed through their front lines. Into this mêlée roared Israeli fighter-bombers, screaming over to release their bombs onto the jumble of armor below. Immediately, the radio was alive with calls for the bombing to cease as they were narrowly missing the Israeli tanks, too. But the Israelis beat off the attack with machine-gun and tank fire, so that the Egyptian infantry soldiers were left streaming back between shattered tanks and glowing columns of oil smoke. As night dimmed the harsh scene, another Egyptian barrage crashed and thundered, its flashes searing across the sullen afterglow and lowering a curtain of smoke to cover their activity along the Canal.

For several days the pattern of warfare was the same, ending with the barrage and smoke. At night, the Egyptian infantry crawled doggedly forward over the chill, abrasive sands to infiltrate to within a mile or so of the Israeli forward positions; on one occasion they went too far and the next morning the Israeli tankers were startled to find Egyptian soldiers dug in behind them. In the morning, when the attacking forces reached the dug-in infantry, they would arise and follow the tanks. Successive waves of infantry would take over from one another as they were decimated by Israeli small arms and artillery fire. As one Israeli mortarman put it, "The determination and courage of those Egyptian soldiers was unbelievable. Time and again they came at us and we chopped them up."

The desert war had reached a stalemate dangerously reminiscent of World War I, in which defenses were replacing tactics, and the daily attacks and counterattacks simply decimated manpower. It seemed that missiles had turned back the clock and attrition was to replace maneuver once again.

Yet, in spite of the carnage, Israel was gradually gaining control of the battlefield as the Egyptian forces broke against their defenses. By Wednesday morning, when Northern Command was driving the Syrians back across the "Purple Line," Southern Command, too, could identify a change of fortune. But the change did little to curtail the stalemate, which, as the Egyptians were well aware, favored the Arabs. Their huge manpower reserves could stand losses indefinitely, whereas Israel, with an army mobilized from her citizens — factory workers, school-teachers, and so on — could not afford a prolonged war without disrupting her precarious economy. When General Gonen inspected the charts in his war room, he could see that Israeli losses were actually falling from their disastrous beginning, while those of Egypt were rising. The reserves were arriving, too, and Israeli strength in tanks and guns was reaching a peak. On the battlefield, the engineers had performed miracles of tank recovery and maintenance. It was therefore inevitable that planning should turn to the next stage of the war, in an endeavor to break the deadlock quickly and give the initiative at last to Israel — an initiative that had been rejected by the policies of static defense lines and attempts to curry world opinion. Given Israel's numerically much weaker forces, clearly the only way in which she could unbalance Egypt and create conditions where her capacity for speed and maneuver could be exploited was by a crossing of the Suez Canal.

Before the Israelis stormed to the Jordan River and the Suez Canal in 1967, they had had no special interest in amphibious operations, and therefore no experience. Following the Six Day War, though, the probability of further Arab confrontations created quite a different situation. With their basic doctrine of carrying the war immediately into enemy territory, some means of crossing the formidable water barriers had to be found.

Since 1968, then, Israeli military doctrine had planned for a counterattack across the Canal. When the daring maneuver eventually took place, the world's press hailed it as a bold exploitation of an Egyptian weakness, and the Israeli communiqués declared that a patrol had found a weak seam between the two Egyptian armies. But, in truth, it was the result of years of foresight, planning, and preparation, although no less daring or imaginative for that.

In the early post-1967 War years, the Israelis tried to purchase up-to-date bridging equipment, but encountered the usual difficulties of supply. They did procure a number of British-made floatable iron cubes known as uni-floats, each of which weighed 3 tons. The cubes—which were some 15 feet long, 8 feet wide, and 4 feet high—could be linked together to create varying-sized platforms to be used as rafts able to carry a tank, or linked together to form a bridge.

In 1969, the chief of doctrine in the Israeli Defense Force's Training Branch organized a bridging demonstration, which highlighted the many technical, tactical, and organizational problems. First, the infantry crossed in rubber dinghies to secure the far bank and hold a bridgehead into which the bridge would be constructed. A convoy of trucks then brought up the uni-floats, which a big crane offloaded straight into the water, where engineers assembled them to the required configuration. The initial task was to create rafts to which engines were attached, that could start ferrying tanks across into the bridgehead. This stage took about an hour. Only when several of these had been fabricated could they begin the job of creating a continuously linked bridge across the entire river.

Although this method was reasonable and used by a number of armies, it had the drawback of obliging the infantry to hold a very narrow bridgehead for too long while the first tanks were got ready for ferrying over to support them. Also, the infantry were able to hold only a limited bridgehead, and that would permit the enemy to maintain a steady fire onto the assembly work. Major General Adan saw the need for a much quicker means of throwing a bridge over a water obstacle, ideally by using assault gear based on tank-towed bridging equipment, which would allow a quick crossing under fire followed by the swift transfer of tanks to the enemy side. Once that had been achieved, the bridgehead could be rapidly expanded.

Adan, who was then commanding the Armored Corps, had their headquarters undertake research and development to evolve a better method. The underlying concept, he writes, "was that the basic element would be the raft, rather than the single uni-

float cube." It was demonstrated that a fully assembled raft, constructed from nine cubes, with two ramps and engines, was approximately 28 yards long and weighed about 60 tons. These preassembled rafts could be towed to the waterline by tanks, then pushed into the water to begin ferrying tanks across immediately. When eleven such rafts were in the water, they would be linked to form a single bridge to span the 200-yard-wide Canal. Experiments showed that when fitted with sledges or huge wheels, the rafts could readily be towed by tanks.

Along the Canal, selected areas had been designated as prospective crossing sites, where the sand ramparts had been made thinner and opening points had been marked. Infrastructure preparations had been made at Kantara; Deversoir, just north of the Bitter Lakes; and north of Suez; and work was still continuing when war began. Prefabricated bridge sections had been moved into Sinai and assembled, while dead-straight roads were constructed toward the Canal to permit the bridges to be towed forward to a specially prepared site, known as the "yard," 150 by 700 yards, with high sand walls constructed around it to facilitate bridge launching.

During the winter of 1972–73, the program was given impetus by an exercise carried out by the Israeli Defense Force. *Exercise Oz*, as it was called, was designed to test many subjects, including the bridging operations, the new structure of the regular armored division against the background of a crossing operation, deep penetration into enemy territory, mobile combat, and the capture of various features. Adan's division was allocated the task of performing the exercise under the aegis of Southern Command, then under Sharon, whose deputy at that time was General Gonen. It had been Sharon's idea to use the small Ruafa'a Dam, enlarged by relatively minor works, which was located in the desert of northern Sinai.

Exercise Oz demonstrated how the operation would proceed. While artillery softened up the far bank, tanks towed in the hastily constructed rafts. Other tanks positioned themselves to support the infantry while they crossed in rubber dinghies; then armored personnel carriers, which had been adapted for amphibious operations, churned across to provide the essential mobile firepower, forcing the "enemy" to keep its head down while the ferrying began. Although the bridging operation took longer than expected, it proved the efficacy of the new methods. Adan was also able to obtain the support of General Tal, the newly appointed deputy chief of staff, who took the problem to seventy-year-old Col. David Lakov of the Engineering Corps, a man of truly innovative abilities.

It was from that meeting that the rolling bridge developed: More than a hundred huge iron rollers, each some 2 yards in diameter, attached to form a single, 200-yard-long rolling bridge. This structure had the enormous advantage that it could be towed to the water's edge ready assembled and shoved into the water until it floated to the far bank. Nevertheless, it also had drawbacks, one being that it weighed a collosal 400 tons and had to be towed by sixteen tanks. It also took three days to assemble. Because of its length, the bridge could only be towed along a dead-straight prepared road. It was totally inflexible, hence in no way adaptable to unforeseen battle conditions and it had never been adequately tested.

The Israeli Defense Force had not limited its experiments to the bridge. The Engineering Corps had managed to purchase in Europe a number of scrap mobile bridging vehicles they named "Gilowas." These were huge wheeled vehicles that could be driven into the water, where they floated, and then linked together to form tank rafts; a number linked together created a floating bridge. The problem was that they were indeed ancient and needed a great deal of repair work, which the Israeli Defense Force could ill afford. Eventually only some eighteen were available for operations.

By the end of the first week of the Yom Kippur War, foremost in the minds of the Israeli Defense Force commanders was that to fulfill their basic doctrine of carrying the war into the enemy's territory, a Canal crossing would have to be made. It was the only way of solving the confrontation problem and

breaking the stalemate that, if left unresolved, would drag endlessly on and destroy Israel's economy. Besides, the Israelis had
spent years preparing for this eventuality, and the existing circumstances were just the kind of situation for which the Canal
crossing had been conceived. Since their successful storming of
the Canal, the Egyptians had firmly established a line along the
East Bank, narrow enough that they could be supported by artillery and antitank weapons from the West Bank, and under the
umbrella of their surface-to-air missiles.

There was no way in which the Israelis could make an attack
around the Egyptian flanks, so they were left with two equally
. distasteful options: either to wait for the Egyptians to break out
of their defensive dispositions far enough to leave the shelter of
the missiles; or to launch a frontal attack straight into the Egyptian defenses. Having considered these possibilities, few doubted
the war could only be concluded after an Israeli Canal crossing
had destroyed the missile sites, opened the air for the Israeli jets,
and isolated the main Egyptian armies.

On October 10, General Bar-Lev arrived by helicopter at
Southern Command headquarters for discussions on the next
stage of the war. At the meeting, Gonen proposed a crossing in
the area of Port Fuad-Port Said, but Bar-Lev shook his head,
declaring they were not yet ready. The chief engineering officer
also made it understood that he could not have the bridging
equipment ready until the 13th at the earliest. The discussions
were continued that evening at a conference of divisional commanders at which Bar-Lev presided. The atmosphere was tense,
yet with a tired expectancy. Mandler again raised the question of
a crossing, and Bar-Lev again demurred, saying that while they
were not prepared to initiate a crossing at that time, the preparations should nevertheless continue.

Southern Command's planning staff had drawn up outline
plans, which they presented to the new commanding officer,
illustrating the moves with maps. They proposed a two-division
attack, with a crossing at Deversoir. This area, they pointed out,
was on the boundary between the Egyptian Second and Third

Armies and contained only weak forces. Bar-Lev listened carefully and approved the concept. In the meantime, Gonen had already instructed that the rolling bridge should be moved forward the previous night. This, the group were informed, was now at the *Yukon* feature, east of Deversoir, where the final assembly was taking palce.

The conference met again the following day to consider the latest developments. For the moment, Egyptian pressure had eased, and it was generally assumed that this portended a buildup for the inevitable Egyptian main offensive, aimed at breaking out of the bridgehead and driving east. So far the attacks, although at brigade strength, had been only probing moves to keep the Israelis off-balance and to test their defensives. Sadat was being urged by President Assad of Syria to begin his offensive quickly in order to take Israeli pressure off his own hard-pressed forces, then being driven off the Golan Heights.

The Egyptians were in their operational hold stage, having consolidated with some pride along the East Bank of the Canal. Israel's last stronghold had surrendered on the 12th, and with much jubilation Egyptian television showed the population the army's continuing success. Nevertheless, some confusion seems to have arisen between the Syrians, who claimed their combined plans had called for the Egyptian's operational hold to begin only when they reached a line 60 miles east of the Canal, and the Egyptians, who disagreed, arguing that their present dispositions were correct.

Underlying their success, the Egyptian High Command had its own problems. The minister of war, Ahmed Ismail, had the reputation of being "every inch a soldier," although he was by nature rather benign and politically unambitious, which no doubt made him attractive to Sadat. Ismail had agreed with Sadat that is was sensible to go to war with whatever was currently available to break the political deadlock, even if it produced only limited results. By contrast, Chief of Staff General Shazli was another charismatic, colorful leader, and a former paratrooper. He had a reputation for arrogance and bravado, which, however, seemed to have deserted him during the 1967 War when he reportedly led the stampede out of Sinai.

In the current campaign, Shazli was all for exploiting the Egyptian advantage and immediately taking the offensive to break through into the Israeli rear areas. But his boss, Ismail, was diametrically opposed to this view, and was determined not to endanger the army in any way. He was acutely aware of the dangers that would confront any initiative in moving large mobile forces deep into Sinai, where they would be very vulnerable to the highly trained and battle-proven Israeli troops without effective air defenses. From his later summary of the war, it is obvious that Ismail was obsessed with the danger of moving his forces beyond the missile cover. Ironically, he seems to have held much the same view as Israel's High Command, preferring to hold his positions and let the Israeli forces dissipate their strength against his army's missiles and tanks. In consequence, the Egyptian offensive plans for Sinai lacked the detailed planning that had gone into their successful Canal crossing.

The stalemate that had developed along the Canal front could not, of course, be allowed to continue. The Israelis, as we have seen, could not afford a prolonged war, and Arab unity, ever a tenuous phenomena, was in danger of cracking as the Syrians began to weaken. Among the Egyptian commanders, too, fears were being voiced that once Syria was defeated, the entire weight of the Israeli Defense Force would be hurled against them.

The trouncing Syria was getting on the Golan Heights made it all the more imperative that a cease-fire should be quickly arranged, before her forces were pushed right out of the area — perhaps even further from the pre-1967 cease-fire lines than they had been on October 5. In his memoirs, Sadat recalls that Syria submitted three requests for a cease-fire to the Soviet Union, all of which were rejected by Egypt. At that time, of course, Egypt was sitting tight under the missile umbrella along the narrow bridgeheads with her forces virtually intact. Moreover, on October 9, Egyptian forces had undeniably inflicted a major defeat on the Israelis. Egyptian confidence was soaring, and it seemed certain that once her forces took the offensive, they would be able to drive deep into Sinai. Then a cease-fire would confirm Egypt's hold on a very substantial slice of liberated territory, leaving no doubts of her new military capability.

In the meantime, Brezhnev contacted President Tito of Yugoslavia in the hope that through his long friendship with Nasser, Tito might persuade Egypt to accept a cease-fire, explaining (according to Sadat) that "President Sadat would precipitate a disaster for the Arab world, progressive regimes everywhere and the world at large." Tito, it seems, declined on the grounds that even personal friendship did not permit him to intervene, as he was of the opinion that Sadat knew what he was doing. At this point Tito supplied Egypt with the 140 tanks. Sadat states that he asked for them as a matter of urgency because of his "experience with the Soviet Union." Other sources state that the tanks were shipped via Yugoslavia *by* the Soviet Union. The Russians were, by then, openly flying in huge volumes of stores in giant Antonov-22 transport aircraft, in what was the biggest military airlift since the Russian invasion of Czechoslovakia in 1968. They were pulling out every stop to replenish Arab supplies of missiles, ammunition, and even tanks, for Syria's depleted force could not have survived without them.

Efforts to bolster the Arab cause were by then taking place anyway, as the initial success incited a resurgent pride in the Arab force of arms, and contingents of varying strengths were arriving from other Arab states, including Algeria, Morocco, Kuwait, Saudi Arabia, Jordan, and Iraq. Of course, with complete duplicity, the Arabs were also warning Western countries not to interfere by aiding Israel. Jordan's King Hussein, who had managed so far to keep his country out of the war, had by then been pushed by his officers to make some gesture toward Arab solidarity. He duly dispatched his 40th Armored Brigade to Syria. Ironically, this same unit had been sent to oppose an expected Syrian invasion of Jordan only a few years previously, when Hussein had expelled the Palestinians. Iraq had mobilized two armored divisions and also placed her substantial air force at

Syria's side. Under this combined Arab pressure, the Egyptian Command, albeit reluctantly, prepared to go over to the offensive. Commenting later on the tank battle that was to take place on October 14, Ismail was to assert that it was much larger than he had intended, and had been launched prematurely because of Syrian pressure upon Egypt to draw off Israeli forces. A few days before, Assad had sent one of his top-ranking generals to Egypt with a message pleading for a major Egyptian offensive.

On Thursday, October 11, just five days after the outbreak of war, the Israeli general headquarters gave Southern Command the go-ahead for the Canal crossing operation. On the following day, General Bar-Lev explained the plan proposed for the night of October 13/14.

The meeting was held in Tel Aviv. It was attended by Elazar and his deputy, General Tal; the director of Military Intelligence, Maj. Gen. Eliahu Zeira; Gen. Rechavam Ye'evi; and Maj. Gens. Aharon Yariv and Benjamin Peled, the air force commander; as well as Gonen and his divisional commanders. Again there were arguments about the location of the crossing. After Gonen had presented his views, both Adan and Sharon expressed reservations and proposed that the crossing should be at one of the other prepared sites. Gonen arose to counter the arguments of his subordinate commanders, maintaining that only at Deversoir was there every possibility the forces could reach the Canal without a prolonged fight, due to the weak Egyptian forces along the seam between their two armies. In fact, just as General Gavish had predicted, the Egyptians had seized a considerable foothold and the Israelis were going to have to fight their way to the Canal. At the other sites, he argued, it would mean forcing a way through the Egyptian positions and would require a major battle to reach the Canal.

Bar-Lev, who had been sitting listening intently to the arguments, then intervened in support of Gonen and Deversoir. He gave a number of reasons. First, he pointed out that the left flank of the crossing would be protected by the Bitter Lakes; second, on the far bank at Deversoir there was only a sweet-water irrigation canal and a narrow agricultural strip to be crossed, which would permit the tanks to fight a battle of maneuver, whereas at Kantara there were many canals and developments. He, too, appreciated the Egyptian weakness along their interarmy boundary.

Peled, the air force commander, was definitely in favor of the crossing, pointing out that the air force was losing so many aircraft to the surface-to-air missiles that it was imperative to cross as quickly as possible in order to eradicate the enemy's air defenses. Major General Zeira also supported the crossing, but General Tal, Elazar's deputy, was just as emphatically against it. He argued that the operation would depend too much on a breakthrough to the Canal, which must incur heavy losses that Israel just could not afford. No, he declared, it was better to engage the enemy in armored warfare on the East Bank before they moved the bulk of their armored forces from the West Bank.

General Elazar was now in a quandary; on balance, he favored the crossing, but thought that the defense minister, Dayan, should take part in the discussion. Dayan was then on the northern front, and although he was requested to come to general headquarters on his return, he wanted the prime minister to make the final decision. Accordingly, the whole conference was moved to the office of the prime minister that afternoon, where they were joined by Mrs. Meir's deputy, Yigal Allon, and Yisrael Galili, the minister without portfolio.

Again the arguments for and against the crossing were put, Tal opposing the crossing and Bar-Lev equally against an indefinite wait for an Egyptian attack. However, at this point, the Egyptians themselves forestalled a decision, for in the middle of the conference word was brought that an Egyptian attack was imminent. All day—intelligence reported—the Egyptians had been making probing attacks. In the circumstances, all present agreed to postpone any action until after the Egyptian attack had been defeated, and only then go for the Canal crossing. Bar-Lev

immediately directed Southern Command to plan the defeat of
the Egyptian offensive, but also to continue with preparations for
the subsequent attack across the the Canal. Elazar fully agreed
with his scheme. In many respects the long-awaited great tank
battle was a relief from the unbearable tension of the previous
week.

First thing on Sunday morning, Elazar flew down to Southern
Command headquarters, and after a brief meeting, went on to
Sharon's advanced headquarters to discuss the plans for the
armored battle, as well as the planned Canal crossing. General
Gonen flew down to Sharon's headquarters in the same helicop-
ter as reserve general Ezer Weizman.

Gonen was anxious to discuss with Albert Mandler the per-
formance of his forces in a battle fought that morning west of
the Giddi Pass. He radioed General Mandler while still in the
air, telling him he would visit him after seeing Sharon. He then
asked Mandler where they should meet. There was a pause, then
Mandler's voice crackled out again, giving a scale point in the
Giddi Pass, and adding, "I suggest we meet at the Giddi-Lateral
Road crossroads." Gonen asked another question, but there was
no reply. According to General Herzog, he turned to Weizman,
saying: "Ezer, Albert has been killed."

"What nonsense, you ass," Weizman retorted.

But Gonen was insistent, sensing some kind of tragedy. "If
Albert doesn't answer me on the radio, he can only be dead."

The radio operator tried again but could get no answer. The
helicopter clattered on and eventually descended in its dust cloud
at Sharon's headquarters. Bar-Lev was also there and Gonen,
Sharon, and Elazar made their way into one of the rooms. Then
the news was brought that Mandler's half-track had received a
direct hit during heavy shelling; he was critically wounded and
was being flown to Refidim. Apparently, he had ignored advice
to wait until the shelling abated because there was so much to
do, and had driven to a crossroads under shellfire. The commanders had barely entered the room when a second message
was relayed to them, that Albert Mandler was dead.

Mandler should have relinquished his command to Brig. Gen.

Kalman Magen just before the outbreak of war, but did not do so because he sensed war was imminent. For a moment there was a stunned silence in the sparse room where the top commanders were meeting. Then it was proposed that Magen be immediately summoned from Baluza to take over divisional command. Three quarters of an hour later, Magen arrived. He was immediately given command, and, there being no rank insignia available, Weizman handed Magen his, which were pinned on by Elazar. Yzhak Sasson was sent to take over Magen's formation in Baluza.

Southern Command's plan for the Egyptian offensive was to let it move deep into Israeli territory, out of range of its own infantry antitank and antiaircraft missiles, before blocking it with an armored force. By this stage of the war, the Israeli tankers had learned that the infantry missiles could be defeated by the fairly simple expedient of hammering the men with machine guns and mortars. Since the resounding success of the Israeli Armored Corps in 1967, the tank concept had dominated Israeli tactics and, as we have seen, resulted in the tanks being deprived of the carrier-borne infantry and mobile mortar batteries that would have played a decisive role early in the Yom Kippur War. By week two, however, lessons had been learned, especially that infantry mounted in M-113 armored personnel carriers and integrated self-propelled artillery working in close cooperation with the tanks offered the best counter to the otherwise lethal Egyptian Sagger tank-killer teams. Similarly, machine guns and mortars mounted in the M-113s gave the essential close support against Egyptian infantrymen when they left their own BRDM carriers.

The divisions of Magen, Sharon, and Sasson were to deploy for containment in their sectors, while Sharon would also hold a brigade in reserve to deal with the eventuality of a localized Egyptian breakthrough. Adan's division was to deploy in the rear, to prepare for the subsequent Canal crossing and act as a mobile reserve striking force to repulse any Egyptian penetration. It was replaced in the line by a brigade under Colonel Yoel.

Washington had reacted extremely cautiously at the outbreak of war. Over the weekend efforts were made to contain the situation, and on Monday evening Kissinger had warned that détente could not survive irresponsibility. Also on Monday, Nixon, at a meeting with the president of the Ivory Coast, urged an end to the fighting, which was, he stressed, inflicting terrible costs on both sides. In these utterances, however, there was no comfort for Israel, for both Americans studiously avoided blaming either Egypt or Syria for starting the war. Only on Tuesday was there a perceptible shift in U.S. policy, after news reached Washington about the Soviet airlift of supplies into Egypt and Syria. The American comments then became more candid, and the State Department warned that if the Soviet airlift became "massive," it would imperil détente by putting a new face on the situation. That same day, the Pentagon confirmed that "very big tonnages" of military supplies were involved. So, by Wednesday, when Nixon met with congressional leaders, there was a definite shift in American attitudes. Nixon still spoke of being "very fair to both sides," but the Senate had already adopted a resolution put forward by the leaders of both parties, demanding that Egypt and Syria pull back their forces to the old armistice lines. The House of Representatives introduced legislation enabling war supplies to be stepped up to Israel in response to the Soviet airlift.

Overall American policy, then, during the first week of the war, had been to play down the extent of Soviet involvement and to refrain from criticism of either the Arabs or the Russians. They were anxious to avoid any pressure that might endanger U.S. oil interests, especially with Saudi Arabia, while criticism of Russia would harm détente, a cornerstone of American foreign policy. There was even a majority view in the State Department that any American aid to Israel should be such as to produce a stalemate in Sinai. This view was shared to a lesser extent by the Pentagon, one of whose officials explained, according to the *New York Times*, "The Arabs have gotten some of their honor back, and we don't want the Israelis to take it away. It's time to settle." The prevailing view was that Egypt was the key to a settlement, and there was not nearly so much concern about an Israeli victory on the Golan Heights. Any military stalemate, in the Pentagon's view, would turn into a cease-fire, and eventually a demilitarization of Sinai, and hopefully the withdrawal of both Egyptian and Israeli forces.

When Kissinger gave a press conference on Friday, October 12, this was very much his line, although correspondents saw little in the approach giving support for Israel. Although Kissinger refrained once again from criticism of the Arabs, he did admit that the Soviet Union had not been entirely helpful in urging other Arab states to support Egypt and Syria. Privately it was admitted by State Department aides that Kissinger was hopping mad at the way the Russians were traipsing around the Mediterranean drumming up military aid for their customers. But in his official accounts, Kissinger's measured statements asserted that Soviet behavior was less threatening, less incendiary, and less geared to military threats than in 1967. He also confirmed that discussions were being held with Israel over arms supplies to replace their losses in aircraft and tanks, but that no decision had been finalized.

Kissinger did, however, venture some barely disguised warnings, cautioning that a prolonged conflict was dangerous because it could increase the possibility of Great Power involvement — the Middle East, as he saw it, was in danger of Balkanizing superpower politics. He was careful, all the same, to assert that to the present time, both the United States and the Soviet Union had endeavored to behave in ways that would avoid confrontation between them. Nevertheless, he saw the Soviet airlift as unhelpful, although not yet a threat to détente, and intoned: "When this point is reached we will in this crisis, as we have in other crises, not hesitate to take a firm stand...," going on to reaffirm America's intention of moderating the conflict.

Behind the public pronouncements, Kissinger was trying to find a common approach with the Soviet Union. Senator Mike Mansfield told the Senate that Kissinger had made approaches to the Soviet leaders, seeking a diplomatic solution "based on no arms shipments to either side." The *Washington Post* reported that the special adviser to President Nixon, Melvin Laird, had confirmed that Kissinger waited four days for signs that the Russians were restraining supplies before acting.

Kissinger's policy was based on several considerations. The most important was that the Soviet Union was prepared to show restraint, although by Friday, October 12, over 3,000 tons of war supplies had already been air-freighted to Syria and Egypt. This figure did not take into account a convoy of transports, which by their progress toward the Arab ports must have left their Black Sea ports before the outbreak of war. The supply tonnage was increasing all the time, and by Monday evening, October 15, when both Arab armies were staggering back in defeat, Cyprus Air Traffic Control reported eighteen Soviet Antonov transports flying over *every hour*. The air traffic was to provoke friction within NATO, for both Greece and Turkey turned a blind eye to the Russian flights while denying the Americans similar facilities. The scene from Beirut, too, looked distinctly menacing by then, for Western observers assumed that America would at least have to match the Soviets to restore the military balance. In addition, they noted that another ten to fifteen Soviet warships had joined the already considerable Mediterranean fleet, bringing it to an all-time maximum of some seventy surface ships.

Also taken into account by America was the reaction of her NATO allies, who were behaving with varying degrees of European perfidy. Britain was refusing to supply Israel with much needed ammunition and spares for the Centurion tanks she had previously issued, as well as other supplies for which there existed contracts. Britain had declared an embargo on military supplies to the combatants, although a small trickle did reach some Arab countries, notably in the Gulf, which no doubt eventually got to Sinai or the Golan. France was still sending arms to Libya, to whom she had already supplied over one hundred Mirage aircraft, and she was also sending arms to Saudi Arabia. West Germany too restrained arms supplies, but protested strongly when American arms were shipped to Israel from bases in West Germany through Bremerhaven. In fact, once the American airlift got going, Portugal alone permitted landing rights for the Americans.

At dawn in Cairo on October 13, the seventh day of the war, President Sadat was awakened with the news that the British ambassador wished to see him straightaway with an urgent message from Prime Minister Edward Heath. Sadat arose and shortly afterward entered the living room, adjoining his bedroom, where the ambassador was waiting. The ambassador had brought a message from Kissinger, passed on through Heath, requesting confirmation that he, Sadat, had indeed accepted a cease-fire, in accordance with what the Russians had told him. Having been energetically working for a cease-fire ever since the war began, Kissinger welcomed the Soviet declaration that Egypt would agree to a cease-fire on the existing lines of October 13.

But Sadat did not confirm the cease-fire agreement. Indeed, he pointedly asked the ambassador to convey the following reply, quoted in Sadat's memoirs: "Please tell Kissinger that this never took place. I haven't agreed to a cease-fire proposed by the Soviet Union or any other party. He should contact Cairo, not Moscow, in respect of anything concerning Egypt. Furthermore, I shall not agree to a cease-fire until the tasks included in the plan have been accomplished."

The ambassador then asked if it was true that Sadat insisted on closing the Red Sea to Israeli shipping. "Yes, indeed," Sadat replied, and when asked what were his terms, he answered promptly: "I am willing to have a cease-fire if Israel agrees to withdraw from the occupied Arab territories."

Only a short while after the British ambassador left to transmit the reply to Kissinger, Sadat received a note from the Soviet Embassy that Premier Alexei Kosygin wanted to call upon him. Sadat assured them that he would be welcome, and Kosygin wasted no time in arriving. The hard-faced Russian came quickly to the point. He wanted Egypt to cease hostilities on the existing lines. According to his memoirs, Sadat replied: "I am not prepared to have a repeat of the 1948 'truce' which was behind our loss of the war."

Kosygin responded: "We'll come in here and guarantee nothing of the sort will happen"—a ready response that smacks of

the Soviets' real objective, to create a situation in which the presence of Russian forces astride the West's oil supply route could
be made legitimate. But Sadat wasn't prepared for that, and
replied contemptuously that it wasn't possible to guarantee anything with Israel.

But his real contention with the tough Russian bureaucrat was
over supplies, and he took the occasion to hammer home this
point. " . . . Where are the tanks I asked for on the second day
of the war?" he demanded, and ranted that the Russian air bridge
was only delivering equipment that should have been delivered
long before. There followed an altercation, during which, Sadat
records, "Kosygin then resorted to his more vicious side." They
argued about the equipment Russia had supplied, especially the
bridges, each of which took five hours to build, while the Russians possessed the latest BMP bridge that could be erected in
only thirty minutes.

The meeting concluded on a sour note when Kosygin
declared that he had not expected Sadat to be "so excited." Kosygin then returned to his embassy, where he remained several days
longer, following the course of the war and only seeing Sadat
briefly in the evenings.

Whether Sadat had briefed the Russians on his long-awaited
offensive into Sinai has not been revealed. Being so reliant on
Soviet aid, one would expect him to have done so, if only to
ensure a flow of replacements and supplies. On the other hand,
Sadat did not let the Russians know, so it is claimed, the date of
the original attack, although the Syrians did inform the Russians.
In all this there is an element of post-event sour grapes and the
truth is hard to perceive. Nevertheless, while Sadat's early morning meetings were taking place, his forces were flowing across
the Canal pontoon bridges and deploying for the following day's
major offensive.

What Sadat did not know was that at seven o'clock that morning, about the time he was talking with Kosygin, American SR-
71A reconnaissance planes—great, futuristically shaped succes-
sors to the notorious U-2 "spy" planes—were flying high over

the Middle East battlefields at an altitude of 15 miles. At that height the sparkling desert air held no secrets from the incredibly sensitive cameras. By late that afternoon the planes' films had been analyzed and showed clearly the Egyptian concentrations. The source of Israel's intelligence reports on the Egyptian build-up has not been fully explained, like so many aspects of this recent war. But this information was undoubtedly passed on to Israel, and confirmed what her own reconnaissance reports were suggesting. Of equal importance, the flights brought home to the hesitant American government the full extent of the Soviet supply, and that in turn began to affect U.S. policy on supplying Israel. Sadat believed that the movement of his 21st Armored Division and his other forces had been observed by an American satellite, which transmitted back the information, and no doubt that was so. The 14-ton United States "Big Bird" satellite was passing over the area regularly, and, unlike the Soviet "Cosmos" satellites, which had to be brought back to earth for their pictures to be recovered, "Big Bird" sent it all back by electronic means.

Saturday was a busy diplomatic morning, which also saw Kissinger meeting Israeli Foreign Minister Eban to explain that he was unhappy about Israeli declarations of the "devastating blows" they were going to deal the Arabs; presumably Arab threats to annihilate Israel were not in the same category. Neither did he like Israel's vaunted drive on Damascus now that they had defeated the Syrians on the Golan Heights. This, he felt sure, would upset the Russians. Kissinger favored a cease-fire that would leave Egypt in possession of both sides of the Canal and the Syrians wherever they happened to halt. He gravely explained that Dobrynin, the Soviet ambassador, would agree to an armistice on this basis, although the Russians were claiming that as they had no leverage in either Cairo or Damascus, they could do little to compel a cease-fire. Russia was against a return to the old cease-fire lines, Kissinger explained slowly and succinctly, as were Britain and France. It was the best Israel could expect.

In the meantime, however, Mrs. Meir had sent a personal

appeal to Nixon, emphasizing the acute Israeli shortages and the urgency with which supplies were needed. Until then, actually, there was still no agreement in Washington about how much help to give Israel, or how they should respond to the Russians' airlift. Some politicians, notably Laird, the President's adviser, were by no means as optimistic as Kissinger about Russian intentions, declaring that they were behaving as if détente didn't exist. The French newspaper *Le Monde* reported that one visitor to the State Department thought himself on a different planet — there was nothing but praise for Sadat's moderation and an assurance that Russia would act judiciously. But there is little doubt that by then Kissinger wanted to send Israel sufficient air-to-air missiles, electronic equipment, and ammunition to ensure her defense against further Arab aggression. By then it was also known that Jordan had raised her small dagger and was reaching around corners through Syria to stab Israel, while prudently avoiding the probability of being given another hiding by the Israelis. Nevertheless, Jordan's action left the Americans uncertain whether or not a third war front was about to be imposed on the already overtaxed Israeli forces.

The Special Action Group met again on Saturday night and held lengthy deliberations, on the level of fighting, Israeli losses, and the huge scale of Soviet supply. There were also reports of North Vietnamese pilots flying for Syria. First thing the next morning, Sunday, Kissinger went to see Nixon, with whom the final decision rested. After listening carefully, the President confirmed the Special Action Group's recommendation to send Phantom fighter-bombers at once and to initiate an air bridge to match the Soviet supply.

Kissinger's original scheme was that the military supplies should be flown to Israel in either their own or hired aircraft, as he did not want American aircraft to be involved. But after a few days that was seen to be quite inadequate to handle the required volume and, after a further urgent appeal from Mrs. Meir to Nixon, the U.S. Air Force took over the task. Soon the world's second biggest airlift was under way as giant C-5 Galaxies (the biggest aircraft in existence) ferried a massive 700 to 800 tons daily, staging through an American air base in the Azores. The size of this airlift was exceeded only by the 1948 Berlin airlift.

At Pease Air Force Base in New Hampshire, the giant aircraft were loaded in bright moonlight. Police had to turn away curious spectators who flocked to see what on earth was going on. Bob Jones, who owns a gas station near the end of the runway, commented that "The only other time you hear that much activity at night is when the reserves fly in." The ground shook from the bellow of another KC-135 tanker as it hurtled along the runway, lifted, then banked away toward the Atlantic Ocean where they would rendezvous with other aircraft in need of refueling. At Dover Air Base in Delaware, arms were loaded by the ton into towering Galaxies, while elsewhere blue and white Israeli 747s lifted off with yet more gear.

By October 17 some three dozen A-4 Skyhawks had been sent, quickly followed by thirty-two combat-ready Phantoms, most from the U.S. Air Force at Seymour Johnson Base in Greensboro, North Carolina, and a few straight off the production line at the McDonnell-Douglas plant in St. Louis. The Phantoms were equipped with electronic countermeasure pods to detect and counter enemy radar by sending out electronic jamming signals; this made up a vital Israeli deficiency. The Phantoms' effectiveness was further increased by a brilliant array of "smart bombs," including "Walleye" TV-guided bombs and laser-guided devices; and "Rockeye" cluster bombs for destroying tanks.

Kissinger's objective was to stabilize the military situation and, above all else, avoid a long war, which would have a detrimental effect on détente and must eventually draw in the superpowers to a greater extent, rather like Spain in the 1930s. The French newspapers *Figaro* and *Le Monde* claimed that the military supplies were conditional on Israel accepting an *in situ* cease-fire that would leave the Egyptians firm on the East Bank.

In Israel, Southern Command's reconnaissance forces were still watching the Egyptian lines and reporting back all troop movements, confirming U.S. Intelligence. All day on the 13th, they were preparing the ground across which the armored divisions would move once they crossed the Canal on their bridges. They laid tapes and made start lines. During the following night, the Egyptian armor began to cross, long queues of tanks, carriers, scout cars, and guns trailed in seemingly endless columns to rattle and sway across the bridges before revving their engines to climb the East Bank through breaches in the high sand embankments. The noise was terrific, and barely drowned by a continuous artillery shoot. By the morning of the 14th, the armor was over and being deployed in the narrow strip they held on the East Bank. Then it was the turn of the support weapons. Soon fourteen antiaircraft batteries, including six mobile SA-6 batteries, were deployed to reinforce and extend the air defense system. More artillery and mortar batteries followed, to swell the already huge forces in the bulging bridgeheads.

All intelligence reports indicated two main efforts on the part of the Egyptians. The 4th Armored Division would lead Third Army's attack and 21st Armored Division would spearhead Second Army. Behind them were massed mechanized divisions, independent tank brigades, and infantry divisions. It appeared likely, intelligence said, that the Egyptians would land commandos again in the Israeli rear to interfere with the communications and generally dissipate Israeli strength. Southern Command was apprehensive. It seemed highly probable that the two Egyptian armored divisions would try for a huge pincer movement aimed at the big base at Refidim (formerly, the Egyptian base of Bir Gafgafa), with Third Army driving for the Mitla and Giddi passes, while Second Army on the northern flank thrust via Tassa. Such a combined attack would concentrate about 1,500 tanks, against which Israeli could only muster 750 along the entire Sinai front. It was a daunting thought.

CHAPTER
12

The Egyptian Offensive

Col. Amnon Reshef's brigade had moved into position at 5:00 A.M. in the Ismailia sector. His tanks had churned across the desert and climbed the sand and stones until they were ranged just below the ridge at the head of a valley leading toward Tassa. They made sure their turrets were below the skyline, and there they waited for the Egyptians to advance. It was already hot and sultry, a heavy, uncomfortable morning.

At dawn, the Egyptian artillery began a massive ninety-minute barrage. As the sound of the big guns died away, thousands of their infantrymen began moving forward to the Israeli positions, followed by hundreds of Soviet-built T-55 and T-62 tanks. In the northern sector the 18th Infantry Division, reinforced by a brigade of T-62 tanks, attacked toward Rumani. A force of commandos whirred into Sinai in Soviet-supplied MIG-18 helicopters and landed among the salt marshes, only to be immediately attacked by Israeli paratroopers and quickly routed.

Col. Mahmoud Montassir, head of military operations of the 21st Armored Division, radioed the commander that its advance from Ismailia was proceeding according to plan. It was strengthened by one of the 23rd Armored Division's tank brigades for the attack. He watched with satisfaction as his tanks, carriers, and guns rumbled along, heading into the shallow valley that led toward the Israeli positions before Tassa on the road to Refidim. Despite their steady progress, however, Montassir was beginning to feel uneasy; he had expected an Israeli reaction to their advance and it had not started. He wondered whether the lack of fire indicated that they might have withdrawn under cover of the dust storm raised by his armored force as they steadily climbed the ridge in blistering heat. Unknown to Montassir, Reshef's reconnaissance company was watching them, and when a group of Egyptian Sagger missile carriers penetrated too far ahead of the main force, the Israelis opened fire and wiped them out. Only later did the advancing armor come across the still-smoking wreckage.

The sky was rent as two Egyptian MIG-17s sped westward after a strafing raid, hotly pursued by several Israeli Mirages. Even as Montassir watched, a MIG flipped onto its back and plunged to the ground beyond the ridge of dunes, leaving only a smudge of oily smoke to mark its crash. He stared in fascinated horror, wondering if there was anything he could do. Beyond the ridge, meanwhile, Reshef had given strict instructions that his force was to hold its fire until the Egyptians closed to a 1,000-yard range. Herzog says that the "Egyptians opened a heavy artillery attack. Suddenly from the Chinese Farm he [Reshef] observed what appeared from a distance to be a vast river of tanks flowing toward him: it was the 1st Brigade of the 21st Armored Division."

It took a lot of discipline for the Israelis to sit it out while such a powerful formation rumbled toward them. They were climbing out of the valley and would soon be within range. Egyptian artillery continued to thunder, pouring shells into Israeli positions along the front, but they had got used to that and only flinched when a shell exploded close enough to rattle their tanks with shrapnel and rocks. Then, at a signal, they edged their Centurions — a type particularly favored by Sharon — up to the ridge and waited tensely, their flat turrets barely visible above the skyline.

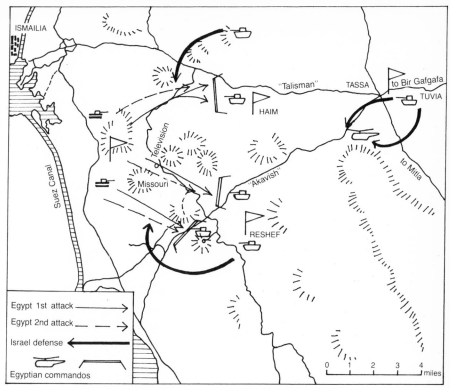

ISMAILIA

"Talisman"   TASSA   to Bir Gafgafa

TUVIA

HAIM

Television

Missouri   "Akavish"

Suez Canal   to Mitla

RESHEF

Egypt 1st attack ⟶
Egypt 2nd attack — ⟶
Israel defense ⟵
Egyptian commandos

0   1   2   3   4 miles

Tassa Opening Action, October 14, 1973 (Egyptian Second Army)

Reshef watched the Egyptians clanking and grinding closer, then commanded: "Fire!" Instantly the whole brigade fired—a terrific rolling crash of tank guns firing almost simultaneously, pouring salvo after salvo down onto the Egyptians. Montassir stared in awe and dismay. Moments before his tanks had been climbing steadily toward the ridge, and the next second they were exploding with horrifying cracks. Tanks disintegrated into instant fireballs. Across the valley echoed the roar of Israeli guns that drowned even the artillery's rumble. The thunder of explosions flung clouds of sand and metal high in the air. Carriers caught in the storm struggled on in bewildered panic, their commanders jamming the radio network as they sought instructions and help. Then they began turning to avoid the Israeli guns, swinging like ships to escape the high-explosive armor-piercing shells already pulverizing their ranks. But on the rocky slopes the ungainly vehicles rocked and many turned over, flinging the unprotected infantrymen out into the already body-strewn sand, where the machine guns and mortars caught them, hurling them in ragged heaps. Others stumbled between the wreckage seeking cover, or threw themselves face down behind burning tanks.

From his forward command post, Montassir valiantly tried to restore order, but the radio was jammed with screams and curses and he could not get through to his battalion commanders. Eventually he managed to organize his own command group and got them moving back down the valley, in an effort to make an orderly withdrawal, from which they could regroup. But by then Reshef's armor had moved rapidly to outflank the Egyptians and block their retreat by holding the ridge to the south. Their long 105mm guns probed over the ridge, waving like antennae as tank commanders selected their prey, then recoiling with the shock as targets exploded.

With a roar, Montassir's artillery commander's car was flung into a hundred flaming pieces by a shell that hit it squarely. Reshef watched from his position half a mile to the east, grimly staring at the Egyptian 1st Tank Brigade as it fled, its retreat disintegrating into a rout. Within thirty minutes, the brigade had been destroyed. The Israelis let them go, watching as they hurried west leaving a trail of burning, smoking hulks.

Maj. Gen. Saad Mahmoun, the commander of the Second Army, had continued to stress the importance of breaking through to Tassa, en route for Refidim. By 8:00 A.M., however, he was anxiously scanning the situation report, which showed all too clearly that the attacks at Kantara and Firdan had failed. He was acutely worried and realized that if his armored forces were not withdrawn to the Canal and the missile defenses there, they would be destroyed, leaving little hope for the reserve forces still west of the Canal. Reluctantly he ordered a retreat. But his subordinate commanders, Brigadier Mohammed Abdul Oraby of 21st Armored and Brigadier Abd Rabb Hafez of the 16th Infantry Division, greeted the orders with dismay. They couldn't retreat, they exclaimed; the battle was only a few hours old. And so, under their combined persuasion, Mahmoun changed his mind and accepted that—provided his forces had sufficient artillery support—a second-line assault could break through the Israeli positions and open the way to Refidim.

Adan's division, which was in reserve while preparing for the crossing, had been called upon to deploy against enemy armor advancing against the *Ma'adim*, *Zrakor*, and *Havraga* features. Gonen had called with the news that the Egyptians had launched attacks along the entire front, and he told Adan to move a brigade south of Tassa immediately ready to counterattack. As Adan records, this left him in a dilemma, for although the Egyptians were exerting great pressure, he was being asked to commit a brigade of only 75 tanks to hold a sector where, in the previous days, 120 had been all but inadequate. He reluctantly split his division, giving Karen command of two brigades and sending the third toward Tassa. But at nine o'clock Gonen was back, demanding that another brigade must be sent to Tassa. This left precious little in reserve for the battle and the crossing operation.

By then the Egyptians had hastily assembled their armored forces for what their Soviet military advisers termed the "second-line assault": A standard Soviet concept of overwhelming defenses with successive waves of infantry massively supported by armor. Although the Egyptians faithfully attacked according to the Soviet practice of the two-echelon assault, its first waves had been repulsed by the longer-range Israeli tank guns. Before the second wave could make its attack, the Israelis had had time to refuel, replenish their ammunition, and still resume their positions.

The attack went in with Hafez's 16th Division infantrymen following their tanks while from the rear the artillery opened fire to pin down the Israeli defenders. But their fire pattern was sporadic and ill coordinated, and soon it fell into an ineffective random shelling that hardly bothered the Israeli tankmen. Deliberately, the remnants of Oraby's 1st and 14th armored brigades advanced against the *Hamutal* and *Hamadia* features where Reshef's troops waited, dry-mouthed and staring. The massed second assault drove at the Israeli positions, but before they could effectively open fire, the Israeli guns again lashed them with a storm of fire at near-point-blank range. The first line of Egyptian tanks was completely wiped out. Shot through, they slewed, collided, and collapsed in their tracks, exuding clouds of flaming smoke through which the desert sun loomed huge and bloody. The chaos threw into confusion the second line of tanks as they tried to squeeze past the flaming hulks, blinded by the smoke and fire, and these were decimated in their turn.

When the news of the calamity reached Mahmoun, he staggered under the impact of a severe heart attack and had to be evacuated by helicopter. Mahmoun's departure caused further extreme confusion. It threw the Egyptian Command out of gear at a crucial time, for without a supreme commander or any clear indication of what was happening on the battlefield, general headquarters in Cairo did not appreciate the pandemonium that reigned in the Sinai hills and let the Second Army's assault continue. Having already been routed, the surviving Egyptian tanks and personnel carriers milled around in total disarray, until in dribs and drabs they began to retreat to the protected bridgeheads along the Canal, harried all the way by Israeli fighter-bombers. The infantry were no better off, and small groups of Egyptian

antitank missile crews were picked off by Israeli machine gunners. It was a merciless fight, and by midday over a hundred
tanks and hundreds of carriers lay shattered. Survivors roamed
the sandy waste, seeking water or just a way out of their thirst-
tortured misery; hundreds surrendered.

While Mahmoun's Second Army was fruitlessly battering its
way to disaster on the route to Tassa, the southern arm of
Egypt's intended pincer movement was also driving eastward.
Maj. Gen. Abdel Munim Wasil's smaller Third Army's crucial
objectives were the Giddi and Mitla passes, and thence a junction
with Second Army at Refidim. Such a juncture would leave
Egypt firmly in control of central Sinai. Wasil had two infantry
divisions well dug in into good defensive positions. On the left,
the 7th had a line 6 miles east of the Canal facing the Giddi Pass
road; and on the right, the 19th faced the Mitla Pass road, with
its front line bellying out at one point to cross the otherwise
Israeli-held Artillery Road.

Wasil planned that his attack would be preceded by a commando helicopter landing in the Giddi area to distract and pin
down Israeli forces. Then, at dawn, the independent 25th
Armored Brigade with a hundred new T-62s would lead the
mechanized element of the 7th Infantry Division's assault on the
Giddi Pass to link up with the commandos. At the same time,
the crack 3rd Armored Brigade—the only brigade of the elite
4th Armored Division east of the Canal—would attack the Mitla
Pass, supported by a tank battalion of 6th Mechanized Division.
The 19th Infantry Division would provide a second assault
wave, while the remaining elements of 6th Mechanized guarded
the flanks of the assaulting troops.

Wasil was quite confident that his attack would succeed. He
knew the Israeli force opposing him was weak, with several of
its tank battalions equipped only with obsolete Shermans and
captured T-55 tanks, although they had been rearmed with the
formidable British 105mm high-velocity tank gun. They also had
numbers of M-60 Pattons, but Wasil was sure his three hundred
tanks could cope with these. If he should need them, he had a
further 150 tanks in reserve on the West Bank, as well as 800

guns to back up his armored brigades. His third advantage was
a narrow front of only 15 miles, compared to Second Army's 40
miles, which meant he could concentrate his armor in a near-
solid phalanx.

Bar-Lev's Southern Command was still adjusting to the sudden loss of Mandler, who had been killed the day before. His
successor, Maj. Gen. Kalman Magen, was very experienced and
had already assumed command of the southernmost division, facing Wassel. Magen's forces were undeniably very limited. To
defeat the Egyptian Third Army, he had a fifty-tank brigade
guarding the junction of the Artillery Road and the Giddi Pass
road. Another brigade, with thirty Shermans, was blocking the
Lateral Road near the Giddi Pass in support of an armored infantry battalion dug in on the actual crossroads. A third armored
brigade, which had a battalion in reserve on the Lateral Road and
two battalions on the Artillery Road near the Mitla Pass road,
was commanded by Col. Dan Shomron. He had had a week's
respite to reorganize his brigade after his earlier desperate battle
that had prevented the Egyptian Marine Brigade from reaching
the passes. He now had sixty-five Patton tanks brought back to
standard with crews ready for another battle. Another two second-line infantry battalions were dug into defensive positions
actually in the Giddi and Mitla passes, while three companies of
first-rate paratroopers held the Wadi Marbouk sector to the
south of the Mitla Pass road. Last, Magen had another good paratrooper battalion at the south end of the Artillery Road and three
battalions of 155mm self-propelled artillery to the south of the
Mitla Pass, well placed to enfilade any force moving toward the
Pass or trying to outflank it to the south.

The Egyptian Third Army's field of battle was an extension
of the northern sector's gently rolling terrain, although the ridges
are further to the east. In this area the Artillery Road is closer to
the Canal, and opposite the Geneifa crossroads, it ran through
Wassel's bridgehead. The main Giddi Pass road ran through
marshy ground, which prevented any traffic from moving off the
road from the Canal to the ravines and ridges to the east. Several
roads ran from the Canal into central Sinai, while others

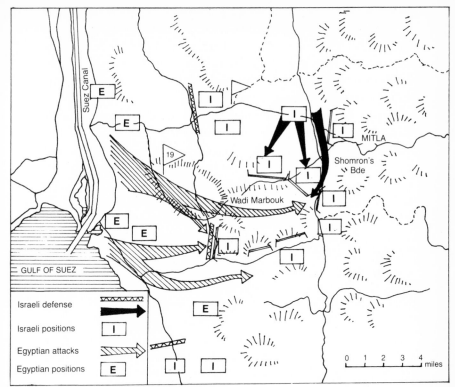

Israeli defense

Israeli positions   I

Egyptian attacks

Egyptian positions   E

GULF OF SUEZ

Suez Canal

E

E

19

I

I

I

I

I

Wadi Marbouk

MITLA

Shomron's
Bde

I

I

E

E

I

I

E

I

I

0 1 2 3 4
miles

Battle of Wadi Marbouk, October 14, 1973 (Egyptian Third Army)

bypassed Suez City to reach the Lateral Road. Following the Six Day War, the Israeli Defense Force had constructed another road from Ein Mussa to the Lateral Road, just south of Wadi Marbouk, and it was this wadi (ravine) that was to become one of the main features of the impending battle. From the Gulf of Suez, Wadi Marbouk climbs gradually eastward to the Lateral Road, between the Ein Mussa and Mitla Pass roads, varying in width from a few dozen to several hundred yards along a sandy and sometimes stony bottom. Close to the Lateral Road, however, the wadi narrows to a steep ravine, dominated by the road itself.

General Wasil believed this area to be Israel's weakest point in western Sinai, basing his analysis on intelligence reports of the weak forces holding the area. Wasil intended to drive a strong force through the wadi to reach the high ground at the Lateral Road, from which point he could outflank the forward Israeli positions and reach the Mitla Pass before their weak forces could halt his advance. He, too, planned a helicopter-borne commando force to land near the passes prior to the attack, with which his forces would then link up.

Magen pondered his problem of holding with one division an attack by so many Egyptian divisions, while not ignoring the likelihood of an airborne landing. It was an obvious military tactic. His 150 tanks would be stretched to the limit to hold both passes, and should the Egyptians decide to launch a third armored force south toward Israel's important oil fields at Ras Sudar, there was nothing he could do to stop them. He decided, therefore, to leave his limited forces along the southern edge of his front while watching Wasil's initial moves. In the meantime, he prepared his own forces to move wherever the Egyptians struck. A wise choice in the circumstances, it required a flexibility of which few armies would be capable; however, the Israeli division, or *Ugda*, is of a much more flexible nature than those in most Western countries. Magen established a network of observation posts along his front commanded by his best officers, alerted to keep their eyes skinned for any signs of the Egyptian offensive.

At 6:30 A.M. a reconnaissance team on a hill overlooking the 19th Infantry Division's base radioed that an armored brigade-sized force was driving toward Wadi Marbouk. The recce team requested permission to withdraw before they were cut off and received approval. But while they carefully pulled back, they still managed to keep a covert watch on the Egyptian force as it advanced into the wadi, heading for the high ground at the Lateral Road. Acting on the recce reports, Colonel Shomron sent a tank company to the high ground along the Lateral Road facing the wadi, ready to block the Egyptians if necessary, while requesting the recce team to maintain its contact and keep reporting as it withdrew eastward. Thus while the Egyptian formation advanced east it was continually under observation, which enabled the Israelis to react in conformity to the enemy's movements.

After also starting at 6:30 A.M., the 25th Armored Brigade had meanwhile advanced its brand-new T-62s toward the Giddi junction, under cover of another great artillery barrage, which hurled shells into the Israeli defenses. The Egyptian Air Force joined in, and a number of sorties were flown by MIG-17s, but they were not pressed home with any conviction and were driven off by Phantoms and Mirages. Colonel Avraham's tanks moved swiftly to block the 25th Brigade's advance. Under accurate Israeli tank fire, the attack faltered and became hopelessly confused. Further south another force was held by the paratroop battalion on the Ein Mussa Road.

By this time it was apparent that the main Egyptian attack was being delivered through Wadi Marbouk, in an attempt to outflank the main road defenses, and was bent on reaching the Mitla Pass. Strangely enough, no paratroop attack had yet taken place—an omission that was never explained in Egyptian communiqués. Two Egyptian forces were, however, moving forward. The 3rd Armored Brigade led the way with 94 T-55s and a 122mm artillery battalion in close support, reinforced by a mechanized reconnaissance group carried in BTR personnel carriers. Behind them was a long column of mechanized infantry and Sagger tank-hunters, with another 122mm artillery battalion at the rear. Simultaneously, the 22nd Armored Brigade with supporting units was moving in echelon formation 6 miles to the south of 3rd Armored's column, heading for the high ground to the east while also protecting 3rd Armored's flank.

Contact was first made when the 3rd Armored's column ran into an Israeli outpost held by a paratroop company, which immediately opened fire with recoilless antitank rifles. It was another David and Goliath encounter, and while the Israelis slowed the attack for a while, it did little to shake 3rd Armored's momentum. But the brief respite enabled Shomron to send two tank companies and antitank platoons to the high ground north and south of the wadi; additional reserves stationed along the Lateral Road were alerted to be ready to move into action. By 7:30 A.M. the first Israeli tank had rolled into position atop the wadi sides, and settled to wait.

Three quarters of an hour later, the battle proper opened when the leading Egyptian tanks rounded a bend near the Artillery Road. Seven Patton tanks were dug in there, hulls down and protected by the sand, and opened fire as the T-55s nosed and swerved into view. Within a few minutes ten of them were burning along the road, exuding oil and flames that effectively blocked the route. The Egyptians responded by opening fire with their 122mm self-propelled guns, but the bubbling black smoke obscured their targets, and most of the shells plunged harmlessly into the sand. While the Egyptians were delayed, more Israeli tanks arrived along the sides of the wadi and began firing on the enemy armor. Wasil then ordered the 22nd Armored to outflank the Israelis from the south while they were kept fully engaged in the wadi.

Ephraim Stein was with a self-propelled artillery unit and recalls, "We saw the Egyptian tanks churning up the desert as they moved parallel to the wadi, then it became obvious they had wheeled northward and were heading straight for us. As they came up the slopes to the ridge, we opened a very accurate fire from our commanding position. It took them completely by surprise, for while several tanks were soon knocked out the rest seemed to falter before moving on, as though they didn't know where the fire was coming from." The Israelis were by then also using antitank missiles, having received quantities of the American TOW missiles that had been flown in by the increasing airlift. The artillery fire and antitank missiles slowed the enemy tanks long enough for a platoon of tanks to reach the ridge and open another tank battle to the south of the one then raging in Wadi Marbouk.

With their tanks held up in Wadi Marbouk, the Egyptian commander sent teams of Sagger troops climbing the steep walls of the wadi. They scrambled close enough to score hits on several Israeli tanks, although the Israeli paratroopers took them on amid the stones and dust of the wadi, fighting a hand-to-hand scrap with Uzi submachine guns and grenades. During this distraction, the Egyptians had meanwhile managed to drag aside some of the wrecked T-55s and began pouring armor through into the wadi. By nine o'clock several tanks were close to the eastern exit. By then, though, Shomron had got a brigade over to the eastern end and had effectively sealed the egress with tanks to the north and south.

While Shomron's tanks moved into position, Israeli armored infantry held the Egyptian spearhead at bay. With 20mm cannon and mortars mounted on M-113 carriers, they slogged it out against Wasil's tanks and BTRs, which were forced to stop while the 122mm guns took over once more, trying to punch a hole through which the tanks would be able to advance. But they were too far back and again were largely ineffective, lacking adequate artillery liaison. Then, while the T-55s opened fire with their 100mm guns, their infantry debouched from their carriers to attack the Israeli defenders. They were at a grave tactical disadvantage, for the T-55s' guns could not elevate sufficiently to reach the Israeli tanks above them on the wadi. BRDM-mounted Sagger teams advanced along the stricken column and desperately attempted to maneuver into position amid the confusion and congestion, but already there was a flowing tide of fear that soon reached panic. Egyptian tanks, infantry, Sagger teams, and carriers were all trying to act individually.

Now the Pattons and Centurions began to show their merits,

for their guns can depress further than the Soviet tanks can, and at 1,000 yards range they slammed round after round into the maelstrom of armor in the bottom of the wadi. The range was soon down to 500 yards, and when they poured fire into the flanks of the stranded Egyptian armor, the Egyptian brigade commander frantically called both division and army headquarters for artillery support. Desperately but with great bravery the Egyptians still forged ahead in the face of growing losses, trying to launch an attack to break through the encircling Israeli tanks and smash their way out of the wadi. Slowly they shoved their way forward until by sheer weight of numbers their force began to tell. Then, just when it looked as though they were going to make it, the air was filled with the piercing shrieks of Israeli Phantoms.

Down they swooped, two flights of shark-shaped fighter-bombers screaming low over the ragged hill crests, and tore into the Egyptian armor with bombs and rockets. Rockeye cluster bombs tumbled from the aircraft, each splitting into many individual projectiles that showered onto the closely packed tanks. Again and again they swept back, their banshee wails ending in the roar of explosions. The Israeli tanks regrouped in the brief respite and once more reorganized their defenses. When, at ten o'clock, the southern force tried to break through to the trapped column in the wadi, they were again blocked by Israeli tanks and antitank weapons and their attack petered out amid the blackened stones.

Newsweek correspondent Arnaud de Borchgrave reported the battle from the Egyptian side:

> The desert turned into a blaze of smoke and fireballs as hundreds of Israeli and Egyptian tanks dueled at point-blank range. At one point four Egyptian tanks surrounded two Israeli tanks. The tanks were so close to each other that in trying to maneuver, an Israeli Centurion backed into an Egyptian T-54. One of the Israeli tanks got off a round that blew off the turret of an Egyptian tank, but minutes later, both Israeli tanks were knocked out by direct hits. A few hundred yards to the north, another Israeli tank crew jumped out of its immobilized Patton

to try to fix a broken tread. As Egyptian artillery shells zeroed in on them, the Israelis gave up their repair effort, jumped onto a passing Israeli tank and fled in a cloud of sand.

Amid the dull thuds of tank cannons, the staccato fire of machine guns, the whine, whistle, and explosions of artillery shells, the eerie sound of men screaming in pain could occasionally be heard. Hundreds must have died during this battle. As the fighting raged, Israeli jets screamed in every minute or two to drop cluster after cluster of 500-pound bombs. Scores of vehicle-mounted SAM-6 missiles whooshed up into the sky in pursuit. During the day-long battle, missiles were seen hitting two Israeli Phantoms, and the planes fell and exploded in the desert several miles away.

In the next two hours two more missions were flown by Phantoms, which returned to rip open the mass of armor milling around in the heat-trap of the wadi. When they finally flew away at noon, Israeli artillery opened up. Magen's divisional artillery had the clear advantage of observers far forward with Shomron's brigade, and under their direction they ranged their 155mm guns onto the wadi bottom. Within a short while the wadi bottom was a roaring inferno through which tanks reeled in desperation. By afternoon, the Egyptian force had been destroyed, and only a very few battered tanks staggered west toward their bridgeheads. From their positions above the wadi the Israelis silently watched them go. Only in the northern sector did the Israelis make an appreciable advance, when an armored unit reestablished contact with the *Budapest* fortification.

After the battle, Israeli tank commanders expressed to reporters a grudging respect for the determination of the Egyptians. Tank battles are usually fought at ranges of 1,500 to 2,500 yards, but much of that day's battle had been fought at 400 to 500 yards. "At that range," an Israeli major told reporter Nicholas Proffitt, "it is often a matter of who chickens out first."

Both sides suffered heavy losses in this battle which, in numbers of tanks engaged, had been outmatched only by the Russian-German battle of Kursk. There is no doubt, though, that the Egyptians got much the worst of the fight. The two Egyptian brigades in the southern sector lost two thirds of their tanks and practically all that entered Wadi Mabouk. Wasil's Third Army had endured a crushing defeat, from which it was not to recover in the traumatic days that followed.

Criticism was subsequently voiced that with the Egyptians reeling back across the desert, the Israeli armor should have exploited its success and pursued them. But, great as this tank battle was, it was only the initial Israeli stroke in the greater strategy of inflicting absolute defeat on the Egyptians. To have pursued them to the Canal would have exposed Israeli forces to the massed air and antitank missiles and would have endangered the armored force that was being prepared for the greater coup of the Canal crossing. Their decision forestalled Egyptian counterattacks and, in effect, besieged the Egyptians in their protected bridgeheads, from which they were reluctant to emerge, hoping to draw the Israelis into their defenses. As Montgomery shepherded his forces after Alam Halfa in preparation for Alamein, so the Israeli commanders showed considerable restraint after the Sinai battles of October 14, and never again lost sight of their real strategic goal—to inflict defeat upon Egypt.

In stopping the Egyptian offensive, Israel kept the Egyptians from reaching the all-important passes that opened the way into the heart of Sinai, and thence to Israel's unprotected borders. U.S. Intelligence reports concluded that had the Egyptians rushed for the passes early in the war, when the battered remains of Israel's armor was still reeling, "They could have overwhelmed the Israeli defenses while they were still weak, taking the desert passes and making some bold armored thrusts to annihilate the Israeli tanks and artillery," as, indeed, Shazli advocated.

But the Egyptian High Command, notably Sadat and Ismail, followed the dictates of cautious Soviet strategy, first consolidating their position along the Canal's East Bank. Then they waited too long to launch their attack and it failed. While they withdrew to re-form and take stock of their losses, the Israelis seized the initiative, drew the right conclusions, and Chief of Staff David Elazar ordered the Canal crossing for the following night.

CHAPTER

13

The Fight to the Canal

Almost without exception the Israeli commanders had realized that the war would be decided only after their forces had landed on the West Bank and eliminated the Egyptians deployed there. It became an obsession with many, born as it had been of several years' tactical thinking and planning, war games and strategy. The answer to Israel's encirclement always was to break through the enemy lines and take the war into their countries. After the breathtaking defeats Israel had experienced in the early days of the war, there was bitterness among the soldiers that their political masters had allowed the Israeli Defense Force to be so constrained as to prevent it from delivering its war-winning preemptive strike, the only answer to Israel's chronic shortage of manpower and equipment. The Canal crossing concept, therefore, became of such paramount importance in their thinking that it imposed a threat to rational strategy. As General Adan put it: "The crossing idea was like some siren song, beckoning the commanders on, teasing them to dare and reach for the prize . . . the clever thing was to withstand the temptation but to watch out for just the *right* moment to cross."

By the second week of the war, pressure was increasing for

227

the crossing to be mounted. Even before the Egyptians' crippling defeat in the October 14 tank battles, it was obvious to the Israeli High Command that they had little time in which to recoup the prestige and reputation they had lost through the Arabs' brilliant invasion and the later skirmishes. The Russians, it was known, were seeking a cease-fire arrangement at the behest of Syria; and while Sadat had so far rejected those overtures, the shattering defeat his armored divisions had since experienced must have caused him to reconsider. Then at 2:00 A.M. on the 13th day, while Bar-Lev was in conference with his generals, news arrived that the United Kingdom was on the point of submitting a cease-fire proposal to the United Nations. There was considerable apprehension that the proposal might be accepted by the United Nations while the military balance was still in the Arabs' favor. One reaction to this bit of news was to suggest an immediate crossing at the northern end of the Canal near Port Said, which had already been proposed on the previous Tuesday.

A crossing at Port Said had actually several advantages. With the sea on one side and several large lagoons on the other, it would be relatively simple to isolate the area from an Egyptian counterattack. However, it had to be remembered that the danger in a water crossing was in the buildup phase when the bridgehead was being consolidated, prior to the breakout. While the area around Port Said could be closed to the Egyptians, they could in turn seal off an Israeli breakout. Furthermore, there was the daunting prospect of the Egyptians turning the full weight of their powerful artillery and missiles onto the bridgehead to eliminate it. A crossing for the Israelis had to offer both the possibilities of surprise in the actual crossing and a rapid breakout on the far side; Port Said did not do so. It was, however, still pointed out that seizing the area would provide a base for attacks on the Egyptian SAM sites, thereby opening a corridor for the Israeli Air Force to support the crossing.

Nevertheless, after all the points had been discussed, it was realized that the Port Said crossing would not contribute decisively to an Egyptian defeat but would only suck in forces that could be better employed elsewhere. There was one point in its favor, which was that in the event of a cease-fire being arranged imminently, retention of Port Said would be a valuable bargaining factor since it gave Israel control of the Suez Canal. But all the discussion was to prove quickly valueless, for not long afterwards on that same morning it became known that Sadat had rejected the cease-fire. The Israelis decided to revert to the original idea of making a crossing at Deversoir, near their *Matzmed* strongpoint.

That same day the crossing equipment was assembled from various places and concentrated in Sharon's sector. The rolling bridge was finally completed, and a tank company learned how to tow the huge assembly. Mobile uni-floats and sixteen self-propelled Gilowa vehicles left Refidim for the Lateral Road. There were another twelve mobile rafts at Baluza, but arguments at Southern Command about whether Sharon or Sasson should detach tanks to tow them so delayed the movement that they eventually arrived late. It was another unfortunate example of the traditional independence of mind of Israel's commanders, which, offering flair and flexibility in battle, produced much confusion and controversy in the more mundane roles of planning and preparation. Israel's commanders led from the front with a charisma that tarnished quickly when the spotlight was not seen to shine so brightly.

During the night of October 13/14, even while preparations were continuing for the decisive battle to contain the Egyptian offensive, Southern Command headquarters issued a written order for Operation *Abirei-Lev* (Valiant). At that stage, it was tentative because no one was then sure if the forthcoming battle was going to be the decisive one that would break the Egyptian armor, or whether the Egyptians were going to make another attack. By the evening of the 14th no such indecision remained, for the surviving Egyptians were reeling back to the Canal. At 10:40 P.M. an oral order was issued to supplement the written order. The crossing attack would start at 5:00 P.M. on October 15—less than nineteen hours away.

The latest Israeli Intelligence reports detailed the Egyptian situation following the day's battles. On the northern sector of the
Canal, Second Army had on the East Bank the 2nd, 16th, and
18th Infantry divisions, the 21st Armored Division, and the 15th
and 24th Tank brigades. On the West Bank they retained only
two mechanized brigades from the 23rd Mechanized Division.
Further south, Third Army deployed on the East Bank the 7th
and 19th Infantry divisions, the 130th Amphibious Brigade, and
the 3rd, 22nd, and 25th Tank brigades. Wassel, Third Army's
commander, had retained on the West Bank the 4th Armored
Division's remaining two tank brigades and the 113th Mechanized Brigade from the 6th Mechanized Division. So the great
bulk of the two armies' forces were on the East Bank by then,
and any Israeli landing on the West Bank would be opposed by
comparatively small forces.

There were, however, a number of other formations on the
western side of the Canal, including a Palestinian brigade and a
Kuwaiti battalion deployed along the west bank of the Bitter
Lakes, while at Cairo were the Egyptian reserves, comprising
two tank brigades, four brigades of paratroopers and commandos,
the Guard of the Republic's tank brigade, several battalions of
the School of Armor, plus several brigades of paratroopers at
Inshas just outside Cairo. There was also the 3rd Mechanized
Division, of which, intelligence admitted, it did not know the
location. But, numerous though these reserves were, they were
of very mixed quality and many were quite long distances from
the proposed crossing sites.

All in all, the Egyptians had between 650 and 750 tanks on the
East Bank, pretty well concentrated in the narrow bridgeheads,
while on the West Bank there were approximately 650 tanks
scattered over a very wide area from Cairo to the Canal. Thus
the Egyptian Army was so deployed west of the Canal as to offer
an excellent chance of the Israelis being able to defeat it piecemeal before it could concentrate forces. Once this had been
accomplished, the Israelis could destroy the Egyptian bridgeheads to the East Bank from the rear and so cut the Third Army

off from its supplies. Seen in this light, the crossing was only a means to knocking out the Egyptian Army. The objective, therefore, was not simply to get a force over the Canal and establish a bridgehead, but to push as large a force as possible across the Canal to break out immediately and begin attacking the missile sites. Once that was done, the Israeli Air Force could operate freely and destroy the enemy armor.

The Israeli Defense Force had four armored divisions to carry out the operation. The two strongest—Sharon's with 240 tanks and Adan's with 200—were to cross the Canal, while Sasson's and Magen's, with 265 tanks between them, would defend the East Bank and the crossing sites against an Egyptian counterattack. Southern Command's intention was to control the area between the Suez Canal and the Sweet Water Canal from the Nile to Ismailia and Mount Ubaid, and south to Suez City—in all about 2,400 square miles, from where it could destroy the Third Army from the rear.

The terrain on the West Bank was examined in detail. From Cairo to the Suez Canal ran the Sweet Water Canal, parallel to the Suez Canal at about 1.5 miles distance near Ismailia. The area was well cultivated, with cornfields and vegetable plots, although it tended to be muddy with irrigation and in places heavily overgrown. It offered excellent cover for infantrymen who, armed with antitank missiles, would be a dangerous threat to tanks trying to break through to the arid plains of Aida beyond. Once there, however, the tanks could rapidly move in all directions. Approximately 9 miles from Deversoir in either direction were two key objectives that needed to be seized as quickly as possible. Northwest of the town were five bridges across the Sweet Water Canal, the possession of which would enable the Israelis to cut off the enemy from the north. Southwest were the Geneifa Hills, dominating the plains in all directions and extending about 18 miles southeast. On the east they presented a range of almost unbroken pink cliffs, although it was possible to cross them and move north and south through clefts and wadis. Intelligence reports, mostly gained by the U.S. "Big Bird" satellite, had located many of the Egyptians' SAM sites in these hills. Between the hills and the Canal there were as well a number of large military camps served by several important roads. In this largely uncompromising desert terrain of sand and stones, the outcome of the war of Yom Kippur was going to be decided.

Operation *Abirei-Lev* was explained in detail to an orders group held at Southern Command at eleven o'clock on Sunday night. It was agreed that Sharon's division would make the first crossing at *Matzmed*, where they would construct bridges across the Canal to seize and secure a bridgehead. On their way to the crossing, Sharon's division would also widen to 3 miles the corridor to the Canal on the East Bank, capturing the Chinese Farm (so named after a Japanese agricultural project) and the *Missouri* stronghold. The corridor would then include the two axis to the Canal: Akavish, a narrow asphalt road; and the dirt track about 2 miles to the north known as Tirtur, which had been specially constructed for towing the rolling bridge.

The first crossing to seize a foothold on the far bank was to be made by a paratroop brigade in inflatable boats, supported by ten tanks crossing on rafts. They would establish a bridgehead on both sides of the Canal, extending at least 2.5 miles northward. Several officers were far from happy at the size of the initial bridgehead, which hardly met the generally accepted rule that a bridgehead should be of sufficient depth to prevent enemy artillery's shelling the bridges. The depth in this case would only be enough to protect the bridges from small arms and mortar fire. Once the bridgehead was held, however, Sharon's division was to rush across a tank force whose task was to grab the bridges over the Sweet Water Canal at Ismailia, thus preventing an Egyptian counterattack. Adan's division was to cross the following morning. It would immediately drive south to capture the Geneifa Hills and to destroy the surface-to-air missiles deployed there, thereby giving the Israeli Air Force air superiority over the crossing area. Meanwhile, Magen's division, which until then would have been defending the East Bank, would take over the bridgehead from Sharon's division, releasing

his forces to break out southward with all speed to take Mount
Ubaid and so prevent an Egyptian counterattack being mounted
from the west.

The morning of the 15th revealed another problem; much of
the bridging equipment was still not ready. By 3:30 P.M., only an
hour and a half before the time set for crossing, Sharon and Brig.
Abrasha Tamir examined the position and concluded the operational timetable could not be met. Sharon therefore suggested
three possible alternatives: Postpone the attack until the 16th;
clear the area up to the Canal during the coming evening but
cross the next day; or carry out the original plan but ignore the
timetable. Bar-Lev was consulted and said he was willing to postpone the crossing until midnight, although Sharon had the feeling that if he had explained he was not capable of adhering to
the timetable, Bar-Lev would have set it back again by twenty-
four hours. Nevertheless, Sharon had got out of his commitment
to the original plan, and in his flamboyant way would deal with
each situation as it arose.

By five o'clock that evening the sun was sinking toward the
western desert in a fireball, turning the Canal to molten gold, for
the clear hot Sinai air produces some of the most spectacular sun-
sets that can be seen. That night, however, it went down largely
unseen by the Israeli soldiers who were gradually moving forward toward the Canal. At exactly 5:00 P.M., the dust-laden air
was pulverized before the muzzles of Israeli artillery opening fire
all along the Canal. The Egyptian defenders, dug in confidently
behind their antiaircraft protection, were sent diving into their
dugouts by the sudden roar and zoom of arriving shells as sand
and rocks erupted in huge gouts of steel slivers and razor-sharp
rock fragments. At the *Televizia* and *Hamutal* features, Egyptian troops were alerted by the sounds of approaching armor as
the brigade of Colonel Tuvia, from Sharon's division, began its
diversionary attack to pin down the defenders and draw off the
21st Armored Division toward the Tassa-to-Ismailia road. This
was to be the first step in driving a corridor from the Israeli
position to the east, through the Egyptian defenses, to carve a

bridgehead on the Canal bank at *Matzmed* between Second and Third armies. Such a bridgehead was inevitably going to be exposed to flank attacks by both Egyptian armies.

An hour later, at about six o'clock, Reshef's brigade moved off along the Caspi Road, led by a reconnaissance unit, followed in turn by three tank battalions and three infantry units, their task being to reach the Canal. The brigade moved cautiously through the shell-torn darkness into the unoccupied seam between the two Egyptian armies, toward the Great Bitter Lake. At the Lexicon axis the column turned north to bypass *Lakekan*, headed by Yoav Brom's paratroop scout units supported by twenty tanks and the same number of armored personnel carriers. Behind them, the rest of the brigade advanced to the Canal, which they finally reached on a front of nearly 2 miles.

Until just after nine o'clock, everything went according to plan, and while Tuvia's brigade drew the enemy away to the east and north, Reshef's brigade penetrated deep into enemy territory on the Lexicon Road. Their progress had already been noticed by Egyptian troops several times as they advanced, but, as the Israelis realized, their daring move was confusing the enemy, who assumed that the force they could hear but only vaguely see must be one of their own. They contacted their headquarters for confirmation, but it took time to get an answer. At about 9:20 P.M., the Egyptians finally put two and two together and realized what was going on. They immediately opened a murderous fire with tanks and Sagger missiles. Within a short while the entire area was involved in a battle of extraordinary confusion. In the yellow light of a full moon, identification was difficult. Egyptian tanks began milling in every direction while the infantrymen darted among them to shoot their missiles. Several Israeli tanks swerved off the Lexicon Road to avoid trouble, but promptly ran over mines that disabled them. In the intensifying battle many tanks and trucks were hit and lit a flaming path toward the Canal.

The sudden firefight had cut Reshef's column in two, with Brom's force of paratroopers at the Canal while Amran's reinforced battalion was left on the Lexicon-Shick junction. Ten tanks of Lieutenant Colonel Almog's battalion, too, were caught along the Tirtur-Lexicon junction and almost completely wiped out. The survivors hurriedly pulled back and evacuated their casualties. Meanwhile, Amran's leading units pressed on from Shick to break into a zone within which the Egyptians had deployed tanks. For a while the battle continued inconclusively, although Amran's troops were getting the worst of it. Reshef, the brigade commander, then instructed Amran to withdraw south and establish a line along the Shick Road, which he managed to do with sixteen tanks, thus forming the southern boundary of the corridor into the bridgehead.

During the past hour the battalion from Tuvia's brigade had opened up the tarmacadam Akavish Road without encountering the enemy. Sharon was so encouraged by this achievement that with his reconnaissance troops controlling nearly 2 miles of Canal, he decided it was time to move ahead with the plan. He therefore ordered forward Col. Danny Matt's paratroop brigade with its rubber boats.

At 11:30 P.M., the brigade moved off in half-tracks, preceded by a tank company from Haim's brigade to secure their route. All went well and they reached the Nahala-Lexicon junction, where the column branched left along Nahala toward *Matzmed* at the very entrance to the Great Bitter Lake. They were progressing steadily through the ethereal moonlight and spasmodic shellbursts, when there was the sound of heavy firing barely half a mile to the north of his column. This prompted Matt to dispatch the escorting tank company northward to protect his flank. Unfortunately, the move resulted in his losing the escort altogether, for before long they were hopelessly involved in a fierce fight with Egyptian forces pressing toward the vital Lexicon-Tirtur junction, through which the roller bridge would have to pass on its way to the crossing site.

Meanwhile, Matt's paratroopers with their precious rubber boats perched tortoise-like upon the half-tracks, pushed on toward the Canal, coming under spasmodic fire from Egyptian units north of the road. They were peppered with small arms fire at several points, none of which did any serious damage, and shortly arrived with two battalions at the *Matzmed* "yard," the sand-enclosed launching site.

Once in the "yard," Matt got his brigade to work readying the rubber boats for the crossing. Yakov Stein was a paratrooper there who recalls that they arrived in the dead of night rather like a freight train at a siding. "We immediately began unloading the boats, which were large and seemed to have a life of their own. Our own commander was impatient to be off, probably because few doubted the Egyptians would soon begin shelling, and to many it seemed safer on the far side. We were well provided with extra machine guns, antitank missiles and projectiles, and it was only with difficulty that we managed to stagger toward the water, so overloaded were we. The water looked very deep in the dark, and seemed to flow very swiftly. To our south was open water, while to the north the dark surface would suddenly light up with reflected gunfire."

At 1:25 A.M. on a dark chill night, the boats were launched. Paratroopers crouched low and dipped their paddles, their heavy round helmets with the chin protectors looking massive in the darkness. Little flotillas began pulling away from the turmoil on the East Bank, heading for the quiet area on the west. All wondered what was awaiting them . . . the Egyptians crouched in the darkness, the machine guns. Yakov writes: "My heart was in my mouth. 'My God,' I thought, 'only ten days ago I was planning to take my family for a seaside holiday at Eilat, now I'm going boating on the Suez Canal.' But as we neared the far bank, straining eyes and ears for the enemy, it seemed deserted and then the boats nudged the bank and we quietly stepped ashore. There was no one waiting for us."

It was a bare few minutes after the paratroopers paddled away that those anxiously waiting at *Matzmed* heard the signal from Matt: "Acapulco!" meaning "We have a hold on the West Bank."

Indeed they had, for incredibly, the Egyptians were quite unaware that the Israelis had landed. There was some shelling across the Canal but that was just a part of the general raking barrage of the East Bank. By 3:00 A.M., Matt's two battalions of paratroopers were dug in along the West Bank, having suffered no losses, and already an effective command post had been established.

The paratroopers are the elite of Israel's infantry, but in the main they had not received the attention that the Armored Corps had. Generally speaking, they were the poor relations in the quality of their recruits and their equipment. One lesson of the Yom Kippur War was that the advent of the infantry antitank missile and the shoulder-fired antiaircraft missile had, for the time being at least, restored the infantryman to importance. It was increasingly apparent that the tank, the "battleship" of the desert, was dangerously exposed, and without its escort of infantry was best used in a sniping role, making the maximum use of cover. Now the paratroopers were showing the mettle that made them an elite force and were consolidating their hold on the West Bank.

By the time the sun was rising with indecent haste over the unholy wreckage, smoke, and flame on the East Bank, the 750 paratroopers had extended their hold to the southern point of the Sweet Water Canal and northward for 2 miles. The Egyptians did not yet know it, but the children of Israel had recrossed the waters back into Egypt.

CHAPTER

14

The Strategy that Must Not Fail

While the paratroopers were crossing the Canal, back along the all-important Tirtur route over which the roller bridge had to be dragged to the crossing, things were far from satisfactory.

Colonel Reshef had personally gone to the Tirtur-Lexicon junction to find the survivors of Almog's battalion struggling to evacuate casualties. The scout force had pressed on, though, and had managed to bypass the junction as far as the Nahala axis, but then had been attacked by a strong Egyptian tank and infantry force and was heavily engaged. That same enemy force had turned on Haim's tanks—left by Matt a few hours previously— and wiped out most of them. The tank company from Tuvia's battalion that had first opened the Akavish Road had driven back again and was now south of the Tirtur-Lexicon junction; and Tuvia by then had another company awaiting the signal to press on along the essential and much disputed Tirtur Road. Meanwhile, their southern flank was protected by a paratroop reconnaissance force under Major Shuneri.

Reshef recognized the first priority to be the clearance of the Tirtur axis—otherwise the roller bridge would not reach the Canal that night—and decided to give the task to Shuneri's force with a tank company in support. Shuneri's paratroopers tried desperately to break the stubborn Egyptian resistance. He left a company equipped with recoilless guns to hold the southern flank of the corridor while two companies of infantry attacked in half-tracks escorted by tanks. But in their haste to secure the axis, the attack was badly coordinated. Shuneri's tanks charged ahead of the infantry, shooting up the enemy tanks guarding the junction, but most of them were in turn hit by Egyptian antitank missiles. The night was pierced by lancing jets of flame from the tank guns and the sudden flare of a tank blowing up. Machine guns screeched and chattered and missiles shrieked; then, suddenly, a couple of Israeli tanks made a break for it, accelerating through the junction on whirling tracks that tore up the stones as they roared away down the Tirtur Road. But they were alone, for the half-tracks carrying the infantry could not get through the junction and fell back in disorder. The two tanks went on into the dark. After some 2.5 miles, both were knocked out by missiles and burned brightly for hours.

By then it was 3:00 A.M., and Matt's paratroopers were across the Canal. In some desperation, Reshef ordered Yoav Brom, whose paratrooper force had been first to break through to the Canal, to leave the Canal bank and attack the Tirtur junction from the western end of the road. But that, too, failed when Brom's tanks were ambushed by the Egyptians, and in the skirmish Brom was killed. The survivors fell back toward the Canal once more. Reshef, however, was under the impression that the enemy tank force had been largely destroyed, although there does not appear to have been any basis for that belief. Israeli commanders throughout the war were too ready to believe the Arab forces would withdraw once attacked, and constantly underestimated the newfound resilience of their opponents. In fact, the Arabs were much more resolute than before and persistently stood their ground, only withdrawing in an orderly manner to new positions when forced to do so.

On this occasion, Reshef again confidently committed Shuneri's force, which advanced with infantry in half-tracks pro-

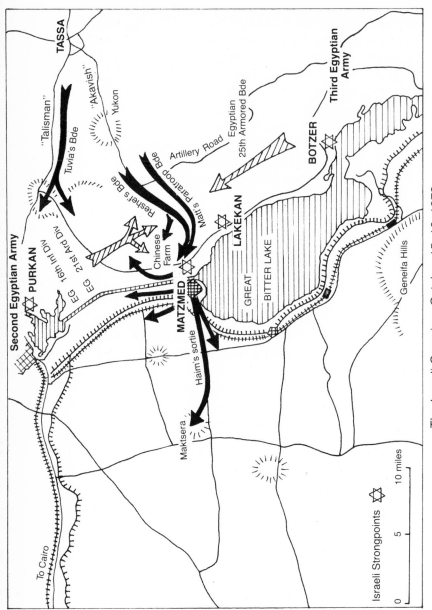

The Israeli Crossing, October 15–16, 1973

tected by a few tanks. But far from withdrawing, the Egyptian infantry were well concealed in ditches alongside the junction with many RPG missiles, awaiting the Israeli approach. The armored infantry and their tanks cautiously drew closer and had actually passed through the junction when the Egyptians opened fire. Missiles streaked from cover ripping open each half-track in turn—all except two that emerged from the junction—and the road was still firmly closed.

While the battle raged for the route to the Canal, Sharon's deputy had been marshaling the bridging equipment along the Akavish route. Although the axis was the solitary paved road from Tassa to the crossing point, it was unfortunately very narrow and flanked by deep, soft sand dunes. The road itself was crammed nose to tail with supply vehicles and engineering equipment, while the dunes to either side bore ample evidence of what happened to the impatient driver who tried to overtake the column. Three forces were moving slowly along the congested route. First came the sixteen tanks that were hauling forward the 400 tons of roller bridge, and with them were engineers and a protecting antiaircraft force. A second force was coping with the massive mobile rafts, while a third engineering force brought forward the giant, wheeled Gilowa vehicles. The entire convoy progressed by inches, and soon all hope faded that the crossing equipment would reach the Canal that night.

Shortly after midnight a conference was convened at Southern Command's headquarters to try to sort out the problem. Both Dayan and Elazar were present. There was a marked feeling of impatience that not one bridge would be in place that night. Following sharp exchanges between Sharon and Bar-Lev, it was decided to hurry on the Gilowas to *Matzmed*, without waiting for the rest of the crossing force. Otherwise, as the conference was told, Danny Matt's paratroopers would be left without tank support when the Egyptians counterattacked them. At that time the conference does not seem to have understood the battering that Sharon's division was taking. Dayan went so far as to suggest that Adan's division should be immediately committed to battle on the East Bank to develop the corridor northward, especially against the Chinese Farm.

Meanwhile the order to get the Gilowas to the Canal reached the crossing force, and these venerable but highly mobile vehicles pulled out of the congestion along the road to set off across the sand dunes with an escort of tanks. By 4:00 A.M. they were at the Canal, where engineers were hard at work breaching the earthen banks. As soon as the bulldozers had finished grading a ramp, the Gilowas edged into the water, where they were assembled into two long ferries able to carry two tanks each trip, backed by a third, single tank ferry.

On the Akavish route, however, things were progressing no better as the sixteen tanks struggled to haul the huge roller bridge westward. Until the point "Akavish 55," the road had been surfaced; but from then on, their route toward Tirtur lay across the southern slopes of the *Hamadia* feature. The tanks revved and heaved the monster bridge along until they reached a long slope toward the Canal. They then began a dangerous descent as the 400-ton load gathered momentum and started to push along the tanks. They used all their massive weight and power to brake the bridge's motion, but the strain was so great that the towing links snapped one after another and the mighty roller bridge broke away. When it finally lurched to a stop amid clouds of sand, a roller connection had broken. It was already five o'clock, and the engineers shook their heads sadly as they examined the damage. It would, they announced bitterly, take them hours to repair.

At 5:15 A.M., in the chill predawn, Tuvia's brigade tried once more to capture the Lexicon-Tirtur junction. Tanks were hit and the deputy brigade commander wounded; the road remained closed. The vital junction, which blocked the final approach to the Canal and through which the bridge had to pass, was on the extreme edge of the Egyptian Second Army's sector. Although the area between there and the northern edge of Third Army was relatively clear, the junction itself was within range of Egyptian artillery and within easy reach of their strong dispositions at the Chinese Farm.

While Reshef was struggling on the East Bank of the Canal, Sharon remained magnificently preoccupied with organizing the crossing to the west. He had ignored the East Bank since ordering Tuvia's attack late the previous evening. Then the tanks had gone too far north, run into minefields between the *Televizia* and *Missouri* features, and spent hours evacuating their wounded and trying to retrieve damaged tanks until forced to abandon many of them. They had therefore contributed little to breaking the Egyptian hold on the flanks of the Akavish-Tirtur axis. Reshef's brigade in that time lost about 120 men and over 60 tanks, and by morning the battalions of both Almog and Amran were confined to the Shick Road, maintaining the bridgehead's northern boundary.

They were exhausted. Any fresh attempts to open the road would have to be made with the remnants of Brom's scout force and some of Tuvia's force that was near *Lakekan*, not far from the junction. Sharon's response was to send a tank battalion from Haim's brigade, and later another from Tuvia, to bolster Reshef's flagging strength. Both battalions were about 6 miles east of Reshef, still on the far side of *Missouri* and the Chinese Farm. Sharon told Reshef to try again to break through and gain control of the road, for he was anxious to send armor across the bridges to reinforce the paratroopers.

At 7:00 A.M., one of Haim's tank battalions mounted an attack from the northeast, but this had not progressed far along the route when it was hit by a salvo of missiles fired from the Chinese Farm and fell back in considerable disorder. Once again, Reshef ordered the force to attack, this time with slender help from an extra six tanks, each commanded by an officer. They made a valiant effort, and penetrated along the road for some way before two tanks were knocked out and the rest retreated, collecting stragglers from Shuneri's force that had been badly defeated during the night.

An hour later the exhausted troops were sent in again, with

simultaneous attacks from north and east of the Tirtur Road. Twenty-two tanks set off. Three were soon hit, and when a force of Egyptian tanks blocked their route, they were forced back. Doggedly, Reshef searched his decimated brigade and scraped together another thirteen tanks, all that remained of Brom's scout force, along with infantry and reconnaissance troops, and sent them in yet again. Tired and disillusioned, the Israelis pressed home their attack by sheer guts, and in the face of this determined attack, the Egyptians at last began to falter. Although they have never disclosed their losses that night, they must have been considerable. Sensing victory, the Israeli tanks increased their pressure and fired round after round into the battered Egyptian positions. By 8:40 that morning the junction fell to the Israelis. The Lexicon-Tirtur junction was littered with charred tanks, carriers, and the debris of battle, but it was in Israeli hands.

Back along the Akavish Road, where engineers were contemplating the broken roller bridge, General Adan passed along on his way to check on two of his brigades that were halted on the Caspi Road near Kishuf, awaiting his orders. His command vehicles pulled up and, although the bridge was not his responsibility, once he found out what was wrong, he refused to accept the hopelessness of the situation. He used his radio to locate Haim Kazan, one of the Armored Corps' top ordnance men, and got him to take a team to repair the bridge.

For several hours Sharon and Bar-Lev had vacillated about whether to direct Haim's escorting tanks from the roller bridge to reinforce the fight for the Tirtur Road. At dawn on the 16th, Southern Command was still not fully informed of the situation along the Canal itself, being only aware that the Akavish Road had been opened and that the Gilowas were ferrying tanks across. But Sharon's persistence in wanting more tanks shipped across gave the impression at command headquarters that the situation on the bank was not that critical. With the bridge halted, at least temporarily, Sharon had left a battalion of tanks under Reshef to carry on the unequal East Bank fight, to break through from the east along the Tirtur axis. Haim's tanks he then directed to get to *Matzmed* as soon as possible, to be ferried over to the West Bank.

Sharon was really doing a "Patton" act, inasmuch as he was committing ever-larger forces to the West Bank to exploit the tenuous (and so far undiscovered) foothold across the Canal while the Egyptians were still unbeaten on the East Bank. They could at any time have closed the axis to the Canal, cutting off the West Bank force. An Israeli officer at the front was to describe the operation to a correspondent: "The strategy is a bold one—brilliant in my mind. But it has its risks. It's the sort of strategy that simply must not fail." However, just as in 1945 Patton audaciously took risks—pushing his armor through the Rhineland without bothering to clear the Germans behind him but simply bypassing them—so "Israel's Patton," the swashbuckling Arik Sharon, was equally quick to exploit an advantage against the enemy.

Sharon had an instinct for the enemy's jugular vein and the one he was now savaging would eventually bleed to death the Egyptian Third Army. Nevertheless, after the war his outspoken bluntness led to an unprecedented public condemnation of his military superiors. That conflict became known as the "war of the generals" as recriminations flew. Grandiloquently, Sharon claimed all the credit for the crossing operation, declaring that months before he had foreseen its necessity and had ordered a weak spot along the Canal to be marked with red bricks. When the time came for the breakthrough, he claimed, his engineers simply located the bricks and swiftly breached the bank. Nor were his outbursts limited to his own achievements, for Sharon went on to deride the Israeli High Command for the delays. "I told the High Command that we were wasting time," he asserted. "I sat for four days doing nothing."

As the sun came up on the 16th, however, these mutual recriminations were still in the future, and Dado Elazar firmly declared that "Sharon . . . will commit his three brigades to battle . . . and will mop up the area northward." This would secure the bridgehead and aid the rafting and bridging operations. Elazar proposed, too, that Matt's paratroopers should quickly deploy northward to seize the nearest Egyptian bridge, or at least deny it to the enemy. Bar-Lev in turn permitted Sharon to reinforce the ten tanks he had across and to begin raiding the missile sites, in the belief that Sharon was committing all his forces on both banks.

But on the East Bank the Egyptians were still far from discouraged. When Haim led a force along the Akavish Road around 9:00 A.M., the Egyptians ambushed it with a salvo of missiles, then poured small arms fire into the half-tracks, tanks, and M-113s—the armored personnel carriers only recently acquired by the Israeli Defense Force. Adan, standing on a hill south of Kishuf, could see Haim's column advancing, and described what happened. "As the column reached a point 2-3 kilometers northwest of our observation site, I suddenly saw four tanks burning. But we heard no firing; Haim's tanks had apparently been hit by Sagger missiles fired from the north. . . . We saw crews jumping out of tanks starting to run in our direction, half-tracks halted as the troops abandoned them to lay down on the ground and other half-tracks turning around and moving back." Leaving four tanks blazing, Haim sent the paratroopers back in the half-tracks, while he led the rest of the tank force and the M-113s south across the sand toward the Canal, in accordance with Sharon's orders. Adan, meanwhile, had ordered Col. Gabi Amir to send armor to the road to help evacuate survivors. As he saw it, "It was now clear that the Akavish Road was totally blocked again."

Despite their counterattacks on the East Bank, incredibly, the Egyptians were still unaware of what was taking place on the west side of the Canal just north of the Deversoir. This was largely because their air force had long since lost control of the airspace over the Canal and was carrying out few if any recce flights. One of the ironies of their air defense system was that it could not distinguish between an Egyptian and an Israeli aircraft. After a few early grotesque errors, the Egyptians had learned to stay out of the way of their own highly dangerous, not-too-discerning missiles. Now the Israeli operations on the West Bank were in fact gaining momentum right under the Egyptians' noses. The tanks that had escorted the Gilowas to the water had crossed after 6:30 A.M. Matt's force had been given seven of these tanks, which he stationed at Deversoir airfield, while others went to block the road over the Sweet Water Canal. They had been met at the *Matzmed* "yard" by Sharon in person, and ordered to cross forthwith, move west, and begin taking out the missile sites. If the Egyptians were still ignorant of what was happening, their indolence was about to be rudely interrupted.

Haim's force was ferried across the Canal quickly and landed on the far bank. After a brief orders session, the twenty-one tanks and seven M-113s were off along the Sakrant Road leading to Cairo. The Egyptians had established sites for their SA-2 and SA-3 missiles at many places on the West Bank. They were hard sites, protected by sandbagged walls, but lightly armed against ground attack. An Egyptian prisoner later recounted what happened next:

> It was midmorning and we had not yet been ordered to fire. The missiles were loaded of course and on their runners, ready to go. Then one of the crew pointed across the desert to a large cloud of dust that seemed to be approaching from the Deversoir direction. An officer came across and stared for a while, but he only shrugged and said it was only more reinforcements patrolling the Canal. We kept our eyes on the force and then someone shouted anxiously that the tanks were fanning out toward us; next moment they opened fire and shells slammed into the defenses, blowing up the sandbagged walls. I heard someone scream, "Israelis!" But I couldn't believe it and we just stared, and they overran us. We did not have time to mount a defense, we just could not understand where they had come from.

The Israelis destroyed the site and went on to knock out four more, engaging them at 1,500 yards with tank guns.

Unaware of what was happening, Sadat addressed a special session of the Peoples' Council in Cairo on October 16, haughtily indicating that Egypt was prepared for a cease-fire based only on an immediate and complete withdrawal by all Israeli forces from Arab territories to the lines of June 5, 1967. Only after this total withdrawal, he asserted bravely, would he be willing to attend a peace conference at the United Nations. Confidently facing his audience, he announced: "We are prepared at this hour, yes even at this moment, to begin clearing the Suez Canal and opening it for international shipping."

His words were greeted with jubilation by the representatives, and the exultant Sadat left triumphantly for the operations room. There, however, the news was disturbing. A small number of Israeli amphibious tanks, he was informed, had managed to cross the Canal at Deversoir to the West Bank. But, he was hastily assured by the military staff, the local commander reported that their destruction was only a matter of time. The Second Army commander had already sent a commando battalion to halt the Israeli intrusion and was engaging the Israeli infantry.

News that the Israelis had crossed the Canal in the Deversoir region only reached the Egyptian Army commander at mid-morning on the 16th, probably by way of signals from missile sites under attack. That was several hours after Matt's paratroopers had landed, and they were by then holding positions near the Sweet Water Canal. All of the reports estimated the Israeli force at nothing more than a reconnaissance group, comprising five amphibious tanks that had supposedly crossed the Great Bitter Lake. According to Palestinian press reports published in Beirut, it was the Palestinian Brigade on the west bank of the lake that first sounded the alarm that three Israeli tanks were operating. It may well be that these were indeed some of the first Israeli tanks to be rafted across, which had then driven south to establish a southern limit to the bridgehead. Later that day, reports began reaching Cairo from their Second Army that Israeli tanks on the West Bank were attacking missile sites in their rear; but these, too, spoke of amphibious tanks. There is no evidence that any amphibious tanks were used, and they must have been rafted across.

However the original Israeli crossing was made, when news

of it reached Egypt's High Command it was greeted with skepticism and dismissed with jocularity. After all, they scoffed, with their own two armies firmly entrenched on the East Bank, what beyond a localized nuisance could the Israelis offer? It would soon be dealt with. The main purpose of the crossing, they reasoned, was to boost Israeli morale at home, which had been severely jolted, and to encourage Zionist support abroad to increase their aid to the tottering Jewish state. President Sadat wrote it off with lofty indifference as a spectacular "television operation."

Sadat is supposed that afternoon to have instructed Shazli, the army commander, to deploy his forces around the bridgehead so that although Israeli forces could enter, they would be unable to leave again. In that way, the entire Israeli force would be captured. However, the subsequent deployments were piecemeal and largely ineffective. Sadat also claimed to have warned his General Staff five days earlier to expect some kind of bold Israeli initiative. Nevertheless, ever since their successful invasion of Sinai ten days previously, the Egyptian command had been caught up by its own achievements and continuously debated what next more should follow. Sadat and Ismail still counseled caution, but Shazli and many of his younger officers advocated that their bridgehead should have been immediately pushed out to the passes, which would have prevented the Israelis carrying out their cross-Canal attack at Deversoir.

There is clearly some truth in that view, echoed by the influential Beirut newspaper *Al Nahar*, which published an article expressing the belief that "had the Egyptian forces advanced in Sinai immediately after the crossing of the Canal and endeavored to capture the Giddi, Mitla, and Bir Gafgafa passes before the arrival of the Israeli reserves, the war in Sinai would not have concluded as it did." Ismail answered critics by explaining that they did not move forward because he was waiting to see what the Israeli reaction would be to their crossing, and because he was unwilling to move forward without strengthening his armor considerably and bringing across the Canal the mobile surface-to-air missiles, the SA-6s. In his summation of the war, Ismail makes it apparent that he would not allow the Egyptian armor to advance beyond the missile cover. Thus what should have been Egypt's greatest advantage became, because of bad deployment and excessive caution, a straitjacket restricting any offensive.

According to the descriptions of these developments as seen by the Egyptian general headquarters, given in postwar interviews and statements by President Sadat and Ismail, the reports from the frontline were linked with overoptimistic accounts of their own commando raids against the Israeli bridgehead, which masked the seriousness of the situation. Third Army confidently reported that its 25th Armored Brigade, having recovered from the trouncing some days before, was advancing to counterattack against the Israeli forces' southern flank, while they were still being heavily engaged by the Second Army. In fact, while the Israeli paratroops were sweeping along the West Bank, attacking antiaircraft batteries, Cairo tried to minimize the significance of the raid, claiming that the seven tanks, which were all the Israelis put across the Canal, had immediately been destroyed. Anyway, they declared, the force was on the verge of being wiped out.

If the Egyptians were outwardly calm at the sudden turn of events, the Russians were aghast. Israel's startling Deversoir bridgehead prompted Kosygin to hasten to see Sadat once more. Apart from the ignominy of another Arab defeat, the Soviets were worried stiff that too many of their latest weapons, which had been supplied euphorically to Egypt and Syria, were falling into Israeli hands and thence to America. That Russia was having a change of heart was manifested by Kosygin's hasty return to Cairo on the 18th to implement Russia's ponderous diplomacy.

Kosygin looked, according to Sadat, extremely gloomy. "With all this counterattacking," Kosygin exclaimed, "you have finally been checked. . . . A threat is now posed to Cairo."

The Egyptian president would have none of this, emphatically denying that any threat would ever be posed to Cairo, even though the Israelis were only a few hours' drive away. "However," he rounded on Kosygin, "where are the tanks I asked you for?"

Kosygin shrugged; they had been concentrating on the Syrians, he replied, who had lost 1,200 tanks in one day. All right, Sadat conceded, Syria needed support and he didn't object to that. But he didn't see why Egypt should be denied the tanks she needed. "You send the tanks and I'll deal with the counterattacks," he proudly insisted.

Nevertheless, the Egyptians were by this time fully aware that the Israelis were fanning out on the West Bank. According to General Ismail, problems had arisen from changes in the local Egyptian command structure just prior to the Israeli attack, which caused some confusion. As a result, reports about the Israeli operations were piecemeal and inadequate. The extent of their encroachment was simply not fully appreciated. Nevertheless, the local commander's report, which was relayed back to Cairo, confidently informed that he had sent a commando battalion against the Israelis and their destruction was just a matter of time. His force, equipped with BMD carriers and supported by tanks, advanced toward the Israelis. But, as General Ismail later explained, the Israelis' tanks were hidden in the dense, jungle-like foliage of the mango plantations along the fertile Canal gardens, and did not arouse the reaction that such a force would have aroused had it been in the open. Whatever reasons are given, the Egyptian force was cut to pieces, losing ten tanks and twenty-five carriers. Haim's raiding force then swept on before returning to the bridgehead that afternoon to refuel.

Three concurrent battles were then being fought. Matt's paratroopers with twenty-eight tanks were fighting to consolidate the West Bank bridgehead. On the East Bank, meanwhile, Sharon's forces were not doing nearly so well as they continued their struggle to clear the approaches to the bridging sites. The Egyptian appreciation of the situation was that the Israelis' West Bank operation was only a strongly mounted raid and could be contained. On the East Bank, though, they had no doubts but that the Israelis were bent on recovering their strongholds and ousting the Egyptian forces from the area. They were determined that this should not happen and were rushing in reinforcements to their units engaged in the battle. The third battle was being fought by Adan's brigade as it exerted pressure to eradicate Second Army's troops barricading the Canal approaches to the north, while also facing south to prevent Third Army from joining in and reinforcing the Second Army. At the same time, Adan's men were pressing westward against the Chinese Farm in a desperate attempt to widen the corridor so as to give protection from enemy shelling to the columns of heavy trucks carrying bridging equipment and supply columns as they drove toward the Canal. It was a bitterly contested battle between two contestants who had both shown their stubbornness and ability. But the Israelis were in the greatest difficulties, for the blocked Akavish Road was choked with their vehicles under constant Egyptian shelling, which was causing great damage. Tanks were abandoned where they were hit.

At this crucial point, with Sharon's West Bank force making itself felt, another crisis of command became apparent, and the strained relations between Sharon and his superiors soured still further. The operational plan had called for two bridges to have been established with two roads serving them by the morning of the 16th. Instead, all that linked the bridgehead was a narrow bypass route from Lakekan across the dunes south of the Akavish-Caspi Road. Sharon's division had exhausted itself against the strong Egyptian forces holding the Tirtur Road and was in danger of being nipped out by a counterattack from Second Army's powerful armored forces. But the implacable General Sharon still stubbornly wanted to exploit the bridgehead immediately. And irrespective of whether or not a bridge was erected, he wanted Adan's division transported forthwith to the West Bank, using rafts if necessary.

Bar-Lev flatly refused this suggestion on the 16th, and again the next day when Sharon persisted. To him it would have been madness to transfer the hundreds of tanks, carriers, guns, and trucks across, even if the highly vulnerable Gilowas were capable of doing so. It was pointed out that these vehicles had rubber flotation sleeves: Once the Egyptians brought their artillery to bear, even a near miss would rip them apart. Neither would he countenance launching a corps-sized attack when not even a supply route had been established. Besides, he emphasized, until the corridor to the Canal on the East Bank, through which supplies would have to flow, had been secured, Adan's division could not be spared.

Southern Command was justifiably anxious at the delays, and Gonen's deputy, Uri Ben-Ari, was flown by helicopter to Adan's command post, which was on high ground overlooking Akavish. He wanted Adan to take over the job of getting the rafts to the Canal, and suggested releasing his own deputy, Brig. Gen. Dov ("Dovik") Tamari and some officers, to supervise the task. Adan wasn't at all keen on the idea, as his division had not been assigned the role, and he demanded to know why the change was being made.

"Bren, for heaven's sake," Ben-Ari retorted, "it's a delicate thing. We'll talk about it after the war."

At that, Adan recalls, he asked no more questions and ordered Tamari to take over the job. Just then another helicopter clattered in; the burly figure of Gonen emerged even before the blades had stopped whirling. He made no bones of the need for Adan's cooperation and complained bitterly about Sharon, who he said was "a disappointment," claiming he "did not know what had happened to Sharon in this war." Adan would not be drawn into the controversy between the two of them and recalls that he discussed with Gonen his own division's inactivity in the past hours. But Gonen stuck steadfastly to his original plan. Shortly afterwards he left with Tamari in a jeep for the Akavish Road.

The two of them drove back along Akavish to the bridges, which they encountered 2 miles east of the Artillery Road. There were half a dozen pontoons on the road and the damaged roller bridge was a short way back. Gonen was assured the bridge would be repaired within half an hour; but, the engineer

added, it couldn't be moved until the road was cleared. Gonen
and Tamari thereupon drove on under intermittent shelling until
Gonen suggested they proceed on foot as they would not present
such a target. They struggled to the crest of a dune from where
they could see the Chinese Farm shimmering in the dazzling
heat, where Israeli tanks were fighting against a constant hail of
missiles. Akavish was obviously held by strong Egyptian
forces—no real progress toward bridging could be made until
they were driven off. There seemed no alternative, Gonen reluctantly concluded. Either the access road had to be secured
quickly, or the operation would have to be canceled, and with it,
Israel's slender chance of decisively defeating the Egyptians.
They would have to stop moving armor across the Canal and
make an all-out effort to secure the East Bank. Gonen then
returned to Adan's advanced headquarters, from where he spoke
to Sharon.

Sharon was ordered to capture the Chinese Farm area at once
and eliminate the Egyptians there before they could launch
another attack against the corridor. Sharon confidently assured
him that he would have the road open in ninety minutes, stoutly
maintaining, though, that the bridge could not be moved. It
could, Gonen contradicted him, and explained that he had just
left the engineers, who had told him it was ready to move.
Adan's division was to open the Akavish and Tirtur routes and
to see that the pontoon bridges got to *Matzmed* without delay.
Tamari would be personally responsible for this. Sharon's deputy, Brig. Yakov ("Jackie") Even, was to be responsible for the
preconstructed roller bridge. Then, and only then, would Sharon
secure the bridgehead while Adan's division crossed to break out
westward to seize the Geneifa Hills. Having told Adan to be
ready to move by noon, Gonen then reported by radio to Bar-
Lev, who in turn confirmed the arrangements to Sharon. Such
was the relationship between Gonen and his commanders.

CHAPTER
15

The Israelis Break Out

Adan received his orders around noon, and in the brazen desert heat he moved his scorching armor down from the hills. The whole area was parched and the shriveled grasses crackled as the tanks cluttered through them toward *Televizia*, then held by Tuvia's forces from Sharon's division. Egyptian troops, hidden in trenches scraped from the hot sand, popped up to loose missiles at the tanks. As Adan still had no infantry protection, it was obviously going to be a difficult operation. Around two o'clock he had word from Southern Command that a paratroop force was being sent to him to launch an attack against the Chinese Farm positions; but although he waited all day, it was night when Uzi's paratroop battalion finally reached him. There seemed to have been a lack of communication.

Having arrived after nightfall, the paratroopers had no opportunity to reconnoiter the positions they were to take, and although Adan's troops could describe the dispositions and show on maps where the main Egyptian forces were holding out, it was still unsatisfactory. Because the preparation had to be done very quickly, when the paratroopers eventually moved off at 11:30 P.M., they did so with very inadequate planning.

Uzi's battalion moved toward the Canal between Akavish and Tirtur, probing along a front nearly a mile wide for some three hours. On the way they passed the logjam of bridges, armor, and pontoons creeping to the Canal with maddening slowness. The paratroop company on the northern flank then came under fire without warning from heavy enfilading machine-gun and artillery fire. Its commander, Major Yaki, promptly ordered his men to storm the enemy positions. But in rushing through the hail of fire he was wounded, a platoon commander was killed, and many men fell dead or wounded. The paratroopers fell back, regrouped, and with almost fanatical determination charged again, firing their machine guns from the hip as they pounded across the sand. In the past such an assault would have set the Egyptians fleeing in panic, but not this time. Inevitably, the Israelis' charge was broken by the machine guns that outweighed their courage and the paratroopers were forced back once more.

A second company then moved forward in support while sending a unit to work its way around the Egyptians' flank. But the enemy positions were strung endlessly along parallel to the road and its flank could not be turned. The Israeli flanking unit, too, was located in the darkness, ripped to pieces by machine guns, mortars, and artillery. The rest of the company rushed in to help them, but only compounded the confusion, for in the dark their close fighting prevented the Israeli artillery from being turned on the enemy, and their company commander was killed. In the novel circumstances of the enemy standing their ground, the Israelis' tactics, though full of *élan*, were as outmoded as Poland's cavalry in 1940.

Adan realized that the paratroopers' task was too extensive, and so ordered them to pull back from the Tirtur route and concentrate only on Akavish. But by then the battle was so intense that the paratroopers could not disengage. They had taken heavy casualties, and it was necessary to send in armored carriers to try to bring out the wounded. Time was fast slipping by, and at 3:00 A.M., not very long before dawn, it became obvious that there was little chance of getting the bridges and pontoons to the Canal. That could only mean another day without the ability to reinforce the West Bank force rapidly and so exploit their one chance.

Adan reluctantly left the paratroopers battling desperately between the two axis, while he directed a recce force of personnel carriers to find out the situation along the Akavish route. To everyone's surprise, the signal came back that the route was clear. With great haste, the wreckage of shelled tanks was pushed off the road, and in the first light of dawn the convoy was unexpectedly advancing. Tamari marshaled his column of pontoons to the lake and thence northward, and before the sun's rays leaped into the sky, they rolled into the "yard."

It was by then apparent to the beleaguered paratroopers still fighting toward the Chinese Farm that they had little hope of clearing the stubborn Egyptians from the positions opposing them. But with the bridging column at last moving toward the Canal, its commander realized they would have to hold their own positions at all costs, occupying and blocking the enemy from interfering with the bridging operation as it gathered momentum again. They were spread along the forward slope of a low dune, pinned down in groups of fifteen to twenty men sprawled in depressions in the terrain. Just about 50 yards away were hundreds of Egyptians with RPG missiles and Russian Kalatchinka rifles. Many had night field glasses. Israeli tanks that approached were challenged by Egyptian tanks coming out to meet them, and when they were driven back, their infantry increased the ferocity of their fire, sending missiles whizzing across the depression. Again and again, individual Israeli soldiers braved the whirlwind of fire to scramble across the sand to drag back wounded. So intense was the fight that another armored unit that tried to reach them to bring out the wounded was driven back.

Hours passed, during which the paratroopers groveled in the stony, dun-colored sand, fighting thirst and heat as much as the enemy, while the wounded of both sides were tormented by flies. A smoke cannister was set off by Yaki's troops to guide tanks to their aid, but instead it brought down a storm of shelling. Eventually tanks did arrive. They advanced toward the

Egyptian positions and the inevitable missile attack; within minutes three tanks were blazing, their oily smoke drifting across the
desert and stinging the soldiers' eyes. Nevertheless, the paratroopers hung on, and would do so for an incredible fourteen
hours against an Egyptian force of division strength, while
behind them the columns of bridging equipment moved to the
Canal. Finally, however, they had to be evacuated. When
Tuvia's tanks eventually pulled them out, they had lost forty
dead and over a hundred wounded.

Correspondent Angus Deming flew across Sinai shortly afterward for *Newsweek*. The scars of battle were evident. The helicopter in which he hitched a ride clattered along at a mere 30
feet to avoid Egyptian gunners. "Skimming over the Sinai," he
wrote, "it was clear from the hundreds of shell holes in the sand
that a tremendous battle had been fought here before the Israelis
smashed their way through to the Egyptian homeland. Orange
flashes and columns of ugly black smoke in the distance indicated
the war was still raging. . . ."

Although the Egyptians still did not understand the implica-
tions of the Israeli crossings, they were only too aware of the
tremendous efforts the Israelis were making to control that corridor to the Canal and their fortifications. On the morning of the
17th, they determined to close that corridor once and for all. In
the previous days, while the battle had been raging along the
Akavish and Tirtur routes, the Egyptian 14th Armored Brigade
had been fighting nonstop against a single Israeli battalion west
of the Chinese Farm; by that evening, it would be almost
destroyed. The Egyptian 16th Infantry and 21st Armored divisions launched two major attacks against Adan's forces at Akavish and Tirtur, driving from the direction of *Missouri* and the
Chinese Farm. Both these attacks were beaten off with heavy
losses, largely by Israeli tanks using their superior gunnery.

At 10:00 A.M. on October 16 Dayan arrived at Adan's
advanced headquarters on the barren hills near Kishuf. Shortly
afterward Bar-Lev, too, arrived. The defense minister wanted to

(ABOVE) *Israeli armored personnel carrier passing burning Egyptian truck in Sinai.* Photo by Terry Fincher, courtesy of Photographers International. (BELOW) *Burned-out Syrian convoy inside Syria.* Photo courtesy of Britain/Israel Public Affairs Committee

(ABOVE) *Israeli 175mm S.P. gun crew resting during Golan battle.* Photo courtesy of Britain/Israel Public Affairs Committee. (BELOW) *Israel's rolling bridge being towed toward the Suez Canal.* Photo courtesy of Israel Government Press Office

"Gilowas" assembling in the Suez Canal. Photo courtesy of Israel Government Press Office

Centurion tank crosses floating rolling bridge. Photo courtesy of Israel Government Press Office

Israeli bridges north of the Great Bitter Lake. Photo courtesy of Israel Government Press Office

Israeli paratroopers driving through groves on the West Bank. Photo by Terry Fincher, courtesy of Photographers International

(ABOVE) *Israeli armored infantry moves into Egypt.* Photo by Terry Fincher, courtesy of Photographers International. (BELOW) *Surface-to-air missiles captured by Israelis in Egypt.* Photo courtesy of Britain/Israel Public Affairs Committee

be taken across to Sharon but very reluctantly gave way to
Adan's dissuasion. Meanwhile a helicopter brought in Elazar, the
chief of staff, and Gonen's deputy, Ben-Ari. Not long after that
a battle-scarred half-track clattered up and from it emerged the
dust-laden, untidy figure of Sharon. His silvery hair sprouted
untidily over the bandages that swathed his forehead where he
had been hit by shell splinters.

This group of determined and brilliant commanders all
crouched in a circle on the sun-drenched hill with their maps, to
decide what to do about the crossings; who was to go over and
when. Sharon poignantly proposed that Adan should deal with
the corridor while he sent his division over the Canal. However,
this didn't suit Adan at all, for he wanted to adhere to the original
plan, whereby Sharon would hold the corridor while his own
division refueled and ammunitioned prior to crossing the Canal.
There is a curious echo in the Israeli generals' clamoring for
roles, recalling nineteenth-century generals insisting on the
honor of the perilous charge. But the bulldog pragmatism of
Elazar held sway. Adan was allocated the crossing. Sharon was
to clean up the corridor and widen it; only then would his division cross to the West Bank. They were still arguing vocifer-
ously when a signal from Amnon Reshef's brigade, which was
reorganizing near Lakekan on the shores of the Great Bitter
Lake, laconically reported that the entire Egyptian 25th
Armored Brigade was moving north toward them.

While Reshef sped south to where he had four dug-in tanks
protecting his southern flank, Adan was hastening from the *al
fresco* conference southward to supervise the battle against the
Egyptian Third Army's attempt to nip out the Israeli corridor.
He rapidly signaled dispositions as he went. Nir's brigade was to
leave one battalion in the Akavish area and to place the rest of
his brigade in an armored ambush to the east of *Lexicon* facing
the lakes; Aryeh Karen was to leave his route south and sweep
across country to reach the *Botzer* fortification southeast of the
Egyptians, cutting off its retreat. Reshef's last signal reported a
huge column of ninety-six T-62 tanks, shepherding along a vast

force of armored personnel carrier, fuel, and supply trucks, all
slowly but deliberately entering a trap. Blocking their path was
Reshef's force; to their left, on the west, was the Great Bitter
Lake with an Israeli minefield between it and the road; to the east
and southeast were Israeli armored brigades.

The battle did not last long. Nir's brigade opened a deadly
accurate fire, panicking a large part of the Egyptian brigade off
the road toward the Great Bitter Lake. It ran into the minefield
and while tanks exploded, others wheeled in confusion as they
tried to turn back on their tracks. The rest of the force had
wheeled right and was heading across the dunes to attack Nir's
forces, but they were well dug in, in hull-down positions, protected by the dunes and operating as static artillery. With long-
range accuracy they picked off the T-62s as they bucked and clattered over the dunes. In the meantime, Karen's brigade had
moved from the Giddi Road and his tanks were coming up
behind the Egyptians. When they, too, opened fire, the Egyptians were boxed in between the lake, the minefield, and surrounding Israelis. They were almost annihilated.

By 5:30 P.M., it was over; of the original force, eighty-six
T-62s had been destroyed. Of the remaining ten, four (including
the commander's) had fled into the *Botzer* fortification. The
entire force of carriers and trucks was wiped out, leaving a dread-
ful pall of smoke and burning rubber to cloud the setting sun.
The Israelis had lost four tanks that had chased the enemy into
their own minefield. It had been a classic tank battle of the sort
that every commander dreamed of.

At two o'clock that same morning, Adan had informed
Sharon's deputy, Brigadier Even, that the Akavish axis was
finally open. Even, who was responsible for the crossing, had
immediately ordered the pontoon convoy to advance to *Lakekan*
to meet Sharon, who would show exactly where the pontoons
were to be launched. The crossing site had by then been pin-
pointed by the Egyptians, who were concentrating artillery fire
upon it. Despite the barrage, engineers continued to labor, duck-
ing when a nearby shellburst showered steel splinters. Wounded

men were evacuated while the damaged rafts were replaced. Roaring bulldozers tore at the banks, ripping open breaches through which supply columns would descend to the bridges. All the while rubber boats and rafts scurried back and forth, sometimes swamped by a gigantic water spout heaved up by a bursting shell.

Dayan writes: "I crossed with Arik [Sharon] to the west bank. Here, unlike the east bank, which is entirely desert, the soil was cultivated and covered with vegetation." He spent only a short while in "Africa"—as Sharon termed the West Bank—before returning to the East Bank, by which time the bridge was finished. An Israeli war correspondent, reporting that Sharon accompanied Dayan on his surprise appearance at the front, said: "The two generals made a striking pair—Dayan with his eye patch and Sharon with his head wrapped in a bandage still stained with spots of blood."

By 7:00 A.M. the long convoy had revved and rattled its way to the site, and a quarter of an hour later the first of the heavy pontoons was pushed into the water.

The battle south of *Lexicon* having ended, the victorious Israeli tanks took on fuel from the trucks while Egyptian artillery fired a heavy barrage, turning its vengeance upon the Israeli positions. But while the battle had been raging, Sharon's engineers had completed the pontoon bridge, and by 4:00 P.M. they were awaiting Adan's division.

At nine o'clock on the evening of the 17th, Adan's division had re-formed and was moving in a long column along the Akavish route toward the crossing area. The advanced headquarters led, with Adan fast asleep in his half-track from sheer exhaustion, followed by the brigades of Amir and Nir in turn. It was a night of brilliant moonlight turning the desert scene to a cold blue that merged with the starlit sky. The Canal waters were mirror-calm, rippled only when the weight of the tanks and carriers flexed the floating bridge. While the men were being ferried across someone pulled out a bottle of whisky, which they passed around for a good swig each. At the far side, the vehicles dipped off the ramp and up onto the track, where they were met by Haim, who yelled for them to carry on to the divisional concentration area at Deversoir airfield. An Israeli driver remembers how relaxed he had felt on the drive, since it was such an unbelievably pleasant night after all they had been through for endless days. "Eventually we reached an airfield where we were ordered to draw up. No sooner had I stopped and the crew clambered out, stretching and groaning, when all hell was let loose. With a terrific crash an Egyptian barrage hit us. We all dived for cover, some under tanks; others, including me, hid behind buildings."

Through the storm of shelling, Amir's brigade was still rumbling over the bridge. Adan asked Haim to send back scouts to guide his brigade through once they were on the West Bank. But the barrage was getting heavier, and then came the frustrating news at 11:45 P.M. that just after Amir's third tank had crossed, the bridge had snapped with the next tank stuck on it. Adan immediately contacted Even to determine how bad was the damage and what arrangements were being made to get the rest of Amir's brigade across. Back came the reply: "We're checking it out." But, Even added, it would take some time. To keep the column moving, he was directing the brigade about 200 yards north where they could be embarked on Gilowas. This was far from satisfactory as the whole area was under a very heavy barrage. The shelling had intensified and been increased by Katyusha rockets, whose blazing fireballs screamed down in a shower of sparks and thunderous explosions. Adan waited impatiently for twenty minutes, then contacted Even again to find out when the bridge would be ready, as his brigade was stranded on the wrong side of the Canal.

It was now a few minutes into the 18th, but Even still could not estimate when the bridge would be repaired, since the engineering experts had not yet arrived at the site. Nine minutes later he called back; the bridge could be repaired, but he still had no estimate of time. There were only five hours of darkness left. Adan recalls that he then had a stroke of luck. He noticed there were two bridge-laying tanks close by his command post. Recalling how they had been used at the Ruafa'a Dam demonstration, he promptly told Even and Amir that he was sending them the bridge-layers. After some frantic searching in the darkness amid crowds of troops, the crews of the tanks were found, and they set off with Haim's deputy.

In the meantime, Amir's tanks were still straggling across on the ancient but invaluable Gilowas, although having to endure the most appalling shell-and-rocket fire. One tank driver slipped while maneuvering aboard a Gilowa and almost sank before he was towed out. Then at 1:35 A.M., the good news came that a bridge-layer had managed to lay its bridge across the damaged roller and traffic was flowing again. This was all the more fortuitous as the Gilowas were far from stable in the turmoil of shell-whipped water. Later a Gilowa received a direct hit from a shell and immediately sank.

By 2:35 A.M. all Amir's tanks were across and a signal was sent to Nir, whose brigade was waiting at *Lakekan*, to get a move on. The bridge was not being used and everyone was getting nervous again. At 3:15 Nir's tanks arrived and began moving over in comparative calm, as the Egyptian barrage had ceased by then. Adan's division was across the Canal, with a battalion of self-propelled guns.

In his discussions, meanwhile, Dayan had suggested that Sharon should launch an attack northward along the East Bank of the Canal, instead of his planned west coast advance. The concept underlying this was that by leaving the West Bank offensive to the brigades already there, and using Sharon's remaining forces on the eastern side of the Canal, the enemy would be rolled up along both banks by mutually supporting firepower. Southern Command was especially anxious that the *Missouri* position should be taken as soon as possible to stop Egyptian artillery emplaced there from firing on the bridgeheads. But yet another bitter disagreement erupted between Sharon and Gonen, who had originated the plan. Gonen insisted on retaining Amnon Reshef's brigade for the attack north, although Sharon wanted the brigade to cross the Canal immediately to strengthen his forces on the West Bank. Angrily, Sharon went over the head of his immediate superior, Gonen, and appealed directly to Bar-Lev. Such was the Israeli command structure that the latter gave Sharon the authority to move his brigade. By that time, Gonen seems to have been in an invidious position in which his remaining authority depended upon Bar-Lev's backing, which was not always forthcoming.

The flamboyant Sharon now had the bit between his teeth and was quite determined to play the major role in the West Bank assault. He went yet again to Bar-Lev, once more proposing a change of plan. Instead of his division pushing south parallel to Adan's division, he argued forcefully, he should be permitted to widen the West Bank bridgehead by driving north to capture the major Egyptian town of Ismailia. Once more the elderly Bar-Lev agreed, and there seems no doubt he was much impressed by the daring and the tactical perception of this most experienced general, although his truculent methods upset most tenets of military order. A reporter wrote of the intransigent Sharon, "His problem was that 'Arik' doesn't care whom he tells to go to hell — and as a matter of fact, I can't think of anyone he hasn't."

Bar-Lev relayed the change of plan to Gonen. General Magen, whose division was to have held the bridgehead, he was informed, would now send his division southward to the west of Adan's division aiming to capture Suez. Sharon would hold the bridgehead in the new plan before he sent his division north to capture Ismailia. This was, in any event, a shrewd tactical move, for there would be Egyptian fuel dumps and supplies in the area; possession of those supplies would greatly ease Israeli expansion. Apart from that consideration, their success would give Israel the vastly important bargaining power of holding both Ismailia and Suez, vital links in the Suez Canal. Gonen had no options but to agree to this proposal, although he remarked rather bitterly to Bar-Lev that life would be much simpler if he had to manage Magen's and Adan's divisions rather than Sharon's. According to Herzog, Gonen found relief in the new command arrangement as it left him commanding forces who would cooperate with him. There would be, he thought, less personal aggravation. In the new plan, Adan would sweep south with his right flank and rear guarded by Magen's division moving to the west.

Early on the 18th, Sharon gave the order to his deputy, Yakov Even, to bring forward the repaired roller bridge. At the crossing sites a very difficult situation had developed: Far from being the surprise success the press reported at the time, the crossing was fiercely opposed by the Egyptians with every means at their disposal. Apart from the deadly artillery and rocket attacks raining explosions all around the narrow crossing, MIG-18 helicopters whirled along the Canal to drop napalm bombs in an attempt to knock out the bridge. They met with little success, however, as a hail of machine-gun and antiaircraft fire from the Israelis brought many down in a bubbling halo of their own napalm. Israeli Phantoms, too, joined in the battle, doing their utmost to keep the crossings open. Nevertheless, the increasing fire being thrown at the crossing made it inevitable that hits would be scored, and the rafts suffered a heavy toll.

The chaos of the Canal made the roller bridge even more important. Slowly, inevitably, it was hauled, yard by yard, toward the crossings. The tanks heaved and boiled as they strained the ungainly mass forward, its enormous rollers flattening a broad swath across the desert in its wake. The structure was easily visible from Egyptian positions at the Chinese Farm, *Missouri*, and from atop the embankments, and spotters directed the Egyptian guns onto the great bridge. Yet although the desert became as pockmarked as the moon in the wake of the bridge, the bridge escaped all but minor hits. But its progress was a nightmare. One of the Israeli soldiers wrote to his cousin in England describing what happened:

> It seemed to go on for ever, and all the time I expected to be killed at any moment—after a while it seemed inevitable that I counted every moment I remained alive as a bonus. The road was a mass of overlapping craters and a couple of bulldozers went

along in front shoving into the craters anything that might fill them, and that included boulders, sand and any wreckage that happened to be in the way. It was awful; I tried to avert my gaze at some stretches, for the road and the surrounding dune were strewn with bodies, some ours and some Egyptians. Their wounds were too ghastly to describe. All the while the shelling went on and men fell wounded or dead. It was like something from a film where the medieval soldiers fell but the siege machine kept going. . . .

Through fire and smoke the bridge crept westward as night fell in a spectacular desert sunset outdone by the fury along the road. They reached the Lexicon crossroads just as the sun dipped, and there, in a redoubled spate of fury, even more shells plastered them. A shell screamed down and exploded close to the bridge, killing Col. Johnny Tanne, the command's chief engineer and the most vital man in the whole operation for he, more than anyone else, knew how to handle and place the bridge. His death threw an unenviable load on the shoulders of Yakov Even, who realized with dismay that he was in deep trouble without Tanne.

Tanne had known every foot of the route, which near the Canal grew increasingly swampy; any false move would irretrievably bog down the 400 tons of bridge. Even also knew the dangers of getting bogged and therefore saw no alternative but to test the way ahead. He set off in the battalion commander's tank, accompanied by an armored personnel carrier. Together they edged forward, proving the firmness of the ground before the rigid structure. Against all odds, they succeeded, and late that evening the tanks slowly and surely shoved the huge bridge out into the Canal. As the watches ticked past midnight into the new day, the bridge became operational. Soon it was echoing to the clatter of more tanks crossing in rapid succession to swell the growing Israeli force on the West Bank.

On that bank, Egyptian attacks were being mounted with increasing force. Matt's paratroop brigade, which had been largely inactive since establishing the initial bridgehead, was subjected to successive Egyptian counterattacks by their commandos ordered to push in the Israeli bridgehead and reach the Canal. That same day, Colonel Shomron moved a tank force north between the Sweet Water Canal and the railroad toward Serafeum on the Ismailia Road. But the Egyptians had acted quickly once the full extent of the Israeli attack had been realized, and by then had established fortified positions blocking any further advance in that direction. A battalion commander and thirteen men were cut off from the main force and attacked by Egyptian infantrymen, who crept close through the dense, luxuriant undergrowth, which enabled hundreds of them to get within yards of the Israeli positions.

The Israelis then withdrew to a bungalow, from where they kept up an accurate fire to hold off the Egyptians. But the Egyptians still came close enough to hurl grenades at them, while bazooka shells blasted holes in the primitive walls. This one-sided battle lasted for hours, during which Egyptian reinforcements were called, and even artillery was used at close range, the gunners laying their weapons over open sites to blow the building to bits. Eventually Israeli relief forces fought their way through to the besieged men. After further heavy fighting through dense undergrowth that was more like Vietnam than the Middle East, they withdrew under cover of darkness, leaving the Egyptians in possession of the positions.

Reshef's brigade had already crossed to the West Bank after leaving a battalion to support the continuing attack against *Missouri*. Once over the Canal, Sharon directed Reshef's force northward to the west of Matt's positions at Serafeum, to take an Egyptian post at Orcha, some 4.5 miles away. The attack, supported by an armored infantry company, went in against prepared Egyptian positions. Once again the enemy put up a fanatical resistance, forcing the Israelis to fight for every yard; it was so determined that Reshef had to send in a paratroop unit. They stormed forward in half-tracks from which machine gunners loosed a continuous stream of fire to keep the defenders' heads down. Then, even before the vehicles had clattered to a halt, the paratroops were leaping over the steel sides to fight their way through the trenches, hacking and slashing and machine-gunning as they went. The enemy commando force gave as good as it got, with antitank guns, antiaircraft guns at depression, and bazookas, forcing a bitter fight for each trench in turn. The savagery was terrible, and darkness closed over a scene of carnage, with the Egyptians having lost many times the Israeli casualties.

The loss of Orcha opened up the Egyptians' northern defense line in that sector and enabled Reshef's troops to rush along through the heavily overgrown agricultural strip, seizing refreshment as they went. Gradually, they were able to swing eastward, which brought them back to the Canal embankments. From there they provided supporting fire for Tuvia's brigade on the East Bank, which was still fighting for control of the *Missouri* positions.

Meanwhile, on the southern sector of the Israeli's West Bank front, Adan's division was attacking along a two-brigade axis, driving down toward the Port of Suez at the head of the Gulf of Suez and controlling the southern end of the Canal. Possession of that area denied to the Egyptians the chances of reinforcing their Third Army by shipping across the Gulf, as Israeli fast missile boats and gunboats began to patrol the narrow waters.

Although in general the Egyptian defenses along the front were crumbling, units of their 4th Armored Division and a mechanized division put up a stiff resistance near Uri, which was only broken after an attack by armored infantry reinforced by paratroopers. In the main, though, defense was limited to isolated groups of troops armed with rockets and missile launchers; at no time on the West Bank did the Egyptians use their considerable tank forces *en masse* in a traditional response to a water-borne invasion. As has been seen, the Arabs had quite significant armored forces within 60 miles or so or the Deversoir bridgehead, as well as various infantry and artillery units. But all their counterattacks were made with small battle groups, which were frittered away against the Israeli forces still concentrated in the bridgehead. It was not hard for the Egyptians to detect by even limited air reconnaissance that the Israelis were in deep trouble with their cumbersome bridges, and there should have been the time for an all-out armored and artillery counterattack against the bridgehead. Instead they preferred, so it would appear, to rely upon the scant and often underestimated reports from local commanders, who perhaps thought the Israelis would go away if left alone.

When Amir moved his brigade south along the Test Road, an Egyptian armored force that was advancing along the parallel road on the left promptly swung west to attack the Israeli column. But the Egyptians became hopelessly bogged in the muddy, irrigated fields, and Amir's tanks turned their guns on them to destroy almost the entire force.

Nir's forces were driving south along the Ismailia-to-Suez road when they, too, were stopped by Egyptian defenses at the Tsach crossroads, which proved too strong for them to overcome. Haim's brigade was at that time moving east of Orcha, where he also ran into an entire infantry brigade with missiles. In the midday heat, both Israeli forces were stopped. An air strike was needed to open both routes, but when Adan radioed headquarters, he was told to send out strong forces to wipe out the SAM sites first. Both Nir and Amir were told in turn to hold a battalion for this task. Nir's force spread out for some 15 miles westward, where they destroyed two positions before returning to base to refuel. Amir's force drove about 6 miles to successfully attack a force of Egyptian tanks sent to block their advance, and also destroy two more missile sites. These joint actions opened a significant gap in the Egyptian air defense system, and into this gap on the following morning streaked Phantoms and Skyhawks. Their way cleared of the SAMs, they knocked out the blocking tanks and gun positions.

The Skyhawks were used especially against Egypt's armor, employing clusters of U.S.-supplied Rockeye projectiles. Their effect was likened to the English longbow on the heavily armored French cavalry at Crecy. The projectiles penetrated inches of armor and wrecked many tanks simultaneously. The Phantoms, too, were operating with electronic wizardry; Walleye TV-guided bombs, radar-seeking bombs, and laser-guided bombs all combined to destroy the Egyptian air defenses. Sadat wrote of the effects of these sophisticated weapons, claiming that whereas persistent Israeli attacks had not seriously damaged his SAMs, the latest weapons knocked them out completely. The appearance of these electronic weapons strengthened Sadat's belief that he was fighting the Americans as well as Israel. It was a significant move toward the frightening escalation the war would soon take.

Now, with full air coverage, Adan's forces swept on, and by midday were attacking the Fayid landing strip. Amir detached a force to cover the airfield, while the remainder of the brigade rolled as fast as they were able toward the Geneifa Hills. Again the Egyptians attempted to block their advance, moving some forty tanks to positions at Mitznefet; but before they were established, they were attacked by Israeli armor and aircraft and forced to pull back. Nir's brigade swept west through an artillery brigade's emplacements, before running into strong enemy forces on the main Cairo-to-Bitter Lake road. But from behind them Karen's brigade came up in support, moved through to keep up the unrelenting pressure, and thundered on protecting Amir's right flank. Each missile site they encountered was destroyed by long-range tank fire, although on one occasion an enterprising Egyptian commander fired an SA-2 missile at maximum depression, sending the 20-foot missile streaking just over the heads of the Israeli attackers to land 400 yards from Adan's advanced headquarters.

The afternoon of the 19th found Adan deep in the Geneifa Hills. Amir's forces were held up east of Mitznefet. Nir and Karen were ordered to continue along the Geneifa Hills, during which they knocked out more missile sites before reaching the lesser Vitamin Road that led down to the lake. Two brigades carried on the drive toward the water.

Magen's division had by then moved from the bridgehead,

through Adan's forces, and was headed west toward Maktsera. It attacked the Egyptian force still blocking the Tsach crossroads, and with its superior strength, succeeded in overcoming Egyptian resistance before driving on to relieve Amir's forces at Mitznefet. By the end of the day, Amir had pushed some way along the Ismailia-to-Suez road, but had been consistently repulsed by heavy Egyptian resistance, which inflicted considerable losses on the Israelis. Elsewhere, though, things went better, and by nightfall the vital Fayid airfield had been captured. This afforded substantial supplies of much needed fuel and gave the Israelis an important air link through which supplies could be ferried from their Sinai bases.

The most significant move in the last two days of fighting had been Adan's dash for the Geneifa Hills, which had guaranteed Israeli success in the breakthrough in their dash toward the Gulf and the Port of Suez. Without command of these hills, the Israeli right flank would have been exposed to an ever-present threat of Arab commando raids, besides providing concealed bases for the Arabs' missiles. Nevertheless, the Egyptian troops defending the hills did not give up easily. Karen's forces continued to have a struggle on their hands as they fought to clear the eastern slopes. Amir, meanwhile, was moving slowly along three roads parallel to the Bitter Lakes. Wasil, the commander of the near-isolated Third Army, hurriedly transported his 22nd Tank Brigade of the 6th Mechanized Division back to the West Bank in an attempt to stem the Israeli advance, but with little effect. Adan had assembled another force — comprising an armored battalion, an armored infantry battalion, a paratroop battalion, and a battalion of engineers. This was slowly making its way south along the Test route, clearing in turn various army camps and coming up against Egyptian, Kuwaiti, and Palestinian units, none of which caused much delay.

Magen's division was still rolling across the open desert toward the Cairo-to-Suez road, a move viewed with considerable alarm by army headquarters in Cairo. On his west flank he had Shomron's tanks, which were by then 17 miles west of the Canal.

The following day, he moved south to Mount Um Katib to take up positions near Mitznefet, where for the next three days his forces were to slug it out against an Egyptian tank brigade. At this time, too, elements of the Egyptian 4th Armored Division were conducting a desperate rearguard action to hold back Nir's brigade south of the Asor Road, for this brigade was already only a mile north of the Cairo-Suez road. Thus, from midday of October 21, fifteen days after the Egyptian attack, their Third Army was cut off from its supplies and faced a terrifying prospect of isolation, surrounded by the victorious Israelis and having no water supply.

Behind the battling front-line troops, Israeli reinforcements were threading across the barren wastes of Sinai. *Time* correspondent Jordan Bonfante described the scene: "Driving south to the Sinai along a road built before the Romans came to Egypt, we found virtually all traffic going one way—toward the Suez Canal. Among the endless columns of military trucks and jeeps were the motley fleets of civilian vehicles mobilized for the war." During the first hectic hours of aggression, Israeli had followed the example of the French General Manoury, who in 1914 had mobilized the Paris garrison and driven it to the front by commandeering all taxis and buses. "Private delivery vans," wrote Bonfante, "called up in the mobilization were now at the front, still bearing the vans markings of the milk or bread companies that they served in peacetime." Many Israeli troops had rushed to their units straight from their Yom Kippur holiday, and Zeiklin, who had been fishing when the recall signals had been broadcast, recalls that "in my own unit most of us had battle jackets and helmets, but down below were every color slacks and socks." Bonfante, too, noted that along the road, "groups of teenagers—some of them Americans visiting Israel—had set up refreshments stands and were offering coffee to the troops."

At one o'clock on the morning of October 19 Sadat was telephoned by Ismail, who asked him to go immediately to the operations room. Even at that late hour, Sadat did as he was asked, and on arrival found Shazli in a state of collapse. He is reputed to have greeted Sadat with the words: "The war is over. A catastrophe has occurred. We must withdraw from Sinai." It was at that juncture that Sadat, probably reluctantly, contacted Soviet Premier Kosygin again. He asked that the Soviet Union should convene the Security Council and order a cease-fire. He also decided then to dismiss Shazli, although for reasons of public morale in the Egyptian forces, this was not made public for some months.

A basic weakness in the Egyptian evaluation is evident in the ways in which their reporting insisted that the Israeli attacks were only minor operations, and concentrated instead upon their own reactions, designed to throw back the invaders. Of course, such reactions have been paralleled many times before; Franco-British assurances in May 1940, the American commanders' reaction to an impending German attack in the Ardennes, and, more pertinently, the Israeli response to the Syrian attack into the Golan Heights. In all these situations there was a kind of cloud-cuckoo hope that the wish would father the result. Clearly, it is important to retain morale, but not when it obscures the perception of command. In this particular case, the Egyptians continued to play down the strength of the Israeli operations, for even as late as the 19th, when two Israeli armored divisions were mopping up the West Bank, Egyptians assumed that no more than one hundred or so enemy tanks were operating.

In spite of the sanguine pronouncements from Cairo, there was an underlying disquiet shown by the Egyptian operational moves. On the 19th the Moroccan Brigade that had been stationed in Cairo, was, according to its commander, suddenly rushed to reinforce the Third Army as reports filtered back of Sharon's division moving resolutely north toward Ismailia. By then, however, Third Army was to all intents cordoned off, and perhaps the Moroccans were really sent to Second Army, where they might have opposed Sharon. At that late date the Egyptians still did not appear to have understood the Israeli strategy, their deep penetration along the West Bank, and the increasing danger to their Third Army.

But when Sadat paid a fleeting visit to army headquarters on the 20th, the Israeli intention could no longer be doubted. A glance at the situation maps showed all too clearly that the enemy's armored columns were fanning out to seal off the area west of the Bitter Lakes, southward toward Suez, and swinging in a great arc to take out the all-important Geneifa Hills missile sites. From that point on, the Egyptians should have had no doubt that the Israelis were deliberately severing all communications and supply routes between Egypt and Wasil's Third Army. But other possibilities existed, too, as a study of maps showed. Supposing, commanders suggested, that the Israelis sent more amphibious tanks west across Lake Timsah, north of the Chinese Farm, to bypass Ismailia on the north. This would give them an important air and supply base which, should it fall to Israel, would provide them with all the fuel and supplies they needed for a drive on Cairo, a mere 60 miles due west along Route 44. Or, as Sadat is reported to have reiterated, the Israelis might launch an amphibious operation across the Gulf of Suez, again bypassing strong Egyptian positions at Suez, which would leave them free to drive the 70 or so miles along Route 33 across open desert to Cairo.

This danger was heightened by the Israelis' success in knocking out so many of the SAM sites, thus opening the way for their planes to begin shooting up all the Egyptian supply columns and armored formations; from then on, all convoys in Third Army's sector had to maintain 300 yards between vehicles. Mohammed Heikal described the atmosphere at the Egyptian High Command, admitting: "It had a considerable effect on strained nerves." It was, he asserted, "a war against our nerves."

Sadat knew from his battlefront reports and his own visits to the operations room that the situation was getting serious. While dissatisfied with the limited extent of Soviet aid to his country, he was nevertheless bitter when America began flying in supplies for Israel. He wrote: "The United States was using us for the air-bridge she now established to save Israel. Al-Arish became an airbase where colossal U.S. transport aircraft landed,

loaded with tanks and sophisticated weapons." He also noted
with despondency that Israel's armored losses were being made
up, although of course so were his. Israel depended solely upon
the aid given by the United States, and that was hindered by the
oil-hungry Europeans. Egypt, on the other hand, was getting aid
from many sources apart from the Soviet Union, including tanks
from Yugoslavia and troops from a dozen Arab states. Even the
president of Bangladesh promised, in a rash moment, to send
50,000 guerillas, although the bravado soon dissipated and Egypt
got 50,000 lbs. of tea instead—perhaps a British legacy.

On October 19, Shazli had returned to Cairo from the front,
in Sadat's words, "a nervous wreck." Shazli wanted Egypt's
forces withdrawn straightway from the East Bank, because of
the threat to their rear by the Israelis on the West Bank. That,
Sadat replied with great perception, was what the Israelis wanted.
Marshal Ali, meanwhile, requested that Sadat go to the command headquarters, where he arrived at midnight.

Ali wanted an important decision from the president in his
capacity as supreme commander. On the East Bank there were
5 Egyptian divisions, with 1,200 tanks, while on the West Bank
only 1 division was to face the growing Israeli strength. There
was in Cairo another division, plus the Republican Guard, that
could be dispatched to the Canal. After pondering the situation,
Sadat called a meeting of all his commanders, who agreed with
his opinion that there was nothing to worry about. Sadat therefore issued a Hitlerian order: There would be no withdrawal at
all, "not a soldier, not a rifle, nothing," from the East Bank of
the Canal to the West. This was followed by an order to the
commander of the armored division on the West Bank that he
should contain the enemy but not engage him until reinforcements could be sent. By then it was a futile gesture, for the Israelis were flooding like the spring Nile and were going to be about
as hard to contain.

CHAPTER

16

Defense Condition Three

By midday on Wednesday, October 10, just four days after Syria launched her devastating attack across the "Purple Line," not a single Syrian tank in fighting condition remained within that line. Two entire brigades had been destroyed in the Hushniyah pocket, and much of the Heights was a graveyard of Syrian tanks, supply trucks, carriers, and hundreds of tons of ammunition. It had been the strategic decision of the Israeli High Command to give priority to the Golan Heights because any Syrian breakthrough could threaten northern Israel, for they had no depth to the front. Following the initial Syrian defeat, the Israeli High Command had conferred with the prime minister and decided that the war should be carried into Syria.

Once on the "Purple Line," they had several options for an attack into Syria. One was based on the advantages of terrain and suggested a drive to the southeast, toward Sheikh Meskin and the 18-mile-wide gap between the great lava sea and the hills overlooking Damascus. Such a move over excellent tank ground would also cut the axis being used by the incoming Jordanian and Iraqi reinforcements. Once the Israelis reached the Kisweh-Abab Hills, they could hit targets in Damascus even with medium artillery. For several days the divisions of Peled and Laner had pursued the Syrians deeper toward Damascus — so much so that the Soviet Union warned the United States it could not allow the Israelis to occupy the Syrian capital. By that time, though, the Israeli cabinet had firmly decided against such a course of action, both to avoid a confrontation with the Russians and because the Israeli forces were not capable of holding so large a city.

On October 11, while the stalemate was enduring on the Sinai front, Laner's division was about to launch a major attack against the Syrians when a large force, which included Centurions, was seen approaching from the southeast. After a flurry of radio calls between Laner and general headquarters, it was realized that this was a powerful Iraqi force coming into the battle. The Iraqis formed the most implacable of all Israel's opponents, with whom a cease-fire agreement had never been concluded even after the 1949 War.

The arrival of so strong an Iraqi force upset the final alignments in Syria. To counter the Iraqi threat to his southern flank, Laner organized his division in a defensive box. He had his 19th and 20th Armored brigades at the Jaba-Tel Shaar crossroads, while the 17th and 79th Armored brigades were at the village of Maatz and its crossroads. When the Iraqis launched their attack late that afternoon, they did so with heavy artillery support and MIG air strikes, but the latter were soon driven off by Israeli jets. For some hours there was skirmishing and maneuvering, and the Israeli 20th Brigade, which had mostly up-gunned Shermans, was nearly caught by advancing Centurions, until a sharp-eyed gunner noticed that the Centurions had the old-fashioned 20-pounder gun, which the Israeli Defense Force no longer possessed. In the nick of time they opened fire with their own 75mm and 105mm guns, and the venerable Shermans drove off a strong Iraqi attack.

There was another sharp engagement during the night, when the Iraqis launched an attack with their infrared equipped tanks, which had the Israelis at a great disadvantage. But the Israelis shut down their engines and called for their infantry support to deluge the area with a mortar attack. Then, by the light of the exploding mortars, they fired point-blank into the confused Iraqis and drove them off.

The Israeli High Command had already decided to play it carefully in Syria, and was more concerned with bringing political and psychological pressure to bear on Damascus than any further territorial gains. It had intended a main effort along the northern and central fronts, but this had been upset by the sudden appearance of a strong Iraqi and Jordanian force on their right flank. It must be admitted that there was never too much coordination among the various Arab forces. There were instances of Iraqi artillery persistently bombarding the Jordanians as they attacked, of grotesque miscalculations in joint attacks so that invariably as one force was going in the other was withdrawing, and of several notable air battles between Syrian and Iraqi aircraft. Nevertheless, the presence of the Iraqis distorted the shape of the closing Golan battles and meant that the Israelis were rebuffed on the central sector.

On the divisional level Laner operated very successfully, but it cost precious time to win the upper hand over the Iraqis, and by then he had lost the initiative elsewhere. An Israeli "bulge" was created in Syria, and they lost a chance on October 12 which they never regained, for while Laner was pursuing the Syrians, Peled's division was stalled at Rafid opposite the Syrian 5th Division, which was nowhere as strong as the Syrian forces further north. If Peled had overcome the Syrians quickly, there would have been time for him to bring his full divisional weight to bear against the Iraqis, and the combined Syrian-Iraqi forces would have been broken. Once the bulge had been formed, the Israelis created a strong defense line and held off successive attacks by combined Syrian, Jordanian, and Iraqi forces.

On Sunday, October 20, Henry Kissinger unexpectedly flew to Moscow following a personal appeal by Brezhnev for him to come immediately. The urgency of his flight was emphasized by the previous two weeks of Soviet indolence. Until two days before, the Soviet leaders had been comforted by the thought that while their clients were not going to win an outright victory, they were, at least, going to finish the war in a position of strength from which to bargain. The news from the Middle East battlefronts had been encouraging if not exactly triumphant; in Syria the Israelis had been halted in their headlong drive toward Damascus, while in Sinai the Egyptians were holding their own. After all, the Soviet leaders must have concurred, had not Mr. Kosygin had talks with Sadat on the 16th, and been assured by the Egyptians that the military situation was excellent? It was true of course, that before Kosygin left Egypt, an Israeli commando raid had penetrated the West Bank. But that was just a minor irritation. Unfortunately, they could reflect on the following Saturday, it had taken the Egyptians a full three days to realize that the Israeli raid was swelling into a major operation, with at least one armored division sweeping to cut off the Third Army.

The Russians seem to have realized the strength of the Israeli offensive a day or two quicker than the Egyptians, informed, no doubt, by their succession of watching Cosmos satellites. But they had not passed this news on to Cairo, much to Sadat's irritation. By the time that Kosygin got back to the Kremlin on Saturday, October 19, the Soviet press was admitting that Israeli units were operating on the West Bank, and, in all probability, preparing its readers for the possibility of some kind of Russian involvement against the "Zionist imperialists." For some days past, too, they had been watching with mounting concern the demonstration of airlift capability as the American C-5 Galaxies pounded down at El Arish. So, by that Saturday evening, in the eyes of the Soviet leaders there was cause for action.

When the Soviet request arrived in Washington that afternoon, Kissinger was just off for dinner and talks with Chinese diplomats in the Mayflower Hotel regarding the momentous visit he was making to Peking on the 26th. Kissinger had his talks with the Chinese, then rushed back for a quick meeting with congressional leaders, although as was later remarked by

Senator Mansfield, "I am not certain Dr. Kissinger had all the details." Certainly, he gave them little information. Nevertheless, Kissinger had an inkling of what was behind the unexpected Soviet summons, because late the day before Dobrynin, the Soviet ambassador, had passed on the Kremlin's latest offer. This demanded an immediate cease-fire and a return to the pre-1967 borders, to be carried out in stages, instead of the immediate Israeli withdrawal previously insisted upon. The American government had greeted these proposals with indifference, which caused Brezhnev, when he heard their response, promptly to invoke the 1971-72 U.S.-Soviet accord, whereby both sides undertook to enter into talks within forty-eight hours if one side regarded a situation as sufficiently dangerous to world peace. Brezhnev's invitation made it clear that his government was very concerned about the Middle East situation and wanted consultations before the Kremlin reached grave decisions.

Two hours after Kissinger's air force plane landed at Vnumovo Airport, swept by winter's first icy blasts, his talks had begun. He had with him Joseph Sisco, Sisco's deputy, Atherton, Kissinger's chief adviser on European and Soviet affairs, Helmut Sonnenfeldt, Winston Lord, head of the State Department's policy planning section, as well as another fifteen aides. After a first brief meeting, later that same morning they got down to a four-hour session. Brezhnev sat down with them, accompanied by President Podgorny, Gromyko—the foreign minister was as stony-faced as ever—and a number of foreign policy experts, although Premier Kosygin was a notable absentee. They all sat along two sides of a long highly polished table in a room heavy with the atmosphere of bureaucracy; each had a blotter and a drinking glass.

Both sides quickly agreed on the need for an immediate cease-fire. That was not the problem. What they could not agree upon was how this should be implemented. The Russians wanted the cease-fire linked expressly to immediate negotiations for a settlement, even naming a time and place for the negotiations. But this the Americans were very reluctant to accept.

According to Michael Elkins, *Newsweek*'s correspondent, the

Russians began the talks with threats, making it clear they "would not permit" Egypt and Syria to suffer a repeat of their 1967 débâcle. To avoid this, the Soviet Union might have to move to a "phase of further involvement with incalculable consequences." Kissinger was taken aback by this Soviet outburst, but regained his composure and stood firm. In his slow, deliberate voice, he insisted the Russians must accept the principle that a settlement must include Arab-Israeli negotiations, demanding on a call for such talks "immediately and concurrently with the cease-fire." The meeting rambled on for six hours all told.

It was followed by a brief Tass statement, curtly announcing that the situation in the Middle East was being examined in detail, and that the leaders had sought possible ways of establishing peace in the area. Within hours of the Moscow meeting, the Security Council was convened and adopted a U.S.-Soviet call for a cease-fire.

In Israel, the general consensus was that Kissinger was only in Moscow for exploratory talks, and therefore they saw no great urgency in the talks and did not expect any startling new developments, at least until he returned to Washington. It came as a bombshell, then, to the Israelis when the Soviet-American agreement was announced. Next, their ambassador in Washington was asked to meet urgently with General Alexander Haig, Nixon's chief of staff, on October 21. At this meeting, Haig showed the Israeli the text of the three-point agreement just signed in Moscow and sent to the Security Council, which said:

The Security Council:

(1)   calls upon all parties to the present fighting to cease all firing and to terminate all military activity immediately, no later than 12 hours after the moment of the adoption of this decision, in the positions they now occupy;

(2)   calls upon the parties concerned to start immediately after the cease-fire the implementation of Security Council Resolution 242 in all of its parts;

(3)   decides that immediately and concurrently with the

cease-fire, negotiations start between the parties concerned under appropriate auspices aimed at establishing a just and durable peace in the Middle East.

The Israeli ambassador went posthaste back to his embassy, from where the message was sent immediately to Tel Aviv. Dayan recalled that he met with the prime minister at 7:00 P.M. to give her a progress report on the successful battle being waged on the West Bank. Then, at nine o'clock, she called him back to her office, whereupon she wasted no time in telling him: "That's it. Cease fire. Tonight, at three A.M. the U.N. Security Council will meet to adopt a resolution jointly presented by the United States and the Soviet Union, calling on both sides to cease fire not later than twelve hours after its adoption." She made it clear that President Nixon had personally asked Israel to accept.

Nixon's message had added that Israel's acceptance would be from a position of strength, and assured Mrs. Meir that American arms shipments to Israel would continue after the cease-fire. It had also evoked from the Soviets the promise of direct negotiations, something that had always eluded Israel in the past.

At midnight, the Israeli cabinet convened and agreed to accept the President's request.

Israel meanwhile was still battling for key positions along her front. At dusk that day an attack had been launched to recapture the Mount Hermon position in the Golan Heights, which gave Israel a commanding oversight of the Syrian front. The battle was fierce but concluded successfully for the Israelis at noon the next day. At the same time, Dayan urged General Bar-Lev to capture Mount Ataka, to the west of the Gulf of Suez, as this would give them an unbroken military line from Ismailia to the Gulf, and completely isolate Egypt's Third Army.

The Israeli government, having unanimously accepted the resolution, notified the U.S. government. Mrs. Meir later said, as quoted in *Newsweek*, "When Washington and Moscow agree upon a cause of action, there isn't a lot of room for us to maneuver." Nevertheless, the Israelis still wanted to isolate Egypt's

Third Army. Before accepting the truce, Mrs. Meir called President Nixon. She told him that Israel would accept the cease-fire, and, using an established mini-hotline to Kissinger's office, asked that Kissinger should stop in Tel Aviv on his way home.

At 2:30 P.M. the next day, October 22, Cairo Radio announced that President Sadat had accepted the cease-fire, which would go into effect at 6:58 P.M. However, the Egyptians also continued their operations through that night and into the next day, with their air force maintaining attacks on Israeli troops on the East Bank of the Canal, where Egyptian troops tried to seize key Israeli positions in the last confused hours. Dayan claims that had the Egyptians and Syrians immediately stopped fighting, they would have also stopped; but this does not agree with the American military view that Israel needed a day or so for mopping-up operations to make certain of her decisive victory. The Syrians finally announced their agreement on October 23 at 6:15 A.M., although it was conditional that Israel could withdraw to the pre-1967 cease-fire lines.

While the talks in Moscow had tried to establish a basis for peace, in the desert the carnage went on. *Newsweek* reporter Arnaud de Borchgrave was in the Egyptian Second Army's sector along the road to El Arish:

> As I rode up to the front in a jeep with an Egyptian brigadier, we passed a desert scene reminiscent of the 1967 slaughter in the Mitla Pass, where to this day you can see mile after mile of burned-out Egyptian trucks and tanks. But this time, the wreckage was Israeli. The Al Arish road was lined with dozens of knocked-out Israeli tanks and half-tracks — some still smoldering, many half melted from exploding ammunition. I looked inside one charred wreck. The bodies of the Israeli tankers had been reduced to ashes and bone fragments.
>
> A few miles farther on, we passed scores of Egyptian troops busily digging in on both sides of the road. Finally, we came to a slight rise where a few Egyptian half-tracks had pulled off to the side. "This is our new second line," the brigadier told me proudly. But in the shifting warfare of the desert, he had made a

terrible mistake. In fact, we were suddenly facing a bristling line
of Israeli tanks. The first round they fired hit the half-track on
our right. As it burst into flames, the brigadier coolly threw our
jeep into reverse and began backing toward the nearest Egyptian
position 300 yards away.

Tank and mortar shells were falling all around us as the brigadier and I leaped from the jeep and made a dive into an Egyptian
foxhole. Heavy-artillery shells were exploding only 20 yards
away. Each earth-shattering explosion covered us with a new
layer of sand. While shell fragments and shrapnel whistled overhead, I burrowed my head into the sand like a mole—a little
deeper with each shell until my mouth was full of sand. Blast
after blast kept filling our position with sand. Our foxhole was
becoming alarmingly shallower. As we tried to scoop out the
sand with our hands, we kept burning ourselves on pieces of
shrapnel.

Mercifully, the shells exploded everywhere except directly on
top of us. We tried to reassure each other that unless we took a
direct hit, we would probably survive. Then suddenly, the whine
of jets could be heard. "Here he comes," cried the brigadier, "diving straight for us!" I rolled over on my back just in time to see
a diving Israeli Skyhawk release its bombs. As the jet pulled out
and began to bank away, two small fireballs streaked toward it—
SAM-6s. One went right past the Israeli plane; the second scored
a direct hit. The Skyhawk disintegrated.

The 500-pound bombs dropped by the plane exploded behind
and in front of us. We couldn't see what damage they did as we
didn't dare raise our heads above ground level. Finally, night
began to fall. Flaming vehicles bathed the flat desert in an eerie
half-light. At last, on a signal from the brigadier, we scrambled
out of the foxhole and raced for the vehicles. The brigadier's jeep
wasn't far away and we jumped into it. I rode clinging to the
fender. Once out of Israeli artillery range, I asked him, could
Egypt continue this war?

"Forever," he replied. "As you can see, morale is very high."

When we finally arrived back at the command post in the
ruins of East Kantara, I turned on the BBC news. The announcer
said a cease-fire had been in effect for eight minutes. Then suddenly, all of East Kantara became a blaze of automatic weapons

fire. Red and white tracers laced the starlit sky. The brigadier grimly juggled two field telephones, trying to get an explanation. After fifteen minutes, it became apparent that it was not an Israeli raid and that all the firing was into the air. "My men are angry," the brigadier explained. "They don't understand the cease-fire and they are protesting. But we soldiers must obey the civilian command." Officers began going down the lines ordering the soldiers to stop shooting. Finally, after the brigadier threatened that any position which continued firing would be mortared, the shooting stopped.

So, for hours longer the desert war dragged on, both sides seeking to establish or reclaim positions that would strengthen their negotiating power. Adan's and Magen's armored divisions rumbled south to surround Suez City and the port of Adabiah, while paratroopers eventually controlled Mount Ataka. This rapid advance brought the Israelis more captured booty, including many brand-new T-62s that had just been abandoned. One Israeli soldier casually dragged a canvas cover off an Egyptian truck to discover four lethal and eagerly sought-after SA-6s.

Possession of Adabiah gave the Israeli Navy — which incidentally had soundly defeated Syrian warships and given the Egyptians a fright earlier in the war — the opportunity to join with the ground forces in sealing off Suez City from the sea, thus finally severing all remaining lines of communications to Third Army. Twenty thousand battered survivors of the Third Army, with no blood for the wounded, little ammunition, and diminishing food and water supplies, were surrounded. An Israeli officer crudely predicted that in a few days they would have them all emerging with their tongues hanging out and their hands up.

Correspondent Nicholas C. Proffitt, who was at the Deversoir bridgehead and walked across the southernmost of the three Israeli pontoon bridges, wrote:

It was obvious from the huge traffic jam that Israel was making an all-out final drive to push its offensive in Egypt as far as possible before the cease-fire. Harried military policemen, sporting red armbands and Uzi submachine guns, stood at the bridge, choking on the dust, trying to funnel the chaos into a single line for crossing. Traffic snaked back into the desert for miles — a caravan of tanks, half-tracks, jeeps, bulldozers, captured Egyptian trucks, milk-trucks filled with water and gaily decorated buses that had been summarily taken off the streets of Tel Aviv and pressed into service carrying Israeli troops to the front.

The bridgehead was quiet then, although yawning gaps in the 195-yard-long wooden platform decking evinced the fierce artillery shelling to which earlier Israeli units had been subjected on their way into the Egyptian heartland. Scores of dead fish, killed by the concussion of shells, floated in the green water, already wafting a putrid smell. Proffitt continued:

> When I stepped onto the west bank of the Canal, an American-made Patton tank rumbled by and its Israeli crew called out in unison, "Welcome to Africa!"
>
> I saw that a crude road had been bulldozed through the steep embankment on the west side, and at the top of the embankment were strongly fortified Egyptian bunkers. The bunkers were now occupied by Israeli troops. The smell of death was heavy in the air, and as I walked down the road into Egypt, forgotten corpses could be seen lying in the ditches. Strewn around the body of one Egyptian soldier were some cheap Arabic paperback books and a grainy photograph of the famous Egyptian singer Oum Koulsoum.
>
> Everywhere I went, Israeli soldiers were huddled around radios, arguing furiously about the impending cease-fire. "It's enough peace," said one recruit. "It is the only peace I've known." But his sergeant snapped: "To hell with that, I've been here sixteen days, and I want a couple more to finish the Egyptians off for good."

At a captured Egyptian airfield west of the Canal, an Israeli colonel pointed out to correspondent Angus Deming the Israeli tanks that ringed the base's perimeter, aiming their guns toward the distant mountains to the west, while Israeli Mirage fighters circled overhead in case of an Egyptian air strike. When Deming requested permission to stay, however, he was adamantly refused. "We're expecting to be hit by Egyptian commando raids," the colonel said. "Cease-fire or no cease-fire, it looks like we're still going to be fighting tonight."

Sadat explained his cease-fire decision by claiming that he had been fighting "entirely alone" against the Americans with their modern weapons, most of which had never been used before. By then he was also very critical of the Soviet Union, which, he wrote, "Stood behind me, ready to stab me in the back if I lost 85 or 90 per cent of my arms, just as in 1967." The Americans, he claimed, were fighting with Israel by supplying all the arms she needed, which was not true. All the same, Sadat may not have been far from the truth in his assessment of Soviet intentions, for the Soviet Union was, indeed still is, seeking an excuse to put into the area a massive force. And, as the world has seen many times in forty years, once in, the Russians are not easily removed.

Kissinger left Moscow when the talks were over and flew on to Tel Aviv, while Russia's peripatetic Premier Kosygin was dispatched to the Middle East for talks with Iraqi and Syrian leaders. There was an audible sigh of relief around the world's capitals in the wake of what seemed a very successful Moscow meeting in true détente spirit. Within forty-eight hours, however, the sign was stifled while the world held its breath as there loomed the most serious crisis since that of the Cuban missiles twelve years before.

Within the Soviet Union, as within the United States, there were both hawks and doves, and the Soviet regime under Brezhnev was nowhere near as monolithic as it had been under Stalin. But Brezhnev, supported by Podgorny and Kosygin, all of whom put their hopes in détente as a way of building Soviet strength to equal at least the Americans, had opened a Pandora's box of Middle East problems. Their early support of the Arabs, their encouragement of third Arab states to participate, and their increasingly strong-worded pronouncements—such as that in the Soviet Army newspaper *Krasnaia Zvesda*, on October 20, which suggested to many Western observers that the very existence of Israel could no longer be taken for granted—were all leading their policy over the brink of détente. During the two weeks of war, too, Soviet statements had begun encouraging the Arabs to use their oil weapon. One Moscow newspaper called upon the Arabs to withdraw their multi-billion dollars from Western banks, which, the paper assured its readers, would play an important, if not a decisive role. The United States was no longer as powerful as it had been at the time of the Six Day War, was the general, if oft-repeated theme. Why, then, asked the Russian "hawks," are we not doing more to aid the Arabs? The Soviet air bridge had been flying in supplies since October 9, even landing at airstrips in the Arab front lines near Israel's northern and southern borders. The Russian heavy cruiser *Admiral Ushakov* was heading with other warships for the Mediterranean, and *Krasnaia Zvesda* was publishing enthusiastic reports about the success of Russian weapons.

By the latter half of October, therefore, the fourth Arab-Israeli war was fast escalating to something infinitely more dangerous. Soviet newspapers, all official Party mouthpieces, ranted that "The military actions of the imperialist states are forcing the countries of socialism to undertake measures to further strengthen their defense capability."

The fighting erupted again on the 22nd, when Israeli forces smashed through Egyptian lines in the south, seized three airfields, and cut the Ismailia-to-Cairo road. In Cairo there was near panic. All men between the ages of twenty-one and thirty-five were called up for service, and there were frenzied calls for Soviet aid, which resulted in a Russian threat to Israel of the most serious consequences.

For three days the United Nations struggled to enforce the cease-fire while the battles raged on. Egypt, especially, was desperately trying to recoup some scrap of her earlier gains, which were fast eroding into another humiliating defeat. Finally, with disaster staring him in the face, Sadat appealed to the Kremlin for help. The Soviet Union turned its fury upon Israel at the

United Nations, deploring Israel's insistent breaches of the cease-fire and accusing her of "pure falsehood" in accepting the United Nations' cease-fire appeal. The Soviet representative, Yakov Malik, demanded that Israel return to the lines she had held on Monday when the cease-fire came into effect. Unfortunately, no one had much idea just where the lines had been on Monday. In an effort to appease Soviet feeling and genuinely stop the fighting, the U.S. ambassador, Kenneth Keating, also made "serious representations" in Tel Aviv.

The real writing, however, was only then about to appear on the wall. It began innocently enough with notes from President Sadat to both Nixon and Brezhnev, requesting that they send forces to the Middle East to enforce a cease-fire on Israel. This was, no doubt, what the wily Russians had long wanted, and finally the pendulum had swung their way. Sadat's request gave them a legitimate reason to move in. But when Nixon was asked about the request, he said that one had not been received and that, anyway, the United States had no intention of sending troops to the Middle East and hoped that no other power would do so either. "The last thing the United States wants to see," a State Department spokesman said, "is Soviet troops in the Middle East. The only worse thing than that would be American troops in the Middle East."

But there were immediate and obvious indications that the Soviets felt otherwise, for both western European and U.S. Intelligence networks gathered signs of Russian military preparations. During the early evening of Tuesday, October 23, U.S. Intelligence Reports began to sound warning notes. First of all, they noted a suspiciously sharp decline in the volume of the hitherto massive Soviet airlift into Egypt and Syria. The Pentagon initially took the optimistic view that this signified a delayed Soviet response to an agreement with the United States to restrict arms supplies. Optimism, however, began to fade when further U.S. Intelligence reports detected indications that Soviet Army and transport units had been placed on the alert. Mobilization had been ordered for two mechanized divisions near the Black Sea. This was followed by news that the Soviet Union had concentrated seven parachute divisions, totaling some 50,000 men, together with their equipment in the south of the country.

It was then realized that the decline in the airlift to the Middle East was so that the huge Antonov-22 aircraft could be retained in readiness. A fleet of Antonov-22s had also been dispersed to Hungary, Bulgaria, and Czechoslovakia, presumably to collect troops or equipment. By Wednesday morning more reports alerted the Americans to other Soviet Air Force and naval movements, including the sending of 6,000 naval infantrymen — Marines — to the *Eskadra*, which was in the Mediterranean with the reinforced Soviet Fleet. Six more ships had joined the fleet. Most alarming of all were reports that Russia had sent SCUD surface-to-surface missiles with atomic warheads to Egypt.

During the day meetings were held between Kissinger and Dobrynin, the Soviet ambassador, and that same evening Dobrynin delivered a "brutal" message from Brezhnev to Nixon. In the harshest wording, the message warned about the grave consequences for Israel and declared that Soviet troops were to be sent unilaterally into the area to enforce the cease-fire.

By that time, though, the Russians had got themselves into a tight spot. The cease-fire had come too late for the Arabs, who were in much weaker positions than they had been a week before. So, despite Soviet promises of aid and the sophisticated weapons and massive support they had been given, Russia's clients were about to go down to the Israelis and their American backers. Soviet anger at Israel knew no bounds in those days, and the Russians would dearly have welcomed the chance to teach them a lesson. They even considered at one point sending their own aircraft to support Egypt's Third Army, in the belief that should the Israelis dare shoot down a Russian plane, they would get the collision they wanted and could intervene in force. It had to be force, however, for even the arrogant Russians recognized that the victorious Israelis were not going to be frightened by the appearance of a single Soviet division, or even two, comprising soldiers who had never actually done any real fighting and were very inexperienced. Until their embroilment in Afghanistan, the Soviets had had an army of "asphalt" soldiers.

Bending to their doctrine of never attacking with less than overwhelming force—a lesson learned in Finland in 1939—the Soviets had mobilized those seven parachute divisions and the two mechanized divisions. So, if they went in, it would be no mere punitive expedition but a massively strong attack. However, in spite of their bluster, the Soviets were realists enough to understand that they could not strike at Israel without knowing exactly how America would react. It has been suggested, therefore, that the saber-rattling was a test of American reaction. If America sought to appease the Soviet Union, or backed away, then it might well have spelled the end of Israel, for there is little doubt that by then the Soviet Union would have stopped at nothing less. Israeli Intelligence believed the Russians planned to land their troops at Cairo and move from there to attack Israeli forces on the West Bank. But even the Russians could have managed that with less than seven divisions. It is more probable that they intended an attack through Syria, perhaps from Iraq. Finally, they may well have planned to coordinate these attacks with the naval landing of the 6,000 naval infantry. But the American response was swift and uncompromising.

Nixon's Special Action Group met in the war room at the White House, and at 12:10 A.M. the first message clacked out on the teleprinters:

... All commands ... Assume ... Def ... Con ... Three ... signed James R. Schlesinger ... Defense Secretary....

Defense Condition Three is the third stage of readiness. Stage "Five" is the normal peacetime readiness, when forces are not expected to be called upon suddenly; "Four" is defined by the Pentagon as "an increased intelligence watch and strengthened security measures," the degree maintained throughout the Vietnam War; "Two" establishes a further increase in force, but is still less than the maximum; and "One" is maximum force readiness—the nation poised on the brink of war. Defense Condition Three had last been called for by President Johnson following the assassination of President Kennedy.

That night, however, in October 1973, it meant that 2,231,000 U.S. military personnel deployed at home and overseas were alerted and ready to move on command. Just before 3:00 P.M., in Okinawa, a sepulchral voice interrupted the regular American Forces program: "This is a recall announcement for the 909th Air Refueling Squadron, 376th Field Maintenance Squadron, 376th Strategic Air Wing, and 82nd Strategic Reconnaissance Squadron . . . I repeat, this is a recall announcement . . .", and the message was repeated.

Around the world at U.S. bases and on ships at sea, speakers crackled and echoed, bringing men to readiness. At the Pacific island of Guam, seventy B-52 strategic bombers were ordered to fly back to U.S. bases to take up their assignments for a nuclear war. Soon the giant camouflaged bombers hurtled away from the blue of the Pacific, thundering off to war. Deep in their silos amid the harvested acres of Kansas and Nebraska, the Minutemen ICBMs were prepared when their mighty covers slid ominously back. In the eastern Atlantic the message reached the bridge of the giant aircraft carrier *John F. Kennedy*, plowing through the whitecaps. Soon she was heeling around in a miles-wide arc with her attendant escorts to join the two attack and two amphibious assault carriers, with 1,800 Marines already on their way to reinforce the U.S. Sixth Fleet.

In the United States itself, the crack 82nd Airborne Division was alerted at Fort Bragg, North Carolina, and thrown into a frenzy of action. Vern E. Smith recalled that it "looked like a shot from a World War II movie. At dawn speeding cars were streaking along Bragg's streets with returning GIs. Long lines of troops filed quickly through hastily improvised tents for inno-culations. There were stacks of machine guns and missile launch-ers piled to await loading. Red-hatted parachute riggers were hurrying across the lawns with packaged parachutes in their hands. And at adjoining Pope Air Force Base, an armada of huge C-141 cargo jets stood lined up, wing tip to wing tip, waiting to take on the machinery of war."

For twenty-four hours the world waited to see what would happen as Soviet and U.S. ships tracked one another across the eastern Mediterranean. The B-52s stood loaded, pilots ready to go, while in the eerie light of the underground silos stood the men who had trained unendingly for the signal that would never come. Perhaps now it had. They knew by heart and by system the routine that preceded the launching of the ICBMs; now they took it as far as it could go short of the final switch being pushed into place at the ultimate command. In Europe, the Soviet forces and the Warsaw Pact allies waited and NATO shadowed them. The RAF pilot of a Nimrod maritime patrol bomber recalls that when they flew out on their great circular route to survey the North Cape for Soviet submarines, they carried their full war stores, including nuclear torpedos. "For us it seemed the real thing, and it seemed a hell of a way from home up there in the Arctic."

Then, on October 26, the tension eased. A new agreement was reached between U.S. and Soviet negotiators, following which the Security Council approved a resolution barring all five permanent members from participating in a peacekeeping force. Fingers gingerly eased off the firing buttons, and like overwound catapults the forces wound down, cautiously and warily, the machines that spelled overkill.

Brezhnev had to have the last word, or almost the last word, and tardily announced that he would send representatives to watch the cease-fire. In due course, seventy Russians in ill-made civilian attire flew in to Cairo.

The greatest crisis since the Cuban missiles dissipated as quickly as it had arisen. Perhaps that is a measure of the force of devastation as opposed to détente. Could all the friendly, right-spirited exchanges have resulted in such a quick realization by both superpowers that the consequences were too terrible to risk?

Why Sadat asked for the Russians and Americans to send troops at all is still far from clear, since it was hardly in his interests to have several Soviet divisions in his country, especially as he can have had few illusions that the Russians preferred someone cast in Nasser's mold and would have liked to see Sadat ousted. In the end, both leaders may have been playing to their galleries. Certainly, Nixon was criticized soon after for what many saw as an action designed to distract people from the latest Watergate scandals; but perhaps they were being unfair, for had he not acted, they conceivably would have had something even more devastating to worry about. As for Brezhnev, he too had hawks to satisfy. Perhaps behind the impenetrable Kremlin walls he turned around and showed them what they might have brought down upon themselves.

If nobody won the war, at least no one lost it either—except the thousands of Arabs and Jews who did not return to their farm or village, town or city, wife and children. The Arabs were left bitter and again defeated, although they had shown their new fighting ability. Israel had learned that she could no longer count on panache and morale to win quick victories. Although many thought her near defeat might ameliorate her attitudes in the future, this doesn't seem to have happened yet. Perhaps the answer to that dilemma is now so deeply embedded in the Jewish nature that it is life and survival itself. Ten million Jews walked unresisting into the death chambers, believing that some great force would surely save them at the last moment. Now they have that great force, and it is beyond belief that they will ever again go pacifically to their doom. Now they fight.

The war did bring Egypt and Israeli together, which was the one favorable outcome. Nevertheless, recent events have shown Syrian-Israeli relations to be as intractable as ever. The spotlight has shifted somewhat, and now Lebanon has become the battleground. It is as though the superpowers have given their errant prodigies a yard of their own in which to play. The Israelis and the Syrians fight it out again, this time through their own small clients. Perhaps they, too, learned a lesson.

Israel remains isolated, but alert and unafraid to do what seems necessary, especially when the other powers can hide behind treaties and alliances that always seem to bend away from Israel's needs. In June 1981, her Phantoms struck at Iraq's nuclear plant, flying in the face of world opinion. But who is to take the chances for Israel if not Israel herself? Who will stop the next Holocaust except the victims of the last?

Postscript

The Middle East has seen many changes since the end of the Yom Kippur War, and yet the fundamental problems remain. Israel still strives for recognition and security and the Palestinians still seek a homeland.

American diplomatic intervention led to the surprising phenomena of Egypt's President Sadat and Israel's Prime Minister Begin visiting each other's countries and eventually signing a peace treaty. President Sadat briefly saw coming true his cherished dream of recovering Egypt's occupied territories. But, alas, such radical peacemaking in a region of age-old hatreds earned him the opprobrium of the hard-line Arabs and he was gunned down before his efforts came to fruition.

Israel has also lost wartime leaders, for both former Prime Minister Mrs. Golda Meir and Defense Minister Moshe Dayan have since died. General Ariel Sharon, however, like many of Israel's military leaders, has turned to politics and is now the country's defense minister.

Superpower influences in the region have been shuffled, too, and while the United States has begun to exert its presence there, paradoxically Israel's hope of a defense treaty with her protector was dashed by Israeli intransigence over her annexation of the Golan Heights. Perhaps she feels that the strategically essential Golan "bird in the hand" is worth more than American defense treaties in the bush. On balance, Israelis have learned to trust their security to no one but themselves.

The most significant and dangerous event since the Yom Kippur War must surely have been the Israeli Air Force's destruction of Iraq's nuclear power complex in June 1981. If the Yom Kippur War had determined anything it was that the Arabs were still unable to defeat Israel in open warfare. If that realization has led to the notion of an Islamic nuclear bomb—probably financed by Libya and engineered by Pakistan—then the world has become an infinitely more dangerous place. Israel's destruction of Iraq's nuclear reactor has incalculably increased the turmoil in the Middle East for it has brought into the open the terrifying prospect of nuclear warfare in the region.

In 1973, as we have seen, Israel failed to use her military strategy of immediate retaliation as a warning that she could defeat her neighbors in war. Israel is certainly ahead of the Arabs in the development of bombs, and so small a country cannot rely on the superpower concept of deterrence by second strike capability. Future Middle Eastern wars are no longer going to be nineday wonders of breathtaking maneuvers and counterattacks. Unless a solution to the region's problems is found very quickly, there may be just one or two awesome bangs heralding the final Armageddon.

Bibliography

Adan, Avraham. *On the Banks of the Suez.* London: Arms & Armour, 1980.

Allon, Yigal. *The Making of Israel's Army.* London: Vallentine, Mitchell, 1970.

Barker, A. J. *Arab-Israeli Wars.* London: Ian Allan, 1980.

———. *Suez: The Seven Day War.* London: Faber & Faber, 1964.

Battle, Nos. 1, 2. London: Ian Allan, 1973.

Begin, M. *The Revolt.* Tel Aviv: Steimatsky, 1952.

Bell, Richard. *The Other Case for Defensible Borders.* Jerusalem: Carta, 1978.

Ben Gurion, D. *Israel: Years of Challenge.* New York: Holt, Rinehart and Winston, 1963.

Cohen, Jack S. *Israel—The Facts.* New York: Youth Institute for Peace in the Middle East, 1978.

Dayan, M. *Diary of the Sinai Campaign.* New York: Schocken, 1967.

———. *The Story of My Life.* London: Weidenfeld & Nicolson, 1976.

Dramit, E., ed. *Born in Battle*, Nos. 8, 13, 15, 16. Israel: Eshel Dramit, 1978.

Eaks, Louis. *Kuneitra: The City Israel Destroyed.* London: Petra.

Eban, Abba. *An Autobiography.* London: Weidenfeld & Nicolson, 1977.

Elston, D. R. *No Alternative. Israel Observed.* London: Hutchinson, 1960.

Herzog, C. *The War of Atonement.* London: Weidenfeld & Nicolson, 1975.

———. *The Yom Kippur War.* Jerusalem: Keter, 1975.

Israel Pocket Library. *History from 1880.* Jerusalem: Keter, 1973.

Lacqueur, N. Z. *The Road to War.* London: Penguin, Harmondsworth, 1969.

Letters from Israel during the Yom Kippur War. Jerusalem: Israel Interfaith Committee, 1973.

Luttwak, E., and D. Horowitz. *The Israeli Army.* London: Allen Lane, 1975.

Middle East Information Services. *Defenceless.* Jerusalem: Ministry for Foreign Affairs, 1973.

———. *Statements and Documents on the October 1973 War.* Jerusalem: Ministry for Foreign Affairs, 1973.

Newsweek, issues from August to December 1973. New York.

O'Ballance, E. *The Sinai Campaign 1956.* London: Faber and Faber, 1959.

Safran, N. *From War to War.* New York: Pegasus, 1971.

Strategic Survey. London: Institute of Strategic Studies, 1971.

Sunday Times Insight Team. *The Yom Kippur War.* London: Deutsch, 1975.

Teveth, S. *Moshe Dayan.* London: Weidenfeld & Nicolson, 1974.

Time, issues from September to December 1973. New York.

The New York Times, editions from May to December 1973.

The Search for Peace. Israel's Foreign Policy. Govt. booklet.

The Times, editions from May to December 1973. London.

Weizman, E. *On Eagles' Wings.* London: Weidenfeld & Nicolson, 1976.

Whetten, Lawrence L. *The Canal War.* Cambridge, Massachusetts: The M.I.T. Press, 1974.

Young, P. *The Israel Campaign, 1967.* London: Kimber, 1968.

Index

counteroffensive against Syria, 172-73, 183-84; and Egyptian offensive, 128-29, 146-48, 212, 218, 220; and penetration raids into Syria, 162-63, 168-70; Sharon and, 252-53; and Soviet-U.S. cease-fire proposal, 287-88; and Suez Canal fortifications, 141; and Syrian and Egyptian victories, 131-32; and Tirtur route battles, 256-58; and underestimation of Arabs, 239; and West Bank battles, 271-77. *See also* Suez Canal crossing
Israeli paratroopers, 234, 235-37, 255-58

Jarring, Dr. Gunnar, 24, 27
Jehani, Col. Tewfiq, 176, 178, 183
Jordan, 5, 9, 10, 35-36, 142, 197, 208, 283
Juhader, 92, 100-101

Kantara, 192, 215
Karen, Col. Aryeh, 148, 150, 154, 185, 186, 215, 264, 265, 275
Katyusha rocket launchers, 152, 177, 188
Khouli, Hassan Sabri al, 35
Kissinger, Dr. Henry, 84, 88, 160-61, 171, 202, 203, 204-5, 208-9, 283-86, 288, 292
Kosygin, Alexei, 205-6, 250-51, 278, 285
Kuneitra, 37, 38, 43, 51-52, 66, 96-97, 100, 105
Kuwait, 197, 230

Laird, Melvin, 203-4, 208
Lakov, Col. David, 193
Laner, Maj. Gen. Dan, 50, 58, 59, 65, 86, 172, 173, 176, 177-78, 183, 282-83
Lexicon-Tirtur junction, 234, 242-43, 244. *See also* Tirtur route
London Institute of Strategic Studies, 24, 131-32

McIntyre, Sir Laurance, 162
Magen, Brig. Gen. Kalman, 119, 146, 148, 201, 218, 220, 225, 231, 232-33, 269, 275-77, 290
Mahmoun, Maj. Gen. Saad, 215, 216, 217
Malik, Yakov, 170-71, 294
Mandler, Maj. Gen. Avraham (Albert), 48, 58, 116, 117, 118-19, 126, 135-37, 142, 144, 146, 200-201, 218
Mansfield, Mike, 203, 284-85
Matt, Col. Danny, 335-36, 238, 239, 241, 246, 247, 271-72
Matzmed fortification, 148, 154, 229, 241
Media, 9, 10, 31, 83, 130-31, 148. *See also* Egyptian media; Israeli media; Soviet media
Meir, Mrs. Golda, 27, 50-51, 54, 82, 88, 144-45, 172, 173, 181, 182, 199, 207-8, 281, 287-88, 300
Meir, Captain "Tiger," 89-91
Messmer, Pierre, 159-60
Mifreket fortification, 119, 124
MIG fighter planes, 4, 7, 29, 60, 102, 212
Mitla Pass, 11, 116, 117, 126, 137, 210, 217
Mitznefet, 275, 276, 277
Montassir, Col. Mahmoud, 211-12, 214
Montgomery, Field Marshal, 143, 153, 172, 180
Morocco, 47, 142, 197
Mount Ataka, 287, 290

Nafekh, 38, 53, 79, 91-93, 97-98, 100, 105, 107, 108-13
Nasser, President, 9-10, 11, 17, 23-24, 25, 26-28, 30
NATO, 18, 204
Newsweek, 31, 125, 129-30, 234-35, 285-86, 288-90
Nir, Col. Natke, 148, 150, 151-52, 153, 154, 155, 179, 185, 187, 188, 264, 265, 266, 268, 274, 275